Rabindranath Tagore

泰戈尔（1861.05.07—1941.07.08）

中国·1924·泰戈尔

重觅师尊的光辉足迹

泰戈尔第一次访华纪实

董友忱·编著

云南人民出版社

图书在版编目（CIP）数据

泰戈尔第一次访华纪实 / 董友忱编著. -- 昆明：云南人民出版社, 2024. 12. -- ISBN 978-7-222-23372-0

Ⅰ . K833.515.6

中国国家版本馆CIP数据核字第20257040Q5号

项目策划：陈　晨
责任编辑：陈　晨
责任印制：代隆参
责任校对：董　毅
装帧设计：张益珲　越凡文化
英文编辑：李妍瑾
助理编辑：李金泽

泰戈尔第一次访华纪实
TAIGEER DI - YI CI FANGHUA JISHI

董友忱　编著

出版	云南人民出版社
发行	云南人民出版社
社址	昆明市环城西路609号
邮编	650034
网址	www.ynpph.com.cn
E-mail	ynrms@sina.com
开本	889mm×1194mm　1/32
印张	11.75
字数	400千
版次	2024年12月第1版第1次印刷
印刷	昆明德厚印刷包装有限公司
书号	ISBN 978-7-222-23372-0
定价	65.00元

版权所有　侵权必究
印装差错　负责调换

如需购买图书，反馈意见，请与我社联系。
图书发行电话：0871-64107659

董友忱教授，中共中央党校文史教研部原副主任，资深翻译家，国际孟加拉学研究会会长（President of Theinternational Society of Bengal Studies）。早年毕业于苏联列宁格勒大学东方系孟加拉语言文学专业，通晓俄语和孟加拉语。他是《泰戈尔作品全集》（33册，人民出版社2015年12月出版）的主编和主译，主编过《泰戈尔小说全译》（7卷本，新华出版社2005年1月出版）和《泰戈尔诗歌精选》（6卷本，外语教学与研究出版社2015年出版）；1994年起享受国务院特殊津贴，2010年5月8日印度泰戈尔文化大学授予董教授荣誉文学博士称号，同年5月9日印度西孟加拉邦文化部授予他泰戈尔纪念奖。主要著作有《泰戈尔画传》《天竺诗人泰戈尔》《诗人之画——泰戈尔绘画欣赏》《心声微语——孟加拉文学论文集》《读解泰戈尔》《泰戈尔第一次访华纪实》等，是当代中国研究泰戈尔最著名的专家。

1924年4—5月诗人泰戈尔访华时的合影
右起：徐志摩、林徽因、泰戈尔、恩厚之、林长民、张歆海、梁思成

右起：徐志摩、泰戈尔、林徽因

泰戈尔

这幅照片是诗人第二次来中国时，即 1929 年 3 月 19 日上午在徐志摩家里拍摄的照片，左侧是胡适的题字，左下角为诗人泰戈尔用英文题写自己的名和姓。

前 言

罗宾德罗纳特·泰戈尔（Rabindranath Tagore, 1861.05.07—1941.08.07），是中国广大读者最熟悉的外国诗人、小说家、音乐家、画家、教育家，也是中国人民真诚的朋友。"泰戈尔"（ঠাকুর）是他家族的姓氏，他的名字为罗宾德罗纳特（রবীন্দ্রনাথ）。他是印度孟加拉族人，出生在印度西孟加拉邦首府加尔各答的焦拉桑科（孟加拉语的意思是"双桥"）小区祖宅。通常，在正式场合孟加拉人一般都称呼他的名字加姓氏：罗宾德罗纳特·泰戈尔，有时称呼他的名字"罗宾德罗纳特"或"罗宾德罗"，不称呼他的姓氏"泰戈尔"，因为姓这个姓氏的人在孟加拉邦很多，若只称呼"泰戈尔"，不知道指何人。他家里人喜欢称呼他的简称"罗比"（রবি）。

泰戈尔家族的发迹，是从他祖父达罗卡纳特·泰戈尔（Dvarakanath Tagore, 1794—1846）开始的。他祖父是当时著名企业家和地主，主要经营蓝靛、茶叶、食糖、煤炭、硝石、矿产等，他还搞远洋运输，拥有一支自己的远洋运输船队，还开设了一家隶属于卡尔—泰戈尔公司名下的"联合银行"。他在孟加拉邦北部和奥里萨邦等地购买了大量的地产。他祖父凭借自己的聪明才智和经营头脑，成为19世纪中叶加尔各答最富有的人，但是他不是我们传统概念中的奸商和恶霸地主，而是一位热衷慈善事业的大商人和同情农民疾苦的善良地主，因此他成为当时孟加拉社会的名人，受到人民的尊敬。

1846年，达罗卡纳特第二次前往欧洲，8月1日客死在英国。从此诗人泰戈尔的父亲代本德罗纳特（Debendranaath，1817—1905）就承担起振兴家业的重担，因为诗人祖父死后，他父亲发现，卡尔—泰戈尔公司已经入不敷出，债台高筑。经过几年的努力，代本德罗纳特还清了公司的债务，卡尔—泰戈尔公司又恢复了昔日的辉煌。不过，在罗宾德罗纳特·泰戈尔出生时他的家庭经济状况已经开始走下坡路。

泰戈尔之家是个大家庭，诗人的母亲莎罗达苏多丽（Saaradasundaree，1827—1875.03.10）共生育了15个孩子，其中第一个女孩和最后一个儿子出生不久就夭亡。在活下来的13个孩子中，诗人泰戈尔是最小的一个，在他上面有7个哥哥和5个姐姐。诗人泰戈尔之家又是书香门第，他的亲人都是有学问的文化人，其中不乏有才华、热爱文学的艺术者。他大哥迪金德罗纳特（1840—1926）是一位热爱文学的诗人、喜欢数学和哲学家，创作了记录歌曲的乐谱；他的二哥绍登德罗纳特（1842—1923）是当时唯一获得研究生学历、在殖民地印度政府工作的人员，用英文和孟加拉文写过诗歌、剧本、回忆录的人；他的五哥久迪林德罗纳特（1849—1925）是位多才多艺的艺术家，他会弹钢琴、吉他，会拉小提琴，会谱写乐曲，会演戏，也会写诗和歌词；他的四姐绍尔诺库玛丽（1856—1932）是女作家，创作过几部长篇小说、剧本、诗集，做过《婆罗蒂》杂志的主编；他的小姐姐波尔诺库玛丽（1859—1943）是位文化素质很高的才女。

在这种家庭环境中成长起来的罗宾德罗纳特，自然拥有良好的家教,这种浓厚文化氛围的熏陶和厚德家风的润染,使其成为那个时代具有优秀品格的伟大诗人。他不仅创作了近10万行诗歌、80多个剧本、15部中长篇小说、96篇短篇小说、大量散文、19卷书信,而且创作了大量歌曲和绘画作品,成为具有革命精神的社会活动家、教育家和厚德人格的一代大师,被孟加拉人尊称为"古鲁代博"(রুদেব——师尊)。

1913年,诗人泰戈尔荣获诺贝尔文学奖,从此他名声大振,世界各国文化人开始阅读和译介他的作品。中国最早接触他作品的英文译本的人,是在日本留学的郭沫若。当时中国国内通晓英语的文化人也开始阅读和译介泰戈尔的作品,并且在中国的报刊上发表,中国最早发表他作品的人是陈独秀,他从《吉檀迦利》中翻译的4首诗发表在1915年10月出版的《新青年》杂志第二期上。此后中国多家出版社也陆续出版他的作品。

世界各国争相邀请诗人泰戈尔前往他们各自的国家访问。中国也不例外,1923年初,北京讲学社[①](Lecture Association)向诗人泰戈尔发出了访华的邀请,他欣然接受中国的邀请,并计划于1923年秋天访华,可是后来他生病了,于是决定推迟访问。随着身体的康复,诗人泰戈尔决定于1924年春天访华。中国方面也做好了迎接诗人泰戈尔来华访问的准备。

1924年3月21日,诗人泰戈尔一行乘坐英国船舶公司的"埃塞俄比亚"号邮轮,从加尔各答出发,前往中国,途中在缅甸、马来亚、新加坡停留,然后改乘日本轮船"热田丸"号(Atsuta-maru)前往香港,于4月12日抵达上海,随后游览杭州、南京、济南,于4月23日晚7时,抵达北京,5月20日夜里离开北京前往山西太原去湖北武汉访

---

① 讲学社——1920年9月,梁启超与蔡元培、林长民、张元济等人在北京成立了讲学社,其目的是增强与国际的文化交流。讲学社的宗旨是聘请国外著名学者来华讲学,计划是以每年董事会基金中的2000元邀请外国学者一人来华讲学。实际上先后共有四位外国著名学者来华讲学:哲学家杜威、罗素、杜里舒和文学家泰戈尔。四人来华讲学,轰动一时,对中外思想文化交流和新文化运动产生了巨大影响。梁启超作为讲学社的实际负责人,在讲学社的酝酿、成立、运作、邀请等重要事项中发挥了关键作用。

问，5月28日回到上海，5月30日离开上海前往日本，诗人泰戈尔结束了第一次访华的行程。

诗人泰戈尔第二次来中国是1929年3月19—21日，当时他前往北美和日本讲学的途中路过上海，在位于福煕路四明村923号徐志摩和陆小曼家里住了3天。这次来中国属于私人访问，他嘱咐徐志摩要保密，只有徐志摩的几位好友知道。19日中午，蒋百里在家里设宴招待诗人泰戈尔，作陪的只有胡适等几位好友。邵洵美携妻子盛佩玉也来徐家拜访过诗人泰戈尔。师尊第三次来中国是同年6月11—13日，即他在结束讲学回国的途中经过上海时，又在徐志摩家里小住了3天。以上是诗人泰戈尔三次访问中国的大体概况。

2024年是诗人泰戈尔第一次访华100周年。为纪念这个具有文化历史意义的日子，我特撰写本书。本书具有与同类书籍不同的两个特点：第一，本书比较翔实地记录了诗人泰戈尔首次访华的行踪，他游览过什么地方，在什么地方会见过何人，在何种场合发表了何种内容的讲话等，也就是说，本书尽力重现诗人泰戈尔访华期间所有活动的场景；第二，本书收录了诗人泰戈尔及接待方主人当时讲话所使用的英语原文。这样，通晓英文的读者就可以欣赏诗人泰戈尔及其接待方主人原汁原味的英语讲话了。

董友忱

2024年5月31日星期五

于北京西郊寓所

目　录

中国邀请和诗人出访前的准备 ··· 001
前往中国途中在缅甸停留 ··· 019
在马来亚停泊 ··· 029
在新加坡和中国香港停留 ··· 037
抵达上海 ··· 043
前往杭州访问 ··· 057
对驻沪日本侨民的讲话 ··· 067
乘船北上南京 ··· 079
访问济南 ··· 093
抵达北京 ··· 097
出席北海静心斋的欢迎会 ··· 103
为欢迎泰戈尔，梁启超在北师大的讲演 ······················ 115
在法源寺观赏丁香花 ··· 141
游览紫禁城和在海军俱乐部的讲话 ······························ 147
在北京先农坛的讲演 ··· 167
参观贵州会馆的画展 ··· 175
在清华大学的讲演 ··· 181
同清华大学同学座谈并宣读《文明与进步》············ 193

出席清华大学欢迎会并与大家交谈……223
在燕京女师大的谈话……231
庆祝泰戈尔的生日……245
在真光剧场的第一次讲演……253
有人散发反对泰戈尔的传单……269
徐志摩的讲话……273
会见俄国代表加拉罕……283
意外遇到北京大学的学生们……291
出席北京大学的送别茶话会……297
参加宗教界人士的欢送会……311
观看《洛神》和出席饯行午宴……327
太原和武汉之行……331
返回上海住进贝纳家里……337
泰戈尔出席告别宴会……349

结束语……353

参考书目……357

中国邀请和诗人出访前的准备

泰戈尔第一次访华纪实

上海 ○
武汉 ○
上海 ○
太原 ○
北京 ○
济南 ○
南京 ○
杭州 ○
上海 ○
香港 ○
新加坡 ○
马来亚 ○
仰光 ○
加尔各答 ○

长期以来，诗人泰戈尔心中一直存有访问中国的梦想。他在童年时就听说过，他的父亲代本德罗纳特·泰戈尔曾经去过中国。

1917年，诗人泰戈尔乘船前往美国访问的时候，顺路去日本的途中在香港码头停留两天。在码头上他第一次目睹了中国工人的劳动场面。看到那种情景，当时诗人泰戈尔简直陶醉了。他写道："首先映入眼帘的，是在轮船停靠的码头上中国工人们的劳动场面。他们每个人都穿一条蓝色裤子，光着上身。这样强壮的身体，没有一点儿多余的累赘之肉。干起活儿来，全身的肌肉有节奏地起伏着。……从头到脚，看不到一点儿疲惫不堪和无精打采的迹象……我从没想到，望着他们在码头上装货卸货，我的心情会如此舒畅。充分使用体力从事劳动，是赏心悦目的，劳动时的每一个动作，美化了身体，与此同时，身体也美化了劳动……目睹这种劳动的力量、劳动的娴熟，我深深地感到，中华民族在全国储存了多大的能量。……长期以来，中国学会了不遗余力地工作，在这种劳动过程中中国的能力全面地展现出来，并且得到了欢乐……中国的这种能力使美国感到恐惧,在工作能力方面美国赢不了中国,所以不要妄图以体力将其征服。如此伟大的力量一旦获得现代载体,也就是说,科学一旦为他们所掌握,世界上还有什么力量能阻止中国呢?……现在那些正在享受世界财富的国家害怕中国的崛起,他们就想阻止这一天的到来。"[①]

这是诗人泰戈尔第一次看到中国人民劳动场面时发出的感慨。当时诗人泰戈尔对中国未来发展的预见,在当今的中国已经成为现实。21世纪,中国的崛起引起美国的恐惧,所以美国当局从各方面打压中国,企图阻止中国的崛起,扼杀中国的发展。这只不过是螳臂当车,是注定要失败的。

诗人泰戈尔一身正气,敢于直言,20岁时就写过一篇文章《在中国的死亡贸易》,谴责英国商人强行向中国销售鸦片,对饱受毒害的中国人民深表同情。1916年,他去日本时看到日本人伤害中国的事件,就愤怒地写了一篇《民族主义》的文章,对其进行批评。

1921年,西方的一位汉语和藏语专家——西洛万·雷维教授来到诗人泰戈尔所创办的国际大学圣蒂尼克坦后,他就决定在国际大学建立汉语和藏语研究中心。他知道,印度的珍贵佛教典籍在印度消失了,可是在中国的汉语和藏语的佛典里却被保存下来。诗人泰戈尔心中存有一个梦想,就是通过翻译重新恢复这批印度文化遗产。

1923年1月11日,诗人泰戈尔在写给拉奴[②]的一封信里说,一位来自中国的贵人请求他去访问,那里的青年人热情地期待他能于当年10月、11月和12月访问中国的北方和南方。

同年春天,诗人泰戈尔派自己的挚友——英国人恩厚之(雷纳德·埃尔姆哈斯特)前往中国联系诗人泰戈尔访华事宜。4月,恩厚

[①] রবীন্দ্র-রচনাবলী দশম খণ্ড পৃ. ৪১৮, চৌষ ১৪১৭. 参阅《泰戈尔作品全集》第10卷,人民出版社2015年版,第583、584页。

[②] 拉奴——拉奴·奥提迦里(1906.10.18—2000.03.15),诗人泰戈尔文学的仰慕者,诗人也视她为自己的女儿一样,经常与之保持通信联系,诗人给她写有大量书信。这些书信后来被收录于《泰戈尔书信集》第18卷出版。

之找到了他的朋友徐志摩，经其周旋，由北京讲学社向诗人泰戈尔转达讲学社邀请诗人泰戈尔来华访问的愿望。于是恩厚之就给诗人泰戈尔写了信，向他传达了这个消息。诗人泰戈尔随后给中国讲学社拍发两封电报，直接发给在北京的恩厚之，请他转达。尽管地址错误，可是恩厚之还是收到了，并把其中的一封电报给讲学社的秘书看了，秘书以梁启超的名义给诗人泰戈尔拍发了回电：

我们刚刚收到从恩厚之先生那里转来的您发给他的电报，得知您已在安排来华访问，我们感到非常高兴。我们毫不怀疑，您也会直接回复我们的，就目前情况而言，您已决定访问中国，对此我们很高兴，这一消息对于所有崇敬您的人来说都是一个巨大的快乐。您也可以直接回复我们，但我们怀疑，由于我们没有提供准确的地址，您发来的消息可能会因某种原因流产。无论如何，我们为您已决定访华而感到高兴，这一消息已使您所有的仰慕者感到极为快乐。我们期待你们能在七月底或八月初到达。您订好船票后，请立即通知我们确切的日期。我们将在一两天内电汇1000美元，以支付贵方第一次航行的费用。

电报地址：liangchichao nanchangchieh, Peking
北京 南长街 梁启超

此后，诗人泰戈尔由于组织他创作的话剧《牺牲》演出，感到身体不适等原因，很多天都没有听到有关他要访华的消息。1923年10月又重新议论起焦格洛基绍尔·比罗拉资助诗人泰戈尔访华之事。10月18日，《华北之星》（*North China Star*）刊登一则消息"印度哲学家将于明年春天在北京进行讲演"：应北京大学的邀请，罗宾德罗纳特·泰戈尔将于明年3月在那里停留一个月，发表讲演。

1923年7月26日，徐志摩又给诗人泰戈尔写了信，向他报告了中国准备欢迎他来中国的情况。

Sung-Po Library,
7 Shi Huh Hutung,
Peking (West)
July 26, 1923

Dear Mr. Tagore,

We are ever so happy that you are arriving in October. The change of date suits us perfectly as the schools will be open then. the only drawback is perhaps the climate; the Peking winter can't be expected to be as warm as that of India though perhaps just as pleasant. You will have to bring all your writer out fits of course. We shall see to it that your lodgings will be properly heated.

The Lecture Association has asked me to be with you during your sojourn in China and to serve as interpreter when and where necessary. I consider the privilege an overwhelming one. But, while fully conscious of my own incompetency for the post. I nevertheless could hardly repress the inmost joy that I should be so very fortunate as to be appointed to wait upon one of the greatest spirits the world has ever seen.

I am supposed to interpret your speeches. But to interpret for a great poet! One might as well try to transcribe the grant roars of a Niagara or the passionate songs of a nightingale! Can there be any more impossible task and impertinent attempt? And yet same sort of arrangement there must be since the audiences that you will attract cannon be expected to comprehend the English language. You can understand the difficulties, can't you? I am also told that generally you have your speeches written out before delivery, in which case it would make my task considerable easier if you would be so kind and considerate as to send us beforehand a copy of whatever you may have already prepared to address our people. I shall try to have the text translated out so as to render the Chinese version, when delivered, if destined to lose all the original charm and beauty, at all events articulate and intelligible. I shall expect to hear from you as soon as possible.

Best wishes from

Tsemou Hsu

Dr.Rabindrath Tagore,

Santiniketan, Bengal

太戈尔①先生：

您准备十月来华，我们快乐极了。这次改期对我们十分合适，因为学校在十月左右都会开课了。唯一不妥的是天气。北京的天气和印度的很有差别，虽然同样的令人愉快。您来时要准备全副冬装才好。我们将在您居住的地方适当地装上暖气。

我已经答应了讲学社，在您逗留中国期间充任您的旅伴和翻译。我认为这是一个莫大的殊荣。虽然自知力薄能渺，但我却因有幸获此良机，得以随侍世上一位伟大无比的人物而难禁内心的欢欣雀跃。

我算是替您做讲台翻译的人，但要为一个伟大诗人做翻译，这是何等的僭妄！这件事若能做得好，人也可以试把尼亚戈拉大瀑布的澎湃激越或夜莺的热情歌唱迻译为文字了！还有比这更难的工作或更不切实际的企图吗？不过安排总是要做一点的，因为来瞻仰您风采的听众不容易听懂英语。您能明白其中的困难的，是不是？人家告诉我，您通常在演说之前把讲稿拟好。要是我所闻不差而您又体谅我的浅陋，盼望能把预备了向我国听众演说的讲稿寄一份来，这样我的工作就不致太困难了。我会把讲稿先译成中文，那么即使在您的讲演中我无能传送美妙动人的神韵，至少也可以做到表达清楚流畅的地步。盼

---

① 当时对诗人姓氏译为"泰古尔""太戈尔""泰戈尔"，后来确定后者。

早获覆音。此候

　　健康

徐志摩敬启
一九二三年七月二十六日
北京石虎胡同七号
松坡图书馆[1]

接到中国发来的邀请函后，诗人泰戈尔开始有些犹豫，他以何种身份访问中国。1924年2月24日，他曾经给罗曼·罗兰写过一封信。他在信中写道："I go to China in what capacity I do not know. It is as a poet or as a bearer of good advice and sound common sence?"[2]

（我不知道，我以什么身份去中国，我是作为一位诗人，还是作为好建议和合理常识的一个传递者呢？）

诗人泰戈尔接到中国邀请的消息，印度大财团的焦戈尔基绍尔·比罗拉知道了，于是1923年10月在加尔各答会见了诗人泰戈尔。他对诗人说，如果能够有几位学者代表印度同诗人同行，比罗拉可以承担他们此行的费用。为此焦戈尔基绍尔决定向他们一次性地捐赠21000卢比。

有了焦戈尔基绍尔·比罗拉的赠款，诗人泰戈尔这次中国之行的费用问题就解决了，因此他决定组成一个印度民间文化代表团前往中国访问，其成员包括国际大学的两位教授，即梵语专家基迪莫洪·森和著名画家依德拉尔·巴苏教授，以及加尔各答大学的佛学专家迦利达斯·纳格博士，同时请恩厚之在这次中国之行中担任诗人泰戈尔的秘书。这样前往中国访问的正式代表团由上述5人组成。除此之外，在诗人泰戈尔振兴农村的实验地——斯里尼克坦工作的美国女士葛玲

---

[1] 韩石山编：《徐志摩书信集》，天津人民出版社2006年版，第370—372页。
[2] প্রভাতকুমার মুখোপাধ্যায়, রবীন্দ্রজীবনী ও রবীন্দ্রসাহিত্য-প্রবেশক, তৃতীয় খণ্ড, ১৭৬ বিশ্বভারতী গ্রন্থনবিভাগ কলকাতা. 普罗帕特库马尔·穆科巴泰：《罗宾德罗传记和罗宾德罗文学导读》第3卷，加尔各答，国际大学图书出版部，第176页。

小姐也与他们一起前往中国,她要顺路横渡过太平洋返回美国去。

11月11日出版的马德拉斯刊物《祖国》(*Swarajya*)发表了一篇提醒性的文章说:"Newspapers report that Rabi Babu's visit to China will do no good either all over China that the people will not listen to himself or the Chinese, as political conditions are so unsettled, and the bandits so active all over China that the people will not listen to the autor of *Gitanjali*.Besides the Chinese are downright materialists today, and Rabi Babu's idealism, which does not promise gold, opium,and concubines is not likely to appeal them."

(报纸报道,罗比先生的中国之行对他自己和中国人都没有好处,政治局势如此不稳定,中国各地的强盗如此活跃,人们不会去聆听《吉檀迦利》作者的讲话。此外,中国人今天是彻头彻尾的物质主义者,而罗比先生的理想主义是不会被重视黄金、鸦片和妻妾的人们青睐的,因而是不太可能吸引他们的。)

事态发展证明,《祖国》刊物的提醒文章并不是完全没有道理的,在美国和英国受过教育的当代中国诗人徐志摩(1896—1931)于1923年12月27日给诗人泰戈尔写了一封信,在简述了一些其他事情的同时对这一说法表达了不同的意见。全文如下:

                      7 Shi-Huh Hutung,

                      Peking,West City,

                      December 27, 1923

Dear Mr.Tagore,

This is already Christmas. I ought to have written to you long long ago. We "Celestials" are notorious for our lethargic habits, and myself. An English friend of mine writing to me last January, said that he would not be surprised if my answer which he expected didn't reach him before end of the year! He understands my wont. And as you know well, men like G. Lowes Dickinson and Bertrand Russell in the West have been lavishing their panegyrics as what is in reality our constitutional laziness, and in what glowing enthusiasm!

Your good letter to me nearly miscarried and didn't get to us till late in October which we were already impatient with expectation. We were very sorry to hear that both yourself and your son had been ill in the summer and that you were not able to come this year, but your kind promise to come over next spring filled us with great joy and gratitude indeed. perhaps India is not well informed of the literary news in China. We have been doing well in preparing ourselves in welcoming you when you arrive .nearby all the leading magazines here have published articles on you and special numbers are issued in honour of your visit. Most of your works in English have appeared in Chinese translation, some in more than one version. Never before has a single writer, eastern or western, excited so much genuine interest in the heart of our young nation ,and few, not even our ancient sages perhaps, have gifted us with sach a vivid and immense inspiration as you have done.Your influence suggests the very return of the spring: as suddenand as marvelous. Our youths, news emancipated, like the tender buds on the stem,need but the embrace of the southern breeze and the kiss of the morning dew to set them a flower; and you have supplied it. Your poems have colored our warp of thinking and feeling;have revealed new possibilities in our otherwise rigid and lurid language. If a creative writer is one whose words have a power to quicken the heart beats of the reader and exact the state of his soul, I have known no better illustration than yourself in the present instance. That is why we so eagerly covet your presence; a presence, we believe, which will lend comfort and calm and joy to this age of gloom and doubt and agitation; a presence which mill further strengthen our faith and hope in larger things in life, which you have helped to install into our minds.

China is relatively at peace these days, one needn't take the newspaper accounts of politics, in China as elsewhere, too seriously. They are nearly always exaggerations, when not flat lies. My own province, Chekiang for instance, is just now being threatened war with its neighbouring provinces which belong to a different political faction, while in reality nothing but fiasco is likely to result. You will enjoy your trip next spring, we are quite certain. Please let me know as early as possible date of sailing and other things which you think we ought to arrange beforehand. Meantime I shall expect manuscripts of your lectures to be rendered into Chinese.

Best wishes from

Tsemou Hsu

太戈尔先生台鉴：

现在已是圣诞节了，我早就应该给您写信。但我们这些"天朝人士"的疲懒恶习是尽人皆知的，我在这方面的疏惰，当内省之际，有时连自己都会大吃一惊。有一位英国友人去年一月写信给我说，他若等到年底才收到我的复信，他也不会感到惊奇！他知道我的习性。您很清楚，狄更生和罗素等人在西方对中国推崇备至的白热化赞词，其对象事实上就是我们的传统惰性！

尊函险遭邮误，在十月下旬才到北京，使我们等得急不可耐。听到您和令郎都在夏季抱疾，因此今年不能启程的消息，我们不胜怅怅，然而您又满怀好意地答应了明春来华访问，真使我们欢欣感谢。印度对这里文学界的动态，可能知之不详。我们已准备停当以俟尊驾莅临。这里几乎所有具有影响力的杂志都刊登有关于您的文章，也有出特刊介绍的。您的英文著作已大部分译成中文，有的还有一种以上的译本。无论是东方的或西方的作家，从来没有一个人像您这样在我们这个国家的年轻人心中引起那么广泛真挚的兴趣。也没有几个作家（连我们古代圣贤也不例外）像您这样把生机勃勃和浩瀚无边的鼓舞力量赐给我们。您的影响使人想到春回大地的光景——是忽尔而临的,也是光明璀璨的。我们青年刚摆脱了旧传统,他们像花枝上鲜嫩的蓓蕾,只候南风的怀抱以及晨露的亲吻,便会开一个满艳;而您是风露之源,您的诗作替我们的思想与感情加添了颜色,也给我们的语言展示了新的远景,不然的话,中文就是一个苍白和僵化的混合体了。如果作家是一个能以语言震撼读者内心并且提升读者灵魂的人物,我就不知道还有哪一位比您更能证明这一点的。这说明我们为什么这样迫切地等候您的光临。我们相信您的出现会给只有一个黑暗的、怀疑和烦躁动乱的世代带来安慰、冷静和喜乐,也会进一步加强我们对伟大事物和生活的信心与希望。这信心和希望是已经通过您的助力而注入了我们的心怀。

中国近日尚算宁静;报纸上关于中国政治的报导不足深信,这种情形在其他方面也是如此。这些报道性的消息即使不是字字谎言,也往往是一些夸张之谈。举例说吧,我的本省浙江目前就有打仗的风声,威胁是来自临近若干不同政府统治的省份。但事实上,除了胡闹一顿之外,大不了的事情是不会发生的。

我们肯定,您明春来华会享受旅游之乐。请尽早让我知道您的船期以及其他您认为我们应该为您安排的一切事务。现在我等候您寄来讲稿,以便先行迻译。

专此敬候

钧安

徐志摩　敬启
一九二三年十二月二十七日
北京城西石虎胡同七号[①]

其实,徐志摩提供的材料并没有言过其实。实际上,当时中国的危机是有原因的,主要是由于两种相互对立的理想主义的冲突。由于

[①] 韩石山编:《徐志摩书信集》,天津人民出版社2006年版,第373—376页。

外国列强的剥削，当时中国的政治、经济、文化方面都遭到破坏，为了改变这种局面，一些接受苏维埃俄国社会主义理想的知识分子和青年中一部分人，决心要改造陈腐的社会制度。

在石什罗库马尔·达什和谭文所写的《引起争论的客人》一书中比较详细地讲述了当时中国的时局。他们写道："罗宾德罗纳特前往中国的时候，改革的风暴正在席卷全国。几年前在语言和文学领域空前的一场革命就开始了。过去的六七年来受过新式教育的社会群体就想在语言、文字书写、宗教思想、政治、社会等方面进行彻底变革。几年前（1919年）就爆发了历史性的五四运动。这期间（1921年）中国共产党成立了。左右两种思想的人都想进行社会改革和政治变革。为了快速变革，一群人就想快速使国家实现工业化。借助于机械打破陈腐的僵化状态，彻底根除陈腐的宗教思想。……为建设中国新社会，他们从日本，而不是从欧美获得了教益。他们追随的目标就是要像日本那样，日本曾借助于机械工业获得了强大的军事力量，中国也要成为这样强盛的主要国家，通过发展经济成为同欧洲国家一样的强国。看到了日本的进步，中国知识分子明白了，中国如果要想强盛起来，就必须依靠机械，只有机械才能摆脱精神枷锁。……西方的哲学，特别是约翰·杜威和伯特兰·罗素的思想鼓舞了这一群人，他们要从根本上改变占统治地位的孔子思想，而另一群人却受到俄国革命和马克思哲学的影响。五四运动之后无数文化组织开始诞生了，出现了外国文学翻译（泰戈尔文学是其中之一），开始详细地介绍马克思的思想，而且激进的政治意识开始觉醒了。"①

1924年1月22日，徐志摩在浙江硖石给恩厚之写过一封信，讲述中国为诗人泰戈尔来华所做的准备工作。

Tsenmou Hsu

---

① শিশিকুমার দাশ ও তান ওয়েন: বিতর্কিত অতিথি (১৯২৮), ১০-১১. 石什罗库马尔·达什和谭文：《引起争论的客人》（1924年），第10—11页。

Yeh Zah, Chijiang

22 January 1924

"Dear Mr. Elmhirst,

    I am glad that you are returned and can come with Mr. Tagore this spring. So we are to have the sage over at last! It would be a jolly delight to meet you here again. We were fully prepared last autumn to receive Mr. Tagore till his letter came further altering place .We had arranged to loan a private house in the west city where we could have steam heat and every modern comfort. We can still have that place if Mr. Tagore has no objection. I had tried to secure that beautiful little round city overlooking the three seas in the palace—the same place you visited, I think, the famous jade Buddha at I didn't succeed, mainly due to the political situation which rendered everything uncertain. In case Mr.Tagore has preferences for typical Chinese house, or even temple sort of thing, do be frank and tell me in time; these won't be much bother at all, you know our eagerness to so provide things as to make our great guest perfectly happy and contented with his trip to China. Do write to me as soon as possible concerning this point especially I expect Mr. Tagore is by now fully recovered from his recent ailments which made all of us very anxious and is strong enough to under take the voyage. You will be a great help in coming over with him.

    I have spent most of my time those months in the south. I lost my dear old granny four months ago and my mother was twice seriously ill, which has detained me here. I am now staying at the foot of our East-hill, a rather quiet and pleasant place amidst ruins and graves which count by hundreds. I am thinking of returning to Peking very soon, but I shall be at Shanghai again to meet you when you arrive. I just heard from Mr.Lowes Dickinson, complaining that you omitted to look him up perhaps you didn't have time .

By the way did you get the packet I sent you containing your seal and other things? I think the address was correct. Mr. Tagore has promised to send over beforehand his manuscript of his lectures to be translated into Chinese. We should be grateful to have them.

Best wishes to Mr. Tagore and Mr. Andrews and all your colleagues from all of us.

Tsemou Zhsu"

厚之先生：

喜悉你已经到步，又知道你和太戈尔先生能于今春来华。这样，我们中国人就将面见圣哲了，能再与你重聚实在是一件喜事。去年秋天我们一切都准备妥当要接待太戈尔先生，可是他来信说要改变行程。那时候我们已经在城西租了一间有暖气和现代设备的私宅。要是太戈尔先生不反对，我们还可以用那个地方的。我曾试借用在故宫内对着三海的团城，我想就是你参观过的那个地方，里面有那尊驰名远近的玉佛，可是我不成功，主要是因为政局不稳，一切事情也就难以确定了。如果太戈尔先生属意传统中国式的房子，或者庙宇之类的住处，请尽早见示，切勿客气。我们绝对没有麻烦，您知道我们一片热诚来备办一切，要使我们的伟大嘉宾在逗留中国期间感到全然喜乐和满足。关于这件事，盼尽早来信。我们相信太戈尔先生现在已完全康复，能够有足够的体力来做这次访问，他生病的消息使我们十分忧急，你能同他一起过来，对各方面都会很有帮助。

数月来我都在南方，四月前祖母谢世，家母也两次患重病，这都是我滞留此地的原因。我现驻东山脚下，周围有的是荒丘古迹，以及数以百计的坟墓，环境很是清静怡人的。我计划快要回北京了，不过我会再到上海。当你们到步之日，我在那边欢迎你们。我刚收到狄更生先生消息，他抱怨说你没有去看他，也许你没有时间。顺便问问你，你收到我寄给你的小邮包没有？包内有一个印章和其他的东西。我相信地址是写得正确的，太戈尔先生已经答应先把他的讲稿寄来，以便迻译为中文，为此先让我表示谢意。

我们这里大家都问候太戈尔先生、安德鲁先生以及你的同仁。

徐志摩启
一九二四年一月二十二日
浙江 硖石"①

徐志摩的这封信里包含一些有关诗人访华的信息：第一，诗人泰戈尔原计划1923年秋天访华，中国方面已经做好迎接诗人的准备，在城西为其租了一栋有暖气的住房，可是诗人因生病推迟了中国之行；第二，诗人泰戈尔已决定于1924年春天来华访问；第三，诗人泰戈尔答应徐志摩将在中国的讲演稿提前寄给徐志摩，以便他翻译成中文；第四，徐志摩近四个月来一直驻浙江硖石老家，因为他祖母病逝，母亲又患重病，尽管如此，他还是许诺，要来上海，欢迎诗人一行的到来。

1924年3月15日，诗人泰戈尔在写给拉奴的信里讲到他为前往中国做准备的情况，他在信中写道："你也许在想，此时我在加尔各答。因为轮船启航的时间临近了，可是现在我被静修院琐事缠身。后天星期二我要乘坐晚车去加尔各答。②这期间我想尽我可能要坐在这里写前往中国时要用的讲演稿。坐在你们那个二层房间里的窗子旁边写完第一个讲稿的最初几张纸。心里想我要把你从房间里赶走多少次，不过不会是很多次。我只写了4张纸，你就不让我继续写下去了。"③

当时的《欢乐市场报》在报道中写道，北京大学（讲学社）将为诗人泰戈尔中国之行提供往返路费。诗人前往其他国家花销以及学者基迪莫洪的路费，由焦格洛基绍尔·比罗拉资助，为此他提供了10000

---

① 韩石山编：《徐志摩书信集》，天津人民出版社2006年版，第303—309页。
② 此处有误，应该是星期六，而不是星期二。
③ রবীন্দ্রনাথ ঠাকুর, চিঠিপত্র ১৮, ১৮০.《泰戈尔书信集》第18卷，第140封信。

卢比资金。除此之外,波洛德殿·达什·比罗拉藩王和焦格洛基绍尔·比罗拉此前已经分别捐给国际大学20000卢比和3000卢比。依德拉尔·巴苏的路费一部分由国际大学支付,一部分由热心于印度绘画艺术的一些有钱人资助。恩厚之、格雷郴·葛玲女士的旅费由苏鲁尔基金会提供。利摩迪尔·垃吉库马尔作为诗人的同行者,他的花费由他个人承担。国际大学秘书写的这篇新闻报道提供的时间是准确的,诗人泰戈尔除了前往中国,他还计划访问日本、印度支那、柬埔寨、暹罗、爪哇,但是这一次除了中国和日本外,并没有再访问其他国家。

得知1923年秋天泰戈尔要来华访问,中国文化界顿时忙碌起来,《东方杂志》第20卷第14号、《小说月报》第14卷第9号和第10号、《佛化新青年》等报刊都出了泰戈尔专号;其他一些报刊,如《时事新报》《民国日报》《晨报》《民铎》《中国青年》等也都登载泰戈尔的翻译作品。

其实从1915年起,中国一些通晓英文的知识分子就开始翻译介绍泰戈尔了。陈独秀最早用文言文翻译发表了《吉檀迦利》中的4首诗,因此泰戈尔的名字已为中国读者所熟悉。通过新闻出版界的宣传,欢迎泰戈尔的气氛很快热了起来。青年诗人徐志摩赞美诗人泰戈尔,将其比喻为泰山日出:"一方的异彩,揭去了满天的睡意,唤醒了四隅的明霞——光明的神驹,在热奋地驰骋。"郑振铎先生在《欢迎泰戈尔》的一文中深情地预言,当诗人泰戈尔到达中国的时候,中国人一定会张开双臂拥抱他,当他做讲演时,人们一定会狂拍着巴掌。后来接触泰戈尔比较多的作家王统照也表达了对诗人泰戈尔的崇敬之情。他说自己在诗人面前总有一种渺小之感,他觉得诗人泰戈尔的"人格过于伟大,精神过于崇高"。

在《引起争论的客人》这本书中作者们用较长的篇幅论述了中国译介诗人泰戈尔的作品及其对中国的影响。

该书的作者们写道，1921年中国共产党成立了，中国知识界深入地学习和研究马克思主义思想，并且在中国呈现出强势的传播态势。当时在中国，除了马克思主义之外，其他外国的任何思想都遭到了怀疑和谴责，诗人泰戈尔也同样遭遇到此种情况。以前那些曾经陶醉于泰戈尔作品并且对其译著大加赞美的人们，学习了马克思主义之后就开始谴责和怀疑泰戈尔的思想，特别是曾经邀请他来中国访问的人们中有人的态度也就发生了变化。中国一部分持有这样观点的青年就对诗人泰戈尔表达不满。恩厚之从中国回到印度后，在他对诗人泰戈尔的汇报中，也没能清楚地说明当时中国政治和文学领域出现的复杂局面，所以诗人泰戈尔就为去中国写讲演稿之事感到难以下笔，因而拖延下来。实际上，诗人泰戈尔对于自己这次中国之行期间讲些什么，特别是对学生和青年人讲些什么，在思想上是处于犹豫的状态。这种犹豫心态在他于1924年2月28日写给罗曼·罗兰的信中表达出来：

"…I myself have a king of civil war constantly going on in my own nature between my personality as a creative artist who necessarity must be solitary and that as an idealist who must realise himself through works of a complex character needing a large field of collaboration with a large body of men… I suppose a proper rhythm is possible to be attained in which both may be harmonist, and my work in the heart of the crowd may find its gracethrough the touch of breath that comes from the solitude of the creative mind…in the meantime I go to China, in what capacity I do not know. Is it as a poet, or as a bearer of good advice and sound common sense?"[1]

（我自己有一个内战的国王，这种内战不断在我自己的本性和我的人格之间进行着。作为一个有创造性的艺术家一定是孤独的，作为一个理想主义者，必须意识到自己作品会扮演一个复杂的角色，需要在一个广大领域与大量人员合作……我想，适当的节奏是可能会获得

[1] 泰戈尔纪念馆保存的泰戈尔手稿。

的，可能和声学家以及我工作中心的人群合作，会发现其优雅的触摸来自于孤独气氛中的创造性思维……在此期间，我去中国，以什么身份，我不知道，是作为一个诗人，还是作为一个好建议和合理常识的传递者？）

3月20日，在阿利普尔气象局办公楼举行了为诗人访华的送别会，诗人泰戈尔在会上发表了讲话，他说，在他即将动身的时候这么多朋友来为他送行，他很感动，因此他就更加自信了。他年龄大了，身体也不好，这次远行对他来说还是有困难的。可是当他接到邀请函的时候，他是不能拒绝的。他觉得，这份邀请函已送达印度，而他作为印度的子孙是应该接受的。贫穷的印度没有任何丰盈的财富，没有任何政治荣耀，没有任何值得骄傲的军事成就，也不能生产大量的物质财富，不能参与列强的竞争。印度知道，只能运用自己精神力量所获得的文明最好结果——印度相信全人类会团结的。他强调地说，他感受到世界万物中都存在着团结，他知道这是真实的。诗人不晓得，中国呼唤他前往有什么期待，但是他只知道这一点，他应该带着这样的话语前往中国。这是一种重要责任，朋友们的美好祝福已赋予他勇气。他相信，他们的这次访问要为中国和印度之间的古老文化和精神关系重新打开交往之门。在两个国家之间如果能够建立起教师和学生的交流机制，那么，他们的这次中国之行就是成功的。[①]

在这一天诗人泰戈尔对新闻记者们说："When the invitation from China reached me I felt it was an invitation to India herself…I am hoping that our visit will reestablish the cultural and spiritual connection between China and India…"[②]

（当我收到中国的邀请时，我觉得这是对印度自己的邀请……我希望我们的访问将重建中印之间文化和精神方面的联系……）

[①] Vlsva-Buarati bulletin, No. part1. *From Calcutta to Peking* [1924] 2.《国际大学新闻简报》，1924年第2期，1号第1部分《从加尔各答到北京》。

[②] Kalidas Nag, *Tagore and China*, P.34. 迦利达斯·纳格：《泰戈尔与中国》，第34页。

泰戈尔第一次访华纪实

前往中国途中在缅甸停留

加尔各答 ○----○ 仰光 ○ 马来亚 ○ 新加坡 ○ 香港 ○ 上海 ○ 杭州 ○ 南京 ○ 济南 ○ 北京 ○ 太原 ○ 武汉 ○ 上海 ○

1924年3月21日上午7点，星期五，诗人泰戈尔一行乘坐英国船舶公司的"埃塞俄比亚"号邮轮前往中国访问。陪同诗人泰戈尔访华的有6个人：格雷梆·葛玲女士、恩厚之（雷纳德·恩厚之）、基迪莫洪·森（ক্ষিতিমোহন সেন）、侬德拉尔·巴苏（নন্দলাল বসু）、迦利达斯·纳格（কালিদাস নাগ），还有利摩迪尔·拉吉库马尔·寇诺沙姆·兴吉（লিমডির রাজকুমার ঘনশ্যাম সিংজি）。美国的研究人员stephen N.Hay曾经写道："泰戈尔一行人从加尔各答乘坐日本客轮'freighter Atsuta Maru'（'热田丸'号货轮）出发。"这种说法肯定是错误的。

　　第二天，诗人泰戈尔给拉奴的另一封信里描写了出发的情况："上午的时候我们来到了恒河的码头，登上轮船。……你爸爸和很多人来为我送行。……轮船大约是在9点的时候启航的。这是我们古老的恒河河岸——在我童年的时候这个河岸给了我多少时日的极大欢乐啊！……昨天多尔节①的圆月出现在恒河的上空。轮船停在沙滩上，等待着海水涨潮，直到晚上7点。如果大海上出现多尔节圆月，那么，这个节日的名称就有价值了——那样的话，摇晃也会出现，我们就会看到洁白与蔚蓝相融、月华与大海交汇的美景。今天早晨，我起来后就看到了轮船在平静的水面上航行，'温馨的和风习习地吹拂着。'今天是星期六。我听说，我们于星期一到达仰光。"②

陪同诗人泰戈尔同行的伙伴们的一项责任，就是给诗人的儿子罗廷德罗纳特写信，向他传达有关诗人泰戈尔的消息。恩厚之是诗人泰戈尔的秘书，他经常向报刊邮寄报道稿，并且利用报道稿和寄来的报道做些摘录，还收集了《国际大学新闻简报》的头两期。除此之外，他为诗人泰戈尔保存那本写有讲演稿的笔记本，并且还要将诗人的讲演稿打印出来，这也是他的日常工作。基迪莫洪·森告诉恩厚之，3月23日诗人泰戈尔已经动手写在中国的演讲稿了，并且说第一部演讲稿很长，诗人泰戈尔要对其进行压缩和润色，改写成第二稿。

跟随诗人泰戈尔访华的迦利达斯·纳格有写日记的习惯，尽管写得很简短，但是在他日记里保存有这次出行的很多细节描写——这些细节描写都收入他撰写的那本于1987年出版的《同诗人在一起100天》的那本书里。利用这记录本，迦利达斯·纳格先生还从《孟加拉之声》《东方来信》《当代评论》上搜集到一些素材，为他后来出版的两本书《罗宾德罗纳特·泰戈尔国际大学的使命》（1924年9月号，第288—301页）和《泰戈尔和中国》（1945年）做准备。

《罗比传记》的作者普罗山多库玛尔·巴尔写道，他知道，诗人泰戈尔每一次国外之行都会写给各种人士书信或日记。可是有关这一次出行的这类材料，他却没有找到，对此他感到很奇怪。现在只好采

---

① 多尔节——即印度的撒红节，印度教徒的霍利节（the Holi festival），孟加拉人称其为"多尔节"（দোল），দোল一词的词义就有"摇晃"之意。
② চিঠিপত্র, ১৮, ২৬৬-২৬৭, পত্র ১৪১,《泰戈尔书信集》第18卷，第141封信，第266—267页。

用诗人泰戈尔写给拉奴的信件来弥补这种缺失。从迦利达斯·纳格的日记里得知，3月22日缅甸总督和驻缅甸华侨团体的邀请电报已经送达诗人泰戈尔所乘坐的轮船上。

1924年3月21日上午，诗人一行乘坐轮船从加尔各答港口出发，在海上航行了3天，于3月24日星期一上午8点，轮船抵达缅甸首都仰光。轮船在码头抛锚之前，缅甸欢迎会的几个特别成员乘坐一艘快艇登上轮船，对诗人泰戈尔表示欢迎。轮船到达码头后，著名商人J.E.K.贾马尔给诗人戴上花环，一名缅甸少女送上一束鲜花，对诗人泰戈尔表示敬爱。然后大家一起前往比甘德特大街的一栋装饰华丽的大楼。缅甸总督哈尔寇特·布特雷先生（Sir Harcourt Butler）设午宴招待诗人泰戈尔一行。

当日晚上5点半，在仰光最大的剧院大厅举行有5000人参加的欢迎大会，大会由U.tuk.kyi（吴图吉——音译）主持，会上宣读了欢迎词。现将其中一部分摘录如下：

> We greet you in the name of that universal culture which you have promoted with admirable devotion and singleness of aim. We greet you in the name of human brotherhood, the inculcation of which in east and west has been with you a consuming passion. We greet you as a votary of truth sensed through beauty. We greet you as one representing the rebirth of Asia, as one who has thrown across the chasm of ignorance and misunderstanding a bridge of future comprehension between Asia and Eur-America. We greet you as the lineal descendant of philosopher-seers of ancient India, who at the dawn of civilization proclaimed the unity of life, and knew humanity for one family transcending barriers of race and clime.[①]

（我们以您那种令人钦佩的献身精神和一心一意推动世界文化的

[①] রবীন্দ্রনাথ ৯/৬১. 孟加拉文版《罗比传记》第9卷，第61页。

名义欢迎您。我们以人类兄弟情谊的名义欢迎您,在东方和西方,这种兄弟情谊一直伴随着您那种强烈的激情。我们欢迎您,是把您看作是一位通过美来感知真理的信仰者。我们欢迎您,因为您代表了亚洲的重生,因为您跨越了无知和误解的鸿沟,在亚洲和欧美之间架起了一座未来理解的桥梁。我们欢迎您,是把您看作是印度古代哲学家和预言家的直系后裔,他们在文明之初就宣布了生命的统一,并知道人类是超越种族和气候障碍的一个大家庭。)

  诗人泰戈尔发表了长篇讲话,作为对欢迎词的回答。他说,世界每一个民族作出的贡献都是全世界人类的共同财富。从前印度同其他国家所建立的关系,不是建立在货物交换和扩展王权的基础之上,而是建立在某种伟大理想的基础之上。这个国家有过值得骄傲的过去,印度的宗教和文化使者穿越高山前往遥远的国家,他们所带去的一切将会成为传播亲情的纽带——传递友谊的理想就是印度对世界历史作出的杰出贡献。①

  3月25日星期三,这里的孟加拉人文学协会刊物《仰光邮报》(Rangoon Mail)的主编内特里彭德罗琼德罗·般多巴泰,主持欢迎诗人泰戈尔一行的大会。摩亚杰姆·阿利在会上宣读了欢迎词。《罗比传记》作者普罗山多库玛尔·巴尔先生写道:"撰写这份欢迎词和组织欢迎大会的,是当地孟加拉人学校校长莫希多库马尔·穆科巴泰和文学家苏提罗琼德罗库玛尔·乔杜里。他们还组织了一场缅甸少女的舞蹈演出。"②莫希多库马尔是缅甸少女舞蹈表演者的长兄。《国际大学新闻简报》报道了有关上述缅甸少女舞蹈及文学晚会的情况:"provided the best entertainment for the poet by organizing a classical Burmese dance party to the accompaniment of Burmese orchestra dominated by a dainty Burmese girl interpreting ten delicate dance rhythms

----

① রবিজীবনী ৯/৬২. 孟加拉文版《罗比传记》第9卷,第62页。
② 参见 রবিজীবনী ৩/১৭৮. 《罗宾德罗传记》第3卷,第178页。

of Burma, which fascinated the poet and provoked the cerebrated artist nandalal bosu to draw a series of quick sketches while the dance was going on."

（文学晚会为诗人提供了最好的娱乐，还组织了一场古典缅甸舞蹈表演，由缅甸管弦乐队伴奏，由一位优雅的缅甸女孩表演，演绎了十种精彩的缅甸舞蹈，这使诗人很着迷。著名艺术家侬德拉尔·巴苏在少女表演舞蹈时画了一些素描画。）

诗人泰戈尔在寄给拉奴的信中也描写那场晚会的盛况："前天晚上一位缅甸姑娘为我表演了舞蹈。她的舞蹈非常迷人，仿佛就像是随着时而从东方时而从南方吹拂的习习和风之波，在多彩多姿的蔓藤上翩翩舞动戏耍。"在文学晚会上诗人泰戈尔发表了讲话，迦利达斯·纳格记录了讲话的全文并将其刊登在《孟加拉之声》杰斯塔月号（第514—516页）上。

3月26日星期三，在仰光城郊区的一所华人学校（Kemmendine School）代表旅居缅甸的华人举行了欢迎诗人泰戈尔的聚会。欢迎会由Tao Sein ko（陶新科——音译）赞助，校长Lim No Chiong（林诺琼——音译）发表了讲话，对诗人泰戈尔一行人表示热烈欢迎，他说："I have no doubt that this mission of Dr. Tagore and illustrious company will mark another epoch of great spiritual influence upon the people of China, such has had been felt in the days of the Tang dynasty when the teaching of Buddha flourished in China… we hope that through his efforts, the best which is in the East and the West may be made to shine side by side and to contribute to the progress, the unity and the perfection of the whole world."

（我毫不怀疑，承担这个使命的泰戈尔博士和他的杰出代表团将会开辟另一个时代，这个时代将为中国人民带来巨大的精神影响，就像在唐朝的岁月感受佛教在中国蓬勃发展一样。……我希望，通过他的努力能呈现出最好的局面,就是东方和西方可以肩并肩绽放光彩,并为整个世界的进步、团结和完美和谐作出贡献。)①

这位校长随后将他代表华人宣读的这份欢迎词装入一个镶嵌着象牙的小盒子里,赠送给诗人泰戈尔。诗人泰戈尔在致答词中说,从前一个时期印度的传道者们带着新的生命哲学理想前往中国,印度和中国双方在文学、艺术和科学领域融洽地开启了伟大的精神交流。诗人指出:"我们出生的这个当今时代的主要特点就是生命力的强大。我们不要对它恐惧。它也会犯错误,也会考验一切"。最后诗人说:"Do not try to keep yourself secure from such blunders by remaining in your tombstones, so the newly awakened China will, through mistakes, find her truth....We in the East have believed in some fundamental reality, some great philosophy of life and if we can keep that truth in the centre of our being, then we have the privilege to walk abroad courting disaster and death and yet attain immortality ...that is the message which I shall take to your country."②

(不要试图通过待在你们的墓碑里来保护自己免于犯错误。新觉醒的中国将通过错误找到她自己的真实形象……我们东方人相信基本的真理和伟大的人生哲学,如果我们能把这个真理放在我们生命的中心,那么,我们就会拥有面对灾难和死亡的特权,从而获得永生……这就是我要带给你们国家的信息。)

诗人泰戈尔回国后,于1924年7月21日在国际大学一个学院举行的欢迎会上谈到了他在仰光的体验,他说:"我在第一个码头下了船,那是缅甸的仰光。你们都知道,在世界历史上仰光不只是属于缅甸人的国家,在那里除了缅甸居民,还有各个国家的人们居住,有很多中国人住在那里。当时我发现,印度人对我都表示尊敬,即使不尊

---

① রবীন্দ্রনাথ ৯/৬২. 孟加拉文版《罗比传记》,第9卷,第62页。
② রবীন্দ্রনাথ ৯/৬২. 孟加拉文版《罗比传记》,第9卷,第62页。

敬,也没有什么关系。然后当中国朋友们邀请我去做客的时候,我内心感到很满足。这是我第一次结识中国人。在那里有一所中国人的学校。为了表示对我的欢迎,这所学校的校长邀请我去他们那里。因此我感到很高兴。那一天我第一次感受到中国人的好客。他们很尊敬地对我说:'你要讲什么,请提前告诉我们,因为我们都不懂英语。我们会立即把你要说的话翻译成中国话。'我说,我现在不能确切地说,我要讲什么。不过大概的情况就是,我去过一些国家,我接到过邀请,我做过讲演,我并非没赢得过尊敬,但是有一种情况我不知道,我现在去中国就是为了了解当前中国的情况,因此这种情况对我很有吸引力。这是一种什么情况?我晓得,在这里我接触人很多。当我接到我们东方国家邀请的时候,我真的受到过热情的款待。我感受到发出邀请的家庭主人的热心友善。我不仅会获得掌声,不仅会获得他们的物质奖赏,我还会获得他们那种火热的心。我就是怀着这种信念去中国的。在他们的家里很多人都受到过热烈的欢迎。在我的命运中是绝不会不受到亲人般的热烈欢迎的,我已经完全感受到了这种热情的欢迎,但是我们的种姓制度是与有亲情的人们没有联系的,他们在语言、情感、宗教和行为方面是有区别的,当亲情从那里涌来,亲情的不朽激流从人性的源泉喷涌而出,冲破一切束缚,冲破笼罩在敌意外面的迷雾的时候,就可以享受到蕴藏在人们内心里的自然之光,即亲情之光,这是值得赞美的。我从你们这里带走这种唯一的希冀而动身,那些侨居在外国的、讲着外国语的人们会把我当成自己国家的人,我也会把他们当成自己的同胞,我会接受他们的热心关爱,人类再也没有比这更珍贵的东西了。"[1]

1924年3月27日星期四上午,诗人泰戈尔给拉奴写了一封信,讲述他在仰光的感受:"今天轮船停在仰光已经三天了。这里的人民群

---

[1] চীন ও জাপানে ভ্রমণবিবরণ, প্রবাসী কার্তিক ১৩৩১,৯৩–৯৮.《中国和日本之行纪实》,《侨民》杂志1924年迦尔迪克月号,第93—94页。

众簇拥着我把我接到陆地上。他们一起成立了一个叫作接待会的组织。这个接待会的人员来到我的身边高喊着欢迎罗宾德罗纳特·泰戈尔的口号,给我戴上花环,请我吃咖喱对虾。在这个城市中心建有一个二层的大厦,在这座大厦里人员和蚊子日夜都在嗡嗡叫着。这个接待会让我下午四点到会,后来又说是五点半到会场,此后在七点才到会,然后在九点半参加宴会,轮番请我吃东西。那个接待会成员扶我登上讲台,让我发表讲话,而宴会的主持人说,我是贤哲诗人、知识渊博的教师、爱国者,等等。听着他的述说,我才相信,他所讲述的那些话语并不完全符合实际,他们只是将所有美好的优点都集中到我的身上,点起一把赞美之火。现在只好让消防队来灭火,若能从涅槃中获得解脱,我就得救了。今天下午二点过后,诗人才能从接待会中解脱出来,就像摆脱了天狗吞日一样。今天是星期四,轮船要在下午4点时启航,我们要在两点之前到达码头。名叫接待会的这个组织——用数百种声音高呼着口号——在我身后撕破喉咙似的喊叫:诗人万岁,罗宾德罗纳特·泰戈尔万岁。"①

当时诗人泰戈尔承载着花环和羞赧的重负,低着头静静地坐在由年轻体壮的两匹马拉着的敞篷马车上,他实在找不到让激动的人群声波平静下来的方法。

在这里他们结识了一位中国女大学生。迦利达斯·纳格在他的日记里写道:"诗尊同一位中国女大学生林贤英(Lin Siang Ying音译)女士进行交谈,感到十分高兴。她提供了很多关于中国的消息,她是位好姑娘。"

3月28日,诗人泰戈尔在写给拉奴的信里也提到这位女士:"在动身的前一天,我同一位中国姑娘进行过交谈。她是北京大学的一位女大学生。她的愿望是去国际大学留学,至少在那里待一年,在我身边研究文学。在这么短的时间内她同我就建立了深厚的感情,这使我

---

① ‍রবীন্দ্র ১৮৷৬৮-২৬৯, পত্র ১৪২. 泰戈尔《书信集》第18卷,第142封信,第268-269页。

感到很惊奇。我到了码头就发现,她已经来到了码头。轮船停在河口中间的不远处,一艘小汽艇成为运送所有乘客的工具。那位姑娘也登上了轮船。她握住我的手说:'您就要走了,我很难过。希望您回来的时候我能再见到您。'当小船靠近我们轮船的时候我说了一声'再见'。她扑到我的怀里——周围的人们都不理解她的行为,于是大家都笑起来。我走进我的舱室洗过脸,在整理东西的时候,她和她的一位男士亲属走进来。她把恩厚之叫来,对他说:'你要特别关照诗人,要注意照看他,不要让他的身体疲惫和生病啊。'恩厚之笑着说:'我不能承担这么繁重的任务,你来代替我吧。'她说:'如果我去方便,我一定会去的,你会看到我是如何关心照顾诗人的。'她一边说着一边用双手握住我的手。当轮船即将启航的时候,她的亲戚才将她拉走。"①

迦利达斯·纳格在日记中写道:"诗人泰戈尔与俄国音乐家普列米兹洛夫夫妇进行了交谈。"

诗人在第二天所写一封信里也写道:"普列米兹洛夫及其夫人为我演奏了小提琴和大提琴,他们都是朴实厚道之人。"诗人泰戈尔在这一封信里也提到了此人和与其同行的其他旅客:"同我们乘坐一艘轮船同行的一位小提琴大师普列米兹洛夫和他的夫人。我们同他们经常聚在一起。还有很多男女乘客,但是我觉得,他们离我很远,仿佛是在大海的对岸。"

恩厚之在寄给诗人泰戈尔的儿子罗廷德罗纳特的信中写道,普列米兹洛夫夫妇在槟榔屿下船,他们希望在北京能再与诗人泰戈尔会面。

----

① 后藏卅1b卷91-292. 第143封信,第271—272页。

泰戈尔第一次访华纪实

在马来亚停泊

加尔各答 ○----仰光 ○----马来亚 ○ 新加坡 ○ 香港 ○ 上海 ○ 杭州 ○ 南京 ○ 济南 ○ 北京 ○ 太原 ○ 武汉 ○ 上海 ○

3月29日晚上，槟榔屿已散发过传单，通告人民群众：明天上午10点著名印度诗人泰戈尔将抵达这座城市。3月30日星期天上午，诗人泰戈尔乘坐的轮船抵达马来亚。当天上午很多人都聚集在码头上。轮船到达码头之前，当地的议会议员P.K.南比亚尔律师和其他几位著名人士乘坐小艇登上轮船向诗人泰戈尔表示欢迎。诗人在这一天写给拉奴的信里也描述了那一天的情况：

"我的天啊，怎么这么多的人呐！我觉得，槟榔屿城所有的男人都聚集在这里了。鼓乐手们站在我的面前吹着唢呐，敲锣打鼓，鼓乐声震天。一群人走过来，将一些大花环戴在我的脖颈上，以此表示对我的欢迎。脖颈上再也没有地方了——花环遮盖了我的半个脸，花环压得我抬不起头来。眼镜都要小心地保护着，呼吸都感到困难。我十分艰难地挤过稠密的人群，坐上了汽车，可是汽车如何能开动呢？数千人在车子右侧挤来挤去，他们想触摸我的脚，要向我行触脚大礼。汽车在骚动的人群中间十分缓慢地行驶着。我乘坐的汽车勉强地开到一座大楼前。……右侧车窗的下面是一条大街。这条大街站满了人,都是为了瞧看我。"①

在诗人泰戈尔的描述中没有一点夸大,《海峡回声报》3月31日报道可以证实这一点:"A party of Indian musicians played weird airs on their sharp-pitched instruments…after the great poet had stepped on to the gangway there was a rush to offer the usual floral tribute…with great difficulty that he was got into a car and home away…the distinguishe guest was driven to residence of the Hon. P. K. Nambyar in Farquhar Street,where large crowds besieged him throughout the day."

(一群印度音乐家用他们尖锐的乐器演奏着奇妙的曲调……这位伟大的诗人踏上舷梯后,人们像往常一样争先恐后地献上鲜花……费了好大的力气他才被扶上汽车,来到主人的家里……这位尊贵的客人被送到法夸尔大街南比亚尔议员的住所,在那里他整天都被一大群人围绕着。)

诗人泰戈尔对于这种表达尊爱的热情从来都不喜欢,所以他在给拉奴的信中写道:"有一种东西直到今天我都不习惯,而且永远都不会习惯。当一群人为表达对我的尊爱仿佛就像暴雨一样挤到我的身边,给我行触脚大礼,我是绝不能接受的。总觉得如此的不可理喻,我的心情就会因此而不愉悦。……我常常为表示反对而企图加以阻止,可是其效果恰恰相反,因为我越谦虚,人们的崇敬就越是强烈。"

诗人泰戈尔整个中午都在这座大楼里休息,而他的同伴们都去山上参观一座佛教寺庙了。后来诗人泰戈尔回到国际大学,在一次讲话中谈到在马来亚的体验时说道:

"我去过很多国家旅游,但是在马来亚我看到一种令人惊奇的景象,使我感到快乐。那就是有一个像码头一样的地方,在那里经常

---

① [孟加拉文] 18卷273—278页, 144封信。泰戈尔《书信集》第18卷,第144封信,第273—274页。

有中国、日本、爪哇、苏门答腊、澳大利亚等国家的人们来来往往。在那里各个不同国家的人们住在一起，尽管如此，他们彼此之间没有任何敌对的意识。……来自中国比较多的是以劳动谋生的人，他们来到马来亚半岛，几乎占据着整个马来亚，本地居民都是不爱劳动的。……来自印度的人都是以劳动谋生，其中多数是马德拉斯人，也有一些旁遮普的锡克人。来自中国的都是华南人……看起来，他们都很富裕，他们拥有土地，拥有大片的橡胶园——中国人从内心都流露出富裕的迹象……而从我们国家来这里的人们，其身上都呈现出贫穷的表情。……马德拉斯苦力是不受尊敬的一类人……这里的人都称呼所有印度人为苦力。他们中百分之三十或四十的人都要拼命地劳动才能长期生活下去，他们都没有剩余钱财。……那些没有一点儿剩余钱财的人们不得不世世代代从事奴隶般的劳动，因此马德拉斯人都是不被尊重的……从马德拉斯来这里的人们虽然都住在一起，但是他们彼此都不能保持相互尊敬。……都企图相互进行剥削。他们在自己内部都在使用上层使用的那种剥削手段相互削弱对方。……

有一群旁遮普的锡克人，他们支持王权政府。当政府镇压其他人的时候，他们就肩负起被人们所憎恨的那种工作重担，其后果也同样悲惨。他们因支持政府而拥有权力，并为此显得傲慢。当一个奴才认为自己是主人并以主人的气势欺压别人和乱用权力的时候，就再也没有像他们这种行为那样恶毒而令人憎恨的了。……我在马来亚半岛并没有看到这种现象，但是在中国却看到了，如此十分可恶的行为是不会再施加给任何其他民族头上的。锡克人抓住中国人的头发用棍棒殴打他们，就连英国警察都不会这样做。他们哪里还有人性和善良悲悯呢，在这种奴才锡克人内心里人性和善良是一点儿也看不到的，他们的行动刺伤了我的心。"①

传来消息说，轮船在3月30日下午6点启航，所以大家于5点半就

---

① প্রবাসী, কার্তিক 1331 ৯৫-৯৬. 《侨民》迦尔迪克月号，第95—96页。

来到了码头，可是又听说，轮船启航的时间推迟到夜里10点钟，所以主人就陪同诗人泰戈尔乘坐汽车参观槟榔屿风景名胜去了。

傍晚大家在南比亚尔先生家里用过晚餐，然后就前往码头登船了。随后轮船就启航了。

1924年3月31日星期一下午1点，轮船抵达库亚拉拉普尔城的码头，接待委员会的几位成员把诗人泰戈尔及其一行人从轮船上接下来，将他们送到位于300英里外的库亚拉拉普尔城，诗人泰戈尔一行被安排在拉姆沙米先生的家里。

下午波雷绍纳特博士、库马尔沙米先生、菲拉斯先生（Mr. H.N.Ferrars）等人组织了一场市民欢迎会，并且承诺要为国际大学募捐。在波雷绍纳特的家里吃过晚餐，大家又回到船上。

晚上7点轮船启航前往新加坡。诗人泰戈尔离开孟加拉邦时没有下雨，那里呈现一片荒凉凄惨的状态，因此诗人很不开心。而在这里雨水充沛，呈现出生机勃勃的景象。他在写给拉奴的信里表达了当时他的欣喜心情：

"……我们乘坐三辆汽车离开码头。道路两旁有的地方是浓密的树林，有的地方是一片橡胶树，中间有华人街区，有的地方是马来亚人的村庄。在任何别的地方都没有见过如此茂密的树木。……蓝天被乌云遮盖着。这种云影与这里的树荫看上去，就像是婚礼上新郎和新娘交换的花环和维系两个人衣襟的纽带一样——碧绿的大地和天空融合在一起。……在离开印度之前很长时间孟加拉邦因为缺少雨水都在苦度艰难的干旱时光。……我想起了《鸠摩罗出世》的故事。天空仿佛就像湿婆一样在进行忘我的可怕苦修。……大地也像在进行苦修的杜尔伽女神一样。我们静修院里的树叶都已经枯黄。大地仿佛都要成为连树叶都不食的苦修的杜尔伽女神。……而在这里当天空的厚重云层中开始电闪雷鸣的时候，透过森林我看到这种宏伟景象，心里就充满了喜悦。当我们接近城市的时候下起了何等大的暴雨啊！简直就是激流在不断地下泄。这样大的暴雨，多少天来我都不曾见过。我无法述说我是何等喜悦啊！我都被淋湿了，可是我并没有因此而苦恼。"①

在第二天，即1924年4月1日，诗人泰戈尔在前往新加坡的轮船上又给拉奴写了一封信。拉奴3月31日开始中级艺术考试。当时诗人泰戈尔正在开往南方的轮船上，在气温逐渐增高的狭小舱室里忙于撰写在中国的讲演稿。诗人泰戈尔将这讲两种情况加以对比时写道："我的考试困难即便小一点儿，也不比你的考试少。我就像回答考试题一样在认真地写着。你可以在考场安逸地写着答卷，我几乎整天坐在舱室内的床铺上撰写着讲演稿。前面一张桌子也没有。3点时西面的阳光还照进舱室里，直到夜里10点钟舱室内的空气都使人厌倦。我的命运不错，舱室里有一台电风扇，这部电风扇日日夜夜在我的头上呼呼地转着，而我就在电扇下按住稿纸在书写着。如果你在试卷纸上像我这样书写，你是否能够通过一级考试，是值得怀疑的。就这样我已经写完了两部讲演稿。第三部讲演稿也写了不少了。总共要写六篇讲演稿。"②

诗人的秘书恩厚之也有记载："gurudev has advanced with his third lecture, in which I believe he is sketching his ideal or drama. I have just finished typing the second one… in spite of lack of convenient writing place gurudev works hard neayly all day sitting propped at on his bunk, and is full of fun at meat times."

"我相信，师尊在他的第三部演讲中更进了一步，他是在描绘他的理想或佛法。我刚打完第二份……尽管缺乏方便的写作场所，师尊几乎整天都坐在他的铺位上努力工作，在吃饭的时候他心里也充满了

---

① রবীন্দ্র, ১৮/২৭৬, পৃষ্ঠা ১৪৫. 泰戈尔《书信集》第18卷，第145封信，第276页。
② রবীন্দ্র, ১৮/২৭৬, পৃষ্ঠা ১৪৬. 泰戈尔《书信集》第18卷，第146封信，第277—278页。

愉悦。"

迦利达斯·纳格在日记中也写道:"诗人在轮船上整天忙于撰写他的讲演稿。"

诗人泰戈尔最初的计划是,访问过中国和日本之后,他打算带领他的一行人去游览印度支那、苏门答腊、爪哇、暹罗国等古代印度教和佛教传播到的国家,他要重新开启印度与这些国家具有悠久历史的文化交流之门。

恩厚之在前往新加坡的途中写给罗廷德罗纳特的信里说,他们准备走一条新的路线:从香港前往印度支那,从那里前往暹罗。如果在暹罗接到邀请,他们就要经过曼谷前往新加坡。已经告知马来亚,诗人泰戈尔在前往爪哇之前要在那里至少度过10—15天。

在新加坡和中国香港停留

泰戈尔第一次访华纪实

加尔各答○--- 仰光○--- 马来亚○--- 新加坡○--- 香港○ 上海○ 杭卅○ 南京○ 济南○ 北京○ 太原○ 武汉○ 上海○

诗人泰戈尔一行乘坐的"埃塞俄比亚"号轮船于4月2日上午9点钟抵达新加坡码头。前来迎接诗人泰戈尔一行的人们早早就在海岸边的码头上等候了。欢迎委员会的秘书长L.G.科兰纳先生热情地欢迎诗人的到来，但是他又深情地说，由于诗人行程计划的原因，新加坡市民们就没有更多一点儿的时间接待泰戈尔先生了，因此他们感到很遗憾。一位名叫Low Kway Song（宋娄宽——音译）的艺术家赠送给诗人泰戈尔一幅油画。Grranville Roberts赠送给诗人泰戈尔一部书的复制本，这本书的作者是宋鸿祥，书名为 *One Hundred Years of the Chinese in Singapore*（《华人在新加坡的一百年》）。

迦利达斯·纳格在日记中写道："印度各界社团的朋友们把我们接走了。住在这里的一位孟买的大人物达武德先生把诗人泰戈尔安排在他的豪华住宅里休息。"达武德先生又请诗人泰戈尔一行在他家里共进午餐。诗人一行在新加坡逗留将近4天。

4月5日下午诗人泰戈尔一行改乘日本的"热田丸"号轮船，前往香港，因为"埃塞俄比亚"号轮船要开往澳大利亚。在这里顺便提一句，一些书刊所写的诗人一行离开新加坡日期有误，例如《国际大学新闻简报》和《罗宾德罗传记》都提到诗人一行离开新加坡是4月7日。

诗人泰戈尔在寄给拉奴的信中这样写道："在新加坡我登上了另一艘轮船。一看名称，我就明白了，这是日本轮船。在这里我所需要的一切都已准备好了。船长对我说，我有什么需要就对他讲，他会提供我所需的一切。早晨其他旅客都在喝茶的时候我还得到了橘子，当时我要求菠萝，于是就送来了菠萝。轮船规定在8点半之前要洗完澡，大家都急忙去洗澡了。我派人告诉船长我要在11点半洗澡，他也满足了我的要求。……他得到消息，在甲板上我的座椅两个扶手上如果放一个长条木板，我写作时就会感到方便，于是他就叫来轮船上的修理工为我安装了一个长条木板。我真的赢得了很多声誉，不过还是应该承认，因为有了一些声誉，也就会有方便之处。"[1]

轮船上各国的旅客很多，船上虽然没有空闲的位置，可是船长还是为诗人泰戈尔提供了一间舱室。

泰戈尔还兴致勃勃地告诉拉奴，在船上举行的舞会上因为缺少女舞伴，恩厚之不得不让利摩迪尔·拉吉库马尔去做舞伴。如果拉奴在场，肯定会让她去做舞伴的。随后他又写道："今天晚上他们还要举行穿着奇异服装的舞会——即被称为化装舞会。我对恩厚之说，应该穿上围裤，围上披肩，打扮成孟加拉人的样子。男青年缠上包头巾，打扮成王子的模样。葛玲小姐毫无顾虑，她脱下纱丽，从马来亚姑娘那里借来服装、首饰等各种华丽的装束。不一会儿工夫，她就穿戴得很华美，看起来超过了当地的所有姑娘。"[2]

---

[1] 孟加拉文，১৮/২৭৬,পৃষ্ঠা ১৪৬．泰戈尔《书信集》第18卷，第147封信，第279—280页。
[2] 孟加拉文，১৮/২৭৬,পৃষ্ঠা ১৪৬．泰戈尔《书信集》第18卷，第147封信，第279—280页。

在新加坡和中国香港停留　039

1924年4月7日，诗人泰戈尔在给他儿媳妇普罗蒂玛的信中写道："今天已接近香港。可是天气很不好。一路很不顺利。海上本来是平静的，从前天起船体开始摇晃——这使得基迪莫洪和侬德拉尔等人感到很不舒服。今天他们都用忐忑不安的目光凝视着大陆的方向。我只是坐在甲板一个角落里写讲演稿——苦命人在天堂也得不到休息啊。"

海上的波涛也使迦利达斯·纳格感到不适。他在4月5日和6日的日记里都记载：sea sickness（晕船）。

4月7日上午10点，轮船在香港码头抛锚停泊。香港虽然是中国的城市，可当时是受英国殖民统治的商业中心。来码头上欢迎诗人泰戈尔的有：新建立的香港大学副校长霍纳尔（W.W.Hornell）、该大学的教务主任马斯金多士（N.T.Maskintosh）、西尼亚尔和久尼亚尔父子、鲁斯彤吉（J.H.Rustomjee）、尼玛兹先生（Mr.Nemazi Bishen Sing）等印度各社团代表。孟加拉邦前教育部部长D.P.I霍内尔是诗人泰戈尔以前认识的熟人，他本来建议在他自己家里接待诗人泰戈尔，可是他也同意其他印度人的要求，于是他们就把诗人泰戈尔接到城外的一个幽静的浅水湾酒店（Repulse Bay Hotel），商人尼玛兹接待了其他客人，他的家就在酒店隔壁。诗人泰戈尔踏上香港的土地之后，附近一些地区部门也来邀请他。厦门大学的副校长Dr.Llm Bong Keng（林伯铿博士——音译）亲自来邀请他前往厦门大学发表演讲，并且提出建议在该大学为研究印度历史和文化为他设置一个教授职位。最高规格的邀请是来自中华民国总统孙中山先生。他在邀请函里写道：

"Dear Mr. Tagore, I should greatly wish to have the privilege of personally welcoming you on your arrival in China. It is an ancient way of ours to show honor to the scholar, but in you I shall greet not only a writer who has added lustre to Indian letters but a rare worker in those fields of endeavor wherein lie the seeds of man's future welfare and spiritual triumphs.May I then have the pleasure of inviting you to canton?"

(亲爱的泰戈尔先生：

我非常希望能有幸亲自欢迎您来到中国。这是我们向学者表示敬意的一种古老方式，但我要向你致敬的不仅因为您是一位为印度文坛增光添彩的作家，而且是一位在为人类未来的幸福和精神胜利而埋下种子的罕见的努力工作者。那我可以邀请你来广州吗？）

诗人泰戈尔没能答应这一邀请，他是应讲学社的邀请来中国讲学的，若去广州，就会耽搁很多时间，他向孙中山的私人秘书讲述了这一原因并表示遗憾，他许诺在返回的途中争取去广州，但是这一许诺也没能实现。当时苏维埃俄国与中国南方共和国签订了友好条约，如果他接受邀请去广州，很可能北京的社会主义者和知识分子反对诗人泰戈尔的情绪就会低落一些。

在香港大学和其他社会团体给诗人发来了很多邀请函，请他去发表演讲。可是由于没有时间他都没能接受。《中国邮报》（China Mail）写道："Tagore goes north to Peking on mission that excites our interest and envy. The North is fortunate, as fortunate as we hope Hongkong may be when the return journey has to be make, in no place than Hongkong is the doctrine of this poet more worthy of preachment and acceptance."（泰戈尔北上北京的使命激发了我们的兴趣和羡慕。北方是幸运的，就像我们希望他在回程时能来香港一样幸运，没有任何地方比香港更值得宣扬和接受这位诗人的学说了。）但是香港居民的这一愿望也没能得到满足。

在离开香港之前，当地锡克社团为诗人泰戈尔一行在锡克教神庙举行了一场颂歌演唱会。诗人泰戈尔出席了这场演唱会。

诗人泰戈尔一行乘坐的轮船，很可能是在4月8日夜里离开香港前往上海的。轮船在海上航行的时候诗人泰戈尔一直在撰写他的讲演稿。迦利达斯·纳格在这一天的日记里写道："我对诗人的第三篇讲演稿进行审读后提出一些建议。"

4月10日，诗人泰戈尔在给拉奴的信中写道："我们正向上海码头航行。今天是星期四，后天星期六上午我们抵达目的地。然后要在陆地上活动一些时间。我们在香港下船，在那里度过两天时光。那个地方很好，但是天空显得抑郁不爽，被云雾阴雨所笼罩。气温比以前降低了，突然降低近20度……越往北走越凉爽。……这么多天来，我坐在轮船甲板上一个寂静的角落里晒太阳。几乎一整天都靠坐在一张宽大的沙发上，凝视着洒落到大海波浪上的太阳光。……今天四周那么一点儿晒太阳角落也消失了。由于阴雨天气寒冷，我被急匆匆地扶回舱室。"①

---

① রচনাবলী ১৮/২৮২-২৮৩, পত্র ১৪৯，泰戈尔《书信集》，第18卷，第148封信，第282—283页。

泰戈尔第一次访华纪实

抵达上海

加尔各答 ○－－－○ 仰光 ○－－－○ 马来亚 ○－－－○ 新加坡 ○－－－○ 香港 ○－－－○ 上海 ○　　杭州 ○　　南京 ○　　济南 ○　　北京 ○　　太原 ○　　武汉 ○　　上海 ○

1924年4月中旬，上海早晨，春寒料峭，乍暖还寒。徐志摩、瞿世英、张君劢、潘公弼[①]、殷志龄、钮立卿等文化界的著名人士和驻沪的外国人聚集在汇山码头，恭候诗人泰戈尔率领的印度文化代表团的到来。

4月12日上午9时许，泰戈尔一行乘坐的"热田丸"号轮船徐徐靠近码头的时候，恭候诗人泰戈尔一行的人群开始骚动起来。徐志摩指着轮船二层甲板激动地说："大家看，那不是泰戈尔吗？戴着红帽，有白色胡子的？"码头上人都踮起脚来，向轮船甲板张望。轮船慢慢靠了岸，人们看见诗人泰戈尔靠在栏杆上，望着江岸，看到欢迎的人群挥手向他致意，便微微俯首，双手合十还礼。

[①] 潘公弼（1895—1961），著名新闻工作者，江苏嘉定人。1914年赴日本留学，入东京政法学校，1916年回国，先后任北京《京报》、上海《商报》等报刊编辑、主笔、总编辑。1926年起先后曾在上海国民大学、沪江大学商学院新闻科任教。1951年去台湾，任《中华日报》顾问兼主笔，病逝于台湾。

诗人泰戈尔所乘坐的轮船抵达上海汇山码头

徐志摩和上海国立自治学院的教授兼教务长瞿世英[①]先生以及几位中国著名文化人士登上轮船，对诗人泰戈尔表示欢迎。前来欢迎诗人的印度侨民们呼喊着"母亲，向你致敬"[②]口号，给诗人泰戈尔戴上花环。H.P.夏斯特里教授也来到码头，向诗人泰戈尔介绍了几位著名的印度和日本人士，并给诗人披上一条绛红色的披肩。诗人泰戈尔在甲板上接受了东方通讯社记者的采访，随后躲避摄影师和其他记者的纠缠，急忙挤上汽车，前往静安寺路沧州别墅（今为南京西路锦沧文华大酒店），下榻23号和24号客房。同诗人泰戈尔一行一起乘船来到上海码头的利默迪尔·拉吉库马尔，没有在上海下船，而要继续乘船前往日本。

当地的印度侨民没经诗人泰戈尔同意就宣布，诗人将在中国青年

---

① 瞿世英（1901—1976），字菊农，江苏省常州人。在1919年"五四"运动中，被推为北京学生联合会代表，赴上海参加全国学生联合会罢课活动。8月，他和瞿秋白、郑振铎、耿济之、许地山等人创办《新社会》旬刊。后他和郑振铎、茅盾、叶圣陶等人发起成立文学研究会。英国哲学家罗素来华讲学，他协助赵元任为罗素翻译；1922年，法国学者杜里舒来华讲学时任翻译。他译过泰戈尔一些作品，1923年任上海国立自治学院教授兼教务长。中华人民共和国成立后先后兼任北京师范大学、北京大学、清华大学、北京女子师范大学等校的哲学教授。

② "母亲，向你致敬"，是孟加拉语作家般吉姆创作诗歌，被定为当时印度的国歌。

基督教协会发表讲演,可是因为诗人泰戈尔反对,他们只能作罢,并表示遗憾。

迦利达斯·纳格关于瞿世英先生的印象有过这样的描写:"此人是位性格温柔和善于思考的人士,喜欢哲学经典,读过《奥义书》,是诗人泰戈尔的《齐德拉》《国王》和《春之循环》(即《初春月圆日》剧本的译者。他很喜欢交谈。"[①](徐志摩是诗人泰戈尔在中国生活期间的翻译,一直陪伴在他身边。后来诗人泰戈尔关于徐志摩写道:"他是陪伴在我身边的一位朋友,承担着把我的英文讲演翻译成中国话的任务,他就站在我身边,他形象英俊,身材比较高,这在中国是很惊人的特点。看到他的优雅和严肃,我很陶醉。"[②])

当日中午,客人们用过午餐后就休息了。下午5点,徐志摩陪同诗人一行游览了位于上海西南郊区的龙华寺。当时龙华古寺、古塔被认定为国宝,可惜年久失修,败落不堪,香火也不旺盛,而且一支军队驻在寺庙里,所以龙华之行给诗人泰戈尔留下了不佳的印象。

4月12日到达上海后,恩厚之将一份最初的旅游计划目录寄给了诗人的长子罗廷德罗纳特。现将其从《国际大学新闻简报》摘录如下:

"北京——4月19-22日,5月16日去山西、汉口。

上海——5月28日离开,去日本6月15日离开。

香港——6月21日;广州和西贡。

曼谷——7月8日。

新加坡——7月22日。

爪哇——7月26日—8月10日。

[①] কালিদাস নাগ, কবির সঙ্গে একশো দিন (১৩৯৮) ১৫. 迦利达斯·纳格:《同诗人一起一百天》,1987年,第15页。
[②] কালিদাস নাগ, কবির সঙ্গে একশো দিন (১৩৯৮) ১৫. 迦利达斯·纳格:《同诗人一起一百天》,1987年,第15页。

仰光——8月15日。

加尔各答——8月18日。

当然，这一切都是暂时的计划，但我们不能冒7月台风季的风险，我想这样我们就可以很容易地逃脱，把所有的事情都安排到日程中。"

可是，诗人泰戈尔从来都不按照旅游计划行动，这一次也是如此。他们从香港出发经仰光，于7月17日就直接返回了加尔各答——这已经是后话了。

4月13日星期天，应犹太人富人俱乐部哈尔顿（也有人译为"哈同"）先生的邀请，诗人一行前往他的花园别墅参观做客。此处的花园就是著名的爱俪园，又被称为"上海大观园"。哈尔顿先生是来自巴格达的犹太富商。这里更吸引诗人泰戈尔的，是这里珍藏的佛教典籍和笃信佛教的哈尔顿夫人罗迦陵女士及其总管宗仰上人。

诗人泰戈尔在与哈尔顿闲聊中谈到了自己办学的理想，哈尔顿先生很欣赏诗人的教育思想，从此就成为国际大学的终身成员，并且对诗人泰戈尔的国际大学多有资助。《罗宾德罗传记》的作者普罗帕特库马尔·穆克巴泰写道：

"雷维教授谈到了哈尔顿先生慷慨捐赠的话题。得知国际大学在学习研究中国语言，我作为国际大学的图书馆管理人员就给哈尔顿先生写了一封信，请求他赠送一套中文版的《三藏经典》。1922年巴乌沙月我从邮局收到了三卷本的《三藏经》。后来他又寄来了一套中国的《二十四史》。"[①]

4月13日中午，驻上海的印度教徒和锡克教徒在闸北的一座锡克寺庙举行欢迎诗人泰戈尔的聚会。诗人泰戈尔对于居住在中国的锡克

----

① প্রভাতকুমার মুখোপাধ্যায়, রবীন্দ্রজীবনী ৩/১৮২, পাদটীকা ২. 普罗帕特库马尔·穆克巴泰，《罗宾德罗传记》第3卷，第182页。脚注2。

居民不是很满意,他在谈到马来亚之行体验时提到了这一点。在这里他又表达了自己对他们很不满的态度。后来他在国际大学一个学院的一次讲话中说:"锡克人邀请我去锡克神庙时,我对他们说,从前从印度来这里的那些人们,都是来传播大爱宗教及其宽宏思想的伟大人物,用各种亲缘纽带把中国、日本与印度连接起来,这在世界史上是罕见的,他们就是这样做的。没有任何商业权利,没有任何国际权利,只是这样来连接友爱纽带。他们只用自己唯一的友爱之心和美好情感把中国、日本变成亲戚,作为他们的后代人——你们却在播撒仇恨。这里的人们就会长期怨恨你们,就会带着仇恨的智慧雄踞在印度人之上,你们已经给印度造成了如此大的损害,你们玷污了先辈们的名誉。你们呼唤我前往锡克教导师的庙宇,导师庙宇为何而设,导师纳那克的咒语是友爱的咒语,大家都是这一位天神的后代,他一直在宣传大爱谏言。如果你们现在不传播这种谏言,导师庙宇又有什么用呢?若不能传播他的教导,那就只有痛苦,不会再有别的什么。这里的人民都是你们的自己人——亚洲人,本应该同他们缔结世代亲情,你们却践踏并扯断了这种亲情纽带。我不知道,我现在说的这番话,你们是否接纳入心。我现在向你们表达痛苦。痛苦在两个方面,一个方面,主人的权威利用奴才展现出自己令人恶心的丑态,这是一个方面的痛苦;而另一方面的痛苦,就是奴才却极其卑躬屈膝地认为,自己所遭受的痛苦、悲惨、侮辱是可以忍受的,这是另一方面的痛苦。这两个方面的痛苦使得印度处于两种黑暗的笼罩之中。印度人都应该永远忘掉这种痛苦。"[1]

  这场欢迎会一开始,姑娘们演唱了印度歌手米拉拜的赞歌《亲爱的,回家吧》,与会者伴随着歌声进行了祈祷。在欢迎会上宣读了一封用印地语写成的感谢信,在信中写道,诗人泰戈尔在这样的年纪长途跋涉,来中国传播印度古老的理想,为此锡克教徒们向他

---

[1] प्रवासी, कार्तिक 1331/26,《侨民》杂志1331年迦尔迪克号,第96页。

表示感谢,并且为了亚洲知识界的团结和世界和平愿意提供相应的帮助。诗人泰戈尔用孟加拉语致答词。基迪莫洪·森将其翻译成印地语。迦利达斯·纳格在日记中写道:"锡克导师的事业是什么呢,为实现导师的教导我们的责任是什么:导师在无限的领域让思想获得解放,并且为实现他的教导把我们的生命充实到无限的旋律之中——在全人类的友爱中获得成功。印度在伟大导师那纳克的格言中获得了新生命。锡克民族和全印度各民族在这一幸福的咒语中获得教益并愿意奉献生命——如果能得到证明,那就是成功。看到那些来到中国的印度人的工作服务理想,中国人就会因心存感激而怀念印度的名字。"①

张君劢(1887—1969)

4月13日下午4点多,由上海自治学院、中国讲学社、中国公学、文学研究会四团体联合发起,在张君劢先生的家——慕尔鸣路(今茂名北路)第37号花园别墅举行茶话会,欢迎诗人泰戈尔。在这里,诗人泰戈尔第一次正式地接触到受过良好教育的中国知识分子。

徐志摩作为中国青年社团的代表,用优美的富有诗意的语言向诗人泰戈尔表示欢迎,他说诗人是在中国处于一个危机的时候来中国访问的,无神论主义和物质主义正在摇摆中前进。他相信,诗人泰戈尔熠熠闪光的人格、深邃的哲学思想和充满活力的诗歌一定会使中国从

---

① কালিদাস নাগ, কবির সঙ্গে একশো দিন (১৩৯৪) ১৩. 迦利达斯·纳格:《同诗人在一起一百天》,1987年,第13页。

这种状态中摆脱出来。泰戈尔致答谢词，这也是他来中国第一次发表讲话。他的讲话全文如下：

It is a day of rejoicing for me that I, who belong to a distant part of Asia, should be invited to this land of yours, and I am deeply thankful that such good fortune has come to me.

I shall make a confession. When I had your invitation I felt nervous; I had read so many conflicting opinions about your religion and your customs that I asked myself:"What is it these people expect when they invite me to their country, and what message is it necessary for me to take for their welfare?"

Before Christmas I had been debating this and putting off the date of my departure, partly because I was unwell, but also, quite frankly, because I could not make up my mind. In the meantime, spring broke out in my own land.

A sense of compulsion had been urging me to sit down and prepare my lectures. Having to write in a language not my own, this preparation was necessary for me and took time. But spring came and the poet heard its call. Day after day tunes came into my mind, songs took shape, and I was lured from what I thought was my duty.

Yes I could not get rid of the trouble in my heart. How was I to stand before my friends in China, after idling away my time doing nothing, or what was perhaps even worse? But surely you don't expect fulfilling of engagements from poets. They are for capturing on their instruments the secret stir of life in the air and giving it voice in the music of prophecy.

Yes, a poet's help is needed at the time of awakening, for only he dares proclaim that, without our knowing it, the ice has given way; that the winter which had its narrow boundaries, its chains of ice,inhospitable and coldly tyrannical, is gone. The world has for long been in its grip—the exclusive winter that keeps the human races within closed doors. But the doors are going to open. Spring has come.

I had my faith, then, that you would understand my idling, my defiance of duty. And it came to my mind: is it not the same thing,your invitation and this invitation of the spring breeze,which was never ignored by your own wayward poets who forgot their duty over the wine-cup? I too had to break my engagements, to lose your respect, and thereby win your love.In other continents they are hard taskmasters; they insist on every pound of flesh; and there, for the"sake"of self-preservation ,I would have done my duty and forgotten my muse.

I say that a poet's mission is to attract the voice which is yet inaudible in the air; to inspire faith in the dream which is unfulfilled; to bring the earliest tidings of the unborn flower to a sceptic world.

So many are there today not believe. They do not know that faith in a great future itself creates that future; that without faith you cannot recognize your opportunities which come again and again, but depart unheeded. Prudent men and unbelievers have created dissensions, but it is the eternal child, the dreamer, the man of simple faith,who has built up great civilizations. This creative genius as you will see in your own past history, had faith which acknowledge no limits.The modern sceptic, who is ever critical, can produce nothing whatever—he can only destroy.

Let us then be glad with a certainty of faith that we are born to this age when the nations are coming together. This bloodshed and misery cannot go on for ever because, as human being,we can never find our souls in turmoil and competition.There are sign that the miracle has happened. That you have asked me to come to you is one of them.

For centuries you have had merchants and soldiers and other undesirable guests, but, till this moment, you never thought of asking a poet. Is not this a great fact—not your recognition of my personality, but the homage you thus pay to the springtime of a new age? Do not, then, ask for a message from me. People use pigeons to carry messages; and, in the war time, men valued their wings not to watch them soar, but because they helped to kill. Do not make use of a poet to carry messages!

Permit me, rather, to share your hope in the stirring of life over this land and I shall join your rejoicing. I am not a philosopher: therefore keep for me room in your heart, not a seat on the public platform.I want to win your heart, now that I am close to you,with the faith that is in me of a great future for you, and for Asia when your country rises and gives expression to its own spirit—a future in the joy of which we shall all share.

Amongst you my mind feels not least apprehension of any undue sense of race feeling, or difference of tradition. I am rather reminded of the day when India claimed you as brothers and sent you her love. That relationship is, I hope still there, hidden in the heart of all of us—the people of East. The path to it may be overgrown with the grass of centuries, but we shall find traces of it still.

When you have succeeded in recalling the things achieved in spite of insuperable difficulties, I hope that some great dreamer will spring from among you and preach a message of love and, there with overcoming all differences, bridge the chasm of passions which has been widening for ages. Age after age, in Asia great dreams have made the world sweet with the showers of their love. Asia is again waiting for such dreamers to come and carry on the work, not of fighting, not of profit-making, but of establishing bonds of spiritual relationship.

The time is at hand when we shall once again be proud to belong to a continent producing the light that radiates through the storm-clouds of trouble and illuminates the path of life.

（我这个来自遥远之邦的亚洲之人，今天应邀来到贵国的土地上，这是一个令人欣喜的日子。我深深地感谢这样的好运降临到我的头上。

我承认，当我收到你们的邀请时我感到很紧张。我读过关于你们的宗教和习俗方面的书籍，了解很多相互矛盾的观点，于是我就问自己："这些人邀请我到他们的国家去，他们希望我做些什么？为了他们的福祉，我又需要传达些什么消息呢？"

圣诞节前，我一直在思考这个问题，于是推迟了出发日期，部分原因是我身体不舒服，但坦率地说，也是因为我拿不定主意。与此同时，春天开始降临到我自己祖国的土地上。

一种冲动的感觉一直催促着我坐下来，撰写我的讲座稿。由于要用非母语写作，讲座的内容日复一日地在我脑海中浮现，歌曲也成形了，于是我被引诱，离开了我正为之劳心的职责。

是的，我无法摆脱心中的烦恼。在无所事事地虚度时光之后，我该如何面对中国朋友们呢？可是你们肯定不会期望诗人们不履行约定。诗人们要用他们的乐器捕捉空气中生命的隐秘颤动，并在所期待的音乐中发出乐音来。

是的，我们清醒时就意识到，诗人的帮助是需要的，因为只有他们敢在我们不知道的情况下宣布，冬天的冰雪已经融化；那种范围狭窄的、冰封成片的、不适宜居住的、冷酷暴虐的冬天已经过去。长久以来，这个世界一直在冬天的控制之下——只有冬天把人类关在紧闭的房间里，但房门会被打开的，因为春天降临了。

那时，我相信你会理解我的闲散、我对职责的蔑视。于是我就在想：你们的邀请和这春风的邀请难道不是一回事吗？你们那些任性的、贪杯的诗人难道从来不会忽视春风的邀请？我也不得不违背我的承诺，不得不失去你们的尊敬，但是我要赢得你们的爱。在其他大陆，诗人们是严厉的监工；他们坚持要称每一磅肉；在那里为了自我保护，我会尽我的责任，忘记我的缪斯。

我说，诗人的使命就是在未实现的梦想中吸引尚未听到的声音，把尚未绽放的鲜花——即将透露的消息最早地带给这个充满怀疑的世界。

今天，会有很多人不相信这一点。他们不知道，怀有美好未来信念本身就能创造出美好的未来；没有信念，你就无法发现机遇，机会一次次到来，又一次次悄然而逝。谨慎的人们和不信教的人们在制造纷争，然而正是那些不断出生的孩子、梦想家和具有单纯信仰的人在创建伟大的文明。这种创造性的天才，你们会在自己过去的历史中看到，他们有信仰，承认创造是无限的。现代的怀疑论者永远持批判的态度，他们什么也不能创造，只会破坏。

因此，让我们满怀信心地感到欣慰，因为我们生在各国团结一致的时代。当前这种流血和苦难不可能永远持续下去，因为作为人类，我们的灵魂不会永远处于动荡和竞争之中。有迹象表明，奇迹已经发生了。你们请我到你们这儿来，就是其中的一个奇迹。

几个世纪以来，你们一直有商人、士兵和其他不受欢迎的客人，但是，直到现在，你们从未想过要邀请一位诗人来。这不是你们对我人格的认可，而是你们对新时代春天的敬意，难道这不是一件了不起的事吗？那么，请不要要求我传递信息。人们用鸽子传递信息，在战争时期人们看重它们的翅膀，不是为了看它们飞翔，而是因为它们帮助杀戮。请不要利用诗人来这样传递信息！

请允许我分享你们对这片动荡土地上的生活所充满的希冀，我要加入到你们的欢乐中来。我不是哲学家，所以请在你们心中给我留一个位置，不是在讲台上。我想赢得你们的心，因为我相信，当你们国家崛起并表现出自己的精气神的时候,你们和亚洲将有一个美好的未来——一个我们大家都将分享的美好未来。

在你们中间,我丝毫不担心会有任何不适当的种族主义感情或传统差异。我情不自禁地想起那一天,印度称你们为兄弟,向你们问好。我希望,这种关系是依然存在的,并且隐藏在我们所有东方人民的心中。在通往友谊的道路上,也许长满了几个世纪以来的青草,但我们仍然会发现它的痕迹。

当你们不顾无法克服的困难,成功地回忆起过去所取得的成就时,我希望你们中间会出现一位伟大的梦想家,向你们宣扬大爱的信息,从而克服一切分歧,弥合多年来不断扩大的鸿沟。一代又一代,在亚洲,伟大的梦想用其大爱的雨滴将世界变得滋润、温馨、甜蜜。亚洲再次等待着这样的梦想家来继承这项事业,不是为了战斗,不是为了牟利,而是为了建立友爱精神关系的纽带。

这样一个时代即将到来的时候,我们自豪地属于一个绽放光明的大陆,这种光明将会穿透危险的风暴雨云,照亮生活的道路。)

诗人泰戈尔在这篇讲话中强调说,他只是一个没有责任意识的诗人,除此之外,他啥都不是,因为他是靠写诗歌来打发时光的,他也应该为来中国而撰写讲演稿。诗人们宛如春风一样毫无功利地来来往往,但是正因为他们的这种毫无功利的目的性格,世界才不会有任何损失。

他说,对于一个居住在亚洲遥远之地的居民来说,这一天是开心的日子,因为他被邀请来到这里。中国想从他那里听到什么话语,他不知道,所以他一开始犹豫不决,而后来他忘掉了春天的幻想,来打发时光。他说:"我不是哲学家,所以请在你们心里给我留一个位置,不要在讲台上。我想赢得你们的心,因为我相信,当你们国家崛起并表现出自己的精气神的时候,你们和亚洲将有一个美好的未来——一个我们大家都将分享的美好未来。"

公历1924年4月14日，是孟加拉历1331年元旦，这一日诗人泰戈尔是在上海度过的。在这里提出了中国和国际大学交流教授和大学生的建议，他因此感到很兴奋。这一天他写给罗廷德罗纳特的信中谈到了此事："在这里我得到很好的关爱，我觉得，我们同这里的人们会相处得很融洽，应该把夏斯特里先生①派到这里来，听了我们的建议②，他们都特别高兴，他们也同意从这里派教授去国际大学，那样的话，在国际大学就能开设中国语言专业了，还便于从中文典籍中翻译那些已经丢失的梵语书籍。关于此事你从现在开始就要与比罗拉兄弟们③谈一谈。除了夏斯特里先生，谁还可以做这项工作？在北京有一位通晓梵文的俄罗斯学者。从我们那里如果能有一个不很重要的人来这里，我就可以把他带走。这位俄国教授在他们的大学里教授梵语课。"

迦利达斯·纳格日记中也写道："新年这一天大家都来向师尊问安，祝贺新年，上午9点乘火车出发前往杭州，中午12点准时抵达。"

为缓解大学的经费困难，波洛德欧达斯·比罗拉藩王捐赠给国际大学2万卢比。国际大学校务委员会决定，用这笔款项为国内外的学者和大学生建造一所客舍。诗人泰戈尔在写给罗廷德罗纳特信中写道："还有一项紧迫的事情就是建设那所比罗拉慈善堂客舍，再不能耽搁了。从这里第一次去国际大学的学生如果由于缺少关怀而处于困境，因而感到生活不方便，那么，就会损坏我们学校的名誉。"诗人泰戈尔想建设这一客舍计划，实际上，并没有实现。

---

① 夏斯特里先生——国际大学教授，诗人泰戈尔的朋友。
② "我们的建议"是指国际大学与杭州的大学交流教授和大学生的建议。
③ 比罗拉兄弟——富商久格尔基绍尔·比罗拉及其兄弟们。

泰戈尔第一次访华纪实

前往杭州访问

加尔各答 ○—— 仰光 ○—— 马来亚 ○—— 新加坡 ○—— 香港 ○—— 上海 ○—— 杭州 ○—— 南京 ○—— 济南 ○—— 北京 ○—— 太原 ○—— 武汉 ○—— 上海 ○

从浙江省杭州市给诗人发来了邀请函，请他到那里去访问。4月14日早晨，在徐志摩和瞿世英的陪同下，诗人泰戈尔一行乘坐火车，前往距离上海110英里远的杭州游览访问。杭州教育界的很多人前往火车站迎接诗人一行，其中有浙江省教育会的副会长李杰、教育厅代表尹志仁、青年会代表美国人士狄耐尔等。列车进站停稳后，李杰登车迎接诗人一行，同诗人泰戈尔交谈片刻，于12点40分陪同诗人下车。诗人泰戈尔与诸位欢迎者一一握手致谢，同车与诗人一起来杭州的还有著名画家侬德拉尔·巴苏、梵语学家基迪莫洪·达斯、佛学家迦利达斯·纳格、英国人恩厚之、美国人葛玲女士以及陪同者徐志摩和瞿世英，共8人。随后乘坐汽车前往刚落成的西湖饭店下榻，分别住进第82号、83号、85号客房。

杭州西湖的美景非常出名，大家住进西湖岸边的一家宾馆。

第二天，即4月15日，诗人的同伴们去杭州近郊一座山上的佛教寺庙参观。传说，一位名叫慧理的印度佛教高僧建造了这座寺庙。

4月16日星期三下午4点，浙江省教育会应各文化团体和学校的要求，在教育会举行一个有1500多人参加的大会，其中多数是大学生，大会由李杰副会长主持。李杰首先讲述了诗人来华访问的宗旨，徐志摩向与会者简单地介绍诗人简历，随后请诗人泰戈尔发表演讲，徐志摩为其翻译。泰戈尔的演讲全文如下：

"You have a temple near by where there is a picture, carved upon the rock, of an Indian monk or sage who came to this country centuries ago. What is most interesting about him is the fact that When he came here he felt that these hills were just like the hills with which he was familiar in his own motherland.It has been said that hill came flying from India to this place ,but the real fact is that the hill which he had known in his own country had a Sanskrit name meaning the Vulture Peak.When he saw a hill here so like the one he had loved in India,he felt a great delight.

When I came, I too saw your beautiful lake and hills around. They did not seem at all strange, for your hills speak the same language as ours, your lake has the same smile as ours lakes, your trees the same physiognomy, with only a slight difference, as our India trees. Therefore when I find myself in the heart of nature here, I realize the unity of different countries in their outer aspect.

Then it comes to me with sadness that, as human beings we have no common language through which we can come close to one another. This perhaps has its advantages; for it makes us pay the price of knowing each other; we begin as strangers and have to win each other's love by strenuous endeavour. The function of true love is to overcome the multitude of obstacles in the way, to spread its sway in spite of them.

This man who centuries ago came to this land, not only discovered a resemblance between the hills here and those of his own land, but found his unity of heart with the people of this country. In one of the pictures a Chines is offering him food—a most beautiful piece of symbolism. I am a descendant of the same ancestors from whom hi came. I also claim the food of human kindness from your hands

I know that many of you do not understand me, but something has drawn you to come and look at me. It is not because you expect any message from me, but, as I believe, because of some memory of that glorious time when India did send her messengers of love to this land—not her merchants nor her soldiers, but the best her children—and they came bearing her gifts across deserts and seas.

This was the great task of Indian in the past, the task of building paths over obstacles. Men, at theirs highest, are pathmakers, paths not for profit or for power, but paths over which the hearts of men can go out to their brothers of different lands. Today the time has arrived when human beings by some chance have found easy to come closer physically. But because that is too easy, therefore it has become really difficult for human races to known each other truly or deeply.

Most of us nowadays are tourists — we come and see only the surface of life. The difficulty Has become all he greater because civilization has produced shells which we carry around with us. Even in distant countries we find food to which we are accustomed; rooms filled with comfort, the comfort which barricades us from the people. We enter big hotels and disappear from the land to which we have come. We come foe some purpose or other, through the mist of which we see but dimly, and we do not see right through.

The man from India who lived and died here, in the midst of those who gathered to accept the gift he had brought, came, not with a sense of race superiority, or of the superiority of his religion, but through an exuberance of love which drove him from is land. Unimaginable difficulties and discomforts he must have experienced, and a strangeness of life that we do not feel today. Science has made it easy for nations to come closer, but the same science has made it easy for us to kill, to exploit; not to known each other, and yet to believe that we know.

The fact of our closer neighbourhood thus remains an external fact of which mankind had no cause to be proud. It always causes evil when we come nearer each other and yet do not establish close relations. We form a crowd, but not community. The time has come when we must do our best to wipeout this shame from which the whole human race is suffering.

My friends, this is my mission. I have come to ask you to re-open the channel of communion which I hope is still there; for though overgrown with weeds of oblivion, its lines can traced. I shall consider myself fortunate if, through this visit, China comes nearer to India and India to China—for no political or commercial purpose but for disinterested human love and for nothing else.

It is not at all difficult for me to love the beauty of your lake and your hills, why then shold it be difficult for me to know you yourselves? Being a man I want to know you as men, not in order to improve your minds or your morals. When we realize this, this unity which is natural only when it is for no ulterior purpose either good or bad, then all the misunderstanding in the human world will be removed. For that I ask your help to make it easy for us. We in India are a defeated race; we have no power, political, military or commercial; we do not know how to help or to injure you materially. But, fortunately we can meet you as your guests, your brothers and your friends. Let that happen.

I invite you to us as you have invited me. I do not know whether you have heard of the institution I have established in my own land. Its one object is to let India welcome the world to its heart. Let what seems to be a barrier become a path and let us unite, not in spite of our differences, but through them. For differences can never be wiped away, and life would be so much the poorer without them, let all human races keep their own personalities, and yet come together, not in a uniformity that is dead, but in a unity that is living."

（你们附近有一座寺庙，那里的岩石上刻着一幅画，所画的是几个世纪前来到这个国家的一位印度高僧或圣人。最有趣的是，当他来到这里时，他觉得这些山就像他在自己祖国所看到的山一样。据说，这座山是从印度飞到这里来的，但事实是，他在自己国家所了解的这座山有一个梵文名字，意思是'秃鹫峰'。当他看到这里有一座山与他在印度所喜爱的那座山如此相似时，他感到非常高兴。

当我来到这里看到了你们美丽的湖泊和周围的小山，就觉得一点也不奇怪，因为你们的山好像和我们的山说着同样的语言，你们的湖也好像和我们的湖绽放着同样的微笑，你们的树和我们的树展现出同样的面貌，只有细微的差别。因此，当我在这里置身于大自然的中心之时，我就意识到，不同国家有着内在的统一性。

然后，我悲伤地想到，作为人类，我们没有共同的语言，可以让我们彼此接近。这也许有它的优点，因为它让我们为相互了解而付出代价；我们从互不相识时开始，必须通过艰苦的努力赢得彼此的真爱。真爱的作用是克服前进道路上的重重障碍，不顾一切地传播爱的力量。

这位几百年前来到这片土地的人，不仅发现了这里的山峦和他自己国家的山峦之间的相似之处，而且发现了他与这个国家人民之心是相通的。在其中的一幅画中一个中国人正在给他提供食物，这是一个最美丽的象征。我是这位祖先的后代。我也要求从你手中得到仁爱的食物。

我知道，你们中的许多人不理解我，但是某种东西吸引着你们来看我。这并不是因为你们期待我能带来什么消息，而是，正如我所相信的——因为你们对那个光荣时代存有一些记忆，当时印度确实向这片土地派遣了她的大爱使者——不是她的商人，也不是她的士兵，而是她最好的孩子，他们带着她的礼物穿越沙漠和海洋来到这里。

这是过去印度人的巨大任务，穿越障碍修筑道路的任务。他们是最高境界道路的开拓者，他们不是为了利益或权力而开拓道路，而是为使人们的心灵可以向不同土地上的兄弟伸展而开拓道路。今天，人类偶然发现，人们在身体上很容易接近的时代已经到来，但是因为这太容易了，所以对于人类来说，真正深入地了解彼此却变得非常困难。

现在我们大多数人都是游客，我们来只是看到生活的表面。困难也变得更大，因为文明生产出我们随身携带的贝壳。即使在遥远的国度，我们也能找到我们习以为常的食物；房间里充满了舒适感——这种舒适使我们与他人隔绝。我们进入大旅馆，就从我们来到的土地上消逝不见了。我们为了这样或那样的目的而来，透过迷雾，我们只能朦胧地观看，我们不能完全明白所观察到的景象。

在这里生活和去世的那位印度人，曾经居住在那些聚集在一起接受他带来的礼物的人群中，他不是带着种族的优越感，也不是带着他的宗教优越感，而是带着一种旺盛的大爱，这种大爱驱使他离开自己的故土，他一定经历过难以想象的艰难困苦，以及我们今天所感受不到的一种陌生环境。科学使国与国之间的亲近变得容易了，但同样的科学也使杀戮和剥削变得容易了；彼此不了解，却相信彼此是了解的。

因此，我们近邻的事实仍然是一个外在的事实，人类没有理由为此感到骄傲。当我们彼此接近，却没有建立亲密关系的时候，总是会产生邪念。我们成为一群人，但不是共同体。这样的时刻已经到来，我们必须尽最大努力消除全人类遭受的这种耻辱。

朋友们，这就是我的使命。我来是请求你们重新打开心灵相通的道路，我希望这条道路仍然存在，虽然它已经被遗忘的杂草所覆盖，但它的线路还是可以追踪到的。如果通过这次访问，中国更接近印度，印度更接近中国，那我认为自己是幸运的——我不是出于政治或商业目的，而是出于无私的人类之爱，别无他求。

对我来说，喜爱你们的湖泊高山的美丽并不难，那么，要我认识你们本人为什么就很难呢？作为一个人，我想了解你们的为人，不是为了改造你们的思想或道德。当我们在实现这一目标——即很自然实现团结——这种团结没有任何不可告人的目的或者没有好坏之分的时候，那么，人类世界的所有误解都将会消散。为此，我请求你们的帮助，这样会使我们实现目标容易些。我们印度是一个失败的种族，我们没有政治、军事或商业方面的力量，我们不知道在物质上如何帮助你们，或者是否会伤害你们。但是，幸运的是，我们可以作为你们的客人、兄弟和朋友，与你们见面。就让这种愿望实现吧。

我邀请你们前往我们国家访问，就像你们邀请我来贵国一样。我不知道，你们是否听说过我在自己的土地上建立的学校，其目的就是让印度欢迎世界进入它的内心。让那些看似障碍的东西变成一条坦途，让我们团结起来，不是无视我们的分歧，而是跨越分歧，因为分歧永远无法消除；没有分歧，生活就会变得单调乏味。让所有人类保持各自的个性，走向团结，但那不是一种僵死的团结，而是一种有生命的团结。)

诗人泰戈尔在谈到上面提到的那位印度高僧时说，他作为我们先辈的一个代表，同样肩负着同一种爱的使命来到这里。这位虔诚的高僧来到这里后看到一座高山就觉得此山仿佛是从他家乡的秃鹫山峰飞过来的——所以两座山峰的景象才如此地相似。"看到这里的这座山上的树木植被，他才想起了一件事，这倒不是因为你们期待我给你捎什么信息，而是，我相信，这是因为对那段光辉岁月的回忆，那时印度的确派遣了她的友爱使者来到这片土地上——他们不是她的商人，也不是她的士兵，而是她最好的孩子，他们带着她的礼物穿越沙漠和海洋来到这里。"

诗人泰戈尔继续讲述到，这条大路的开辟是古代印度完成的——不是为了经商，不是为了争霸，而是为了将宗教谏言送达遥远国家兄弟们的心里。今天在科学的帮助下遥远的距离变得容易来往了，可是彼此间建立轻松友好关系的目的却丧失了。当我们近在咫尺的时候，却没能联合起来，这是一个损失。在这方面我们要形成一个群体，但不是一个社区。随后诗人泰戈尔用清楚的语言讲述了这次来中国的目的："朋友们，这是我的使命。我来是请求你们重新打开心灵相通的通道，我希望这个通道还是存在的。如果通过这次访问，中国更接近印度，印度更接近中国——不是出于政治或商业目的，而是出于无私的人类之爱，别无其他目的，那我就认为自己是幸运。"

恩厚之用铅笔记录下诗人的这次即兴讲话，并且打印出来，经诗人修改后，被收录《在中国的讲话》（*Talks in China*）一书的第二篇讲话，标题是《在杭州对大学生们的讲话》（*To Students at Hangzhou*）。

虽然当天下雨，但是会场坐满大学生。他们听了徐志摩的翻译，一次又一次多次欢呼起来。诗人泰戈尔讲演持续到5点30分结束，然后李杰邀请各界代表在二层小会议室举行小型茶话会，诗人泰戈尔会见了浙江省的一些著名的教育家，同他们一边喝茶一边交谈，回答他们提出的问题。茶话会持续到6点30分才结束。

诗人泰戈尔一行在杭州逗留将近4天。在这期间他还会见清末民国初年的知名诗人陈三立。1923年至1925年，陈三立住在杭州。

前往杭州访问　065

1924年4月，印度诗人泰戈尔来中国杭州时，徐志摩等陪同诗人泰戈尔来到风光旖旎的杭州，在西湖之畔的净慈寺泰戈尔特地拜会了陈三立。两位不同国籍的老诗人，通过徐志摩的翻译，各道仰慕之情，互赠诗作。泰戈尔以印度诗坛代表的身份，赠给陈三立一部自己的诗集，并希望陈三立也同样以中国诗坛代表的身份，回赠他一部诗集。陈三立接受书赠后，深表感谢。他对印度诗人谦逊地说："您是世界闻名的大诗人，是足以代表贵国诗坛。而我呢，不敢以中国诗人代表自居。"随后两位诗人比肩合影，传为中印文化交流史上的一段佳话。

4月17日，诗人泰戈尔一行乘火车，返回上海。

对驻沪日本侨民的讲话

泰戈尔第二次访华纪实

加尔各答○----仰光○----马来亚○----新加坡○----香港○----上海○----杭州○----南京○----济南○----北京○----太原○----武汉○----上海○

4月17日星期四上午8点，诗人泰戈尔一行乘坐火车返回上海，一路上在谈论杭州之行的各种观感，接近中午回到上海。

当天晚上日本侨民在上海四川北路的一所日本人的学校举行欢迎会，欢迎诗人泰戈尔一行。欢迎会的主人首先致欢迎词，然后诗人泰戈尔致答词，恩厚之记录了他的答词讲话。记录稿经诗人修改后收录在《在中国的讲演集》，标题是 *Talk to the Japanese Community of China*（对在华日本社团的讲话）。诗人泰戈尔在讲话中回忆起1916年访问日本的体验。他说，在那里他住在日本人的家里，感受到了他们的关爱，好客是日本的传统。但是他也看到了在欧洲学校接受过教育的现代日本人，他直言不讳地说："I had some glimpses also of political Japan and the Japan that was intent upon profit-making and augmenting political power—rigid, exclusive, suspicous, lacking in humanity."

（我也隐约看到了政治上的日本和一个一心追求利润和扩大

政治权力的日本——僵化、排外、多疑、缺乏人性。）当然，造成这种现象不是日本一个国家的责任。"Power is rampant in the human world today, the power of money, of machine guns and of bomb-dropping aeroplanes, and the primitive in us stands once more, in awe of that which is neither spiritual nor moral."

（今天权力在人类世界泛滥，金钱的权力、机枪的权力、投掷炸弹的飞机的权力，我们人类的原始本性又站起来，对那些既非精神也非道德方面的东西感到敬畏了。）

诗人泰戈尔讲话的全文如下：

"When I was invited to this place by the Japanese community of this city, I was glad to accept the opportunity of meeting the people of your country. Not being a speaker by nature or training, and English not being the language to which I was born, I always feel nervous and shy when expected to address a big meeting in that language. What gave me courage was the thought that you did not seriously expect a speech, you wanted, rather, to see me and to hear my voice.

I believe some of you present here were in Japan at the time I arrived there and possibly took part in the wonderful reception I had at Tokyo station, but that was not the most important thing that happened to me. I came to know your people intimately. I lived in their houses as one of them, and though I had read in books that they were reserved by nature, I found no difficulty in knowing them and, through intimate knowledge, in loving them.

The happy memories of those days have attracted me to this meeting; but, I must add, I was also induced to accept this invitation for the sake of the dignity of my vocation as a poet. You accord me welcome because I am a poet. I do not take this as a personal merit, but I know in the East the poet's place is still held in reverence and God himself is described in the

Upanishad as the Supreme Poet. In spite of the fact that most of you do not know my work, and some have only read parts of it through a translation, always inadequate, my reputation as a poet has given me a place of honour in your hearts. This makes me feel proud, not in a personal way, but because such reverence reveals the heart of your civilization.

But men in the East are rapidly borrowing the culture and manner of the West, even their mental vision, and therefore I feel some misgivings about the reason which has persuaded you to invite me. I see that you know that by some stroke of luck I have gained a reputation in the West, that I won the Nobel Prize. Also, I find that you have been misinformed about the wealth I had, and when you mention a gift of ten million dollars to my institution you make me giddy at the very thought. It has set me debating whether these facts have not influenced your decision in offering me your welcome. But I hope my doubts are groundless.

In the East, poets have been loved and venerated, and prophets have not been stoned to death, a fact quite evident when you remember those great sages who came from India carrying their message of truth and love found their way into the heart of your people. They were able to live among you and to preach a religion that was strange to your land.

To those men you opened your doors. You didn't passed the law prohibiting their entry into your land. They lived amongst you and died happy. According to us the obligation of hospitality is civilization. I know that among the simple people of the East there still persists this faith in such an ideal, even in a world that has been poisoned with race hatred and national egoism.

When I went to your country, I met also the sophisticated modern Japan, schooled in the Western manner. I had some glimpses also of political

Japan and the Japan that was intent upon profit-making and argumenting political power-rigid, exclusive, suspicious, lacking in humanity. I do not blame only Japan for this. It is the same in other countries where a great part of humanity has become mechanical and dead, with that monotonous uniformity which dead things have in common.

The political and commercial Japan is not the true Japan, the living Japan. Masks, like mail armour, can be made of the same type and in the same mould, and the political and commercial lives are masks. You may see the same thing in New York, in Calcutta, in Shanghai and Hongkong, everywhere these stiff lifeless make-believes, with their angular gestures of greed, of inhospitality.

So I should not be surprised if I, in my turn, were to be excluded, and prevented from receiving your hospitality by the political spirit of your country, just as I should not be surprised if in England, or America, or anywhere else in the West, the politicians and prosperous people should shut their doors in my face, because they know that ideals have their explosive power. Is it not their age-long custom to treat idealists in this manner, and even to put them in prison? They would have crucified Christ just the same today, for would not Christ have preached pacifism had he come even in the middle of the most terrible fight in human history.

We, also, have our long list of sages whose preaching was not popular, for it was directed against prevalent creed and custom, yet they were venerated by the people of the age. This spirit is, I hope, still living in the East, and therefore I am glad you have asked me here, you who do not know me, but have only heard of my reputation.

I have seen in the West what a tremendous excitement of admiration is aroused when they meet some successful boxer or cinema actress, how they strain their necks to see some one who has the reputation of being a multi-millionaire. We in the East hope to be saved from this great calamity of vulgarism. This species of power worship, when it attracts our admiration, shows something in us which is crudely primitive and purely individualistic.

There is nothing moral or social about the boxer who has skill and music tremendously developed. But the poet, or prophet, or sage dwells in the lives of men and women, uniting heart to heart. These are the men who have built up this wonderful creation, called civilization, whose visions became symbols of beauty that spoke of the reconciliation of conflicting interests. They should claim our admiration, and not one who can play cricket to perfection.

Things frightful or powerful in nature have a great fascination for the primitive man and for this reason our worship and religion began in a sense of awe for all things that produced terror. Power is rampant in the human world today, the power of money, of machine guns and of bomb-dropping aeroplanes, and the primitive in us stands once more, in awe of that which is neither spiritual nor moral. The shrine of this demon of power you will find here in the city of Shanghai, and as in the days when men offered human sacrifice to their fetish, so today men are offering human sacrifices to this demon of greed.

There did come a time of old when the human races developed a spiritual religion, based on moral idealism and when they lost the sense of awe for mere destructive forces. We are waiting today for a revival of that moral ideal, of a spiritual standard of life, to save us from this demon worship of power.

Therefore I entreat you, friends, do not bring me your homage of welcome words because I have been successful. That will be impure, and if it is that, I shall not accept it. If you have faith in ideals, and if you think the mission of a poet is to uphold this faith in the face of antagonism, and if you want to offer your love and respect to a poet who believes in the spirituality of man, I shall humbly and proudly accept such offering."

（我接受了驻沪日本侨民社团的邀请。有机会与贵国人士见面，我感到很高兴。我不是天生的演说家，也不是受过训练的演说家，英语也不是我的母语，所以当我要用英语在一个大型会议上发表讲话的时候，我总是感到紧张和羞赧。有一种想法给了我勇气，你们并不是认真地期待我的演讲，相反，你们是想看一看我，想听一听我的声音。

我相信，在座的一些人在我昔日访问日本的时候就在日本，可能还参加了在东京站对我的热烈欢迎，但那并不是发生在我身上的最重要的事情。我很了解你们日本人。我像他们中的一员一样，也曾经住在他们的家里，虽然我通过读书知道他们生来就性格矜持，但我能毫不费力地了解他们，并通过对他们的深入了解，也爱上了他们。

那些美好的回忆吸引着我来参加这次会议，但是我必须补充一点，我接受这次邀请也是出于我作为诗人这一职业的尊严。你们欢迎我，因为我是一个诗人。我不认为这是个人的优点，但我知道，在东方，诗人的地位仍然受到尊敬，天神本人在《奥义书》中曾经被描述为至高无上的诗人。尽管你们中的大多数人不晓得我的作品，有些人只通过翻译读过其中的一部分，而且总是不够充分，但我作为诗人的声誉使我在你们心中占有荣耀的地位。这让我感到自豪，不是出于个人原因，而是因为这种尊敬揭示了你们文明的核心。

可是，东方人正在迅速地借鉴西方的文化和生活方式，甚至借助于他们的思维方式，因此，我对于你们邀请我的原因感到有些疑虑。我想你们一定知道，由于某种运气，我在西方获得了声誉，获得了诺贝尔奖。此外，我发现你们对我的财富有错误的认知，当你们提到向我的机构捐赠1000万美元的时候，你们就会想到，这会让我高兴得头晕目眩。我在想，这些事实是否影响到你们对我表示欢迎的决心。不过我希望我的怀疑是没有根据的。

在东方，诗人受到爱戴和尊敬，而先知们却没有受到这种爱戴和尊敬，但是先知们也没有被石头砸死。当你们想起那些从印度来的伟大圣贤，他们把真理和爱的信息带来，真理和爱已进入你们人民的心中，这个事实是显而易见的。印度古代圣贤能够住在你们中间，并且传播你们国家所不熟悉的宗教。

你们为他们敞开了大门。你们并没有通过法律禁止他们进入你们的土地。他们就生活在你们中间，并且快乐地死去。在我们看来，好客的礼仪就是文明。我知道，即使在一个被种族仇恨和民族利己主义所毒害的世界，在东方纯朴的人民中间，仍然坚守着这种理想信念。

当我去你们国家访问的时候，我也遇到了以西方教育方式而变得成熟的现代日本。我也瞥见了一个政治化的日本，以及一个一心追求利益和政治权力的日本——僵化、排外、多疑、缺乏人性。因此我并不只是责怪日本，在其他国家，情况也是如此，那里的大部分人已经变得机械呆板、毫无鲜活气息，与死气沉沉的东西一样，单调乏味。

政治化和商业化的日本不是真正的日本，不是活生生的日本。面具和锁子甲一样，可以用相同的模型和模具造出来，政治化和商业化的生活就是面具。你们可以在纽约、加尔各答、上海和香港看到同样的情况，到处都是这些僵硬的、毫无生气的伪装，以及他们那种贪婪、冷漠、棱角分明的姿态。

因此，如果你们国家的政治精神把我排除在外，不让我接受你们的款待，我也不会感到惊讶，正如在英国、美国或西方其他任何地方的政客和有钱人如果把我拒之门外，我不会感到惊讶一样。因为他们知道，理想具有爆炸性的力量。这样对待理想主义者，甚至把他们关进监狱，难道不是他们长久以来习惯的做法吗？他们今天也会把基督钉在十字架上，如果基督在人类历史上最可怕的战斗中出现，那样他就不会宣扬和平主义了。

我们也有一长串圣人的名单，他们的布道不受欢迎，因为他们反对流行的信条和习俗，然而他们受到了那个时代人们的尊敬。我希望这种精神还活在东方,因此你们邀请我来这里,我是很高兴的,你们不认识我,只是听说过我的名字和声誉。

我曾在西方看到,当他们遇到一些成功的拳击手或电影女演员时,会激起一种巨大的钦佩之情,他们是如何伸长脖子去瞧看那些以百万富翁而闻名的人士。我们东方人希望能从这种粗俗的大灾难中解脱出来。当这种对权力的崇拜引起我们的钦佩的时候,就显示出我们内在的某种粗俗的原始性和纯粹的个人主义陋习。

拳击手的技巧和音乐的极大发展与道德和社会无关。但诗人、先知或圣贤却寓于人们的生活之中,同他们心连心。正是这些人创造了这个被称为文明的奇妙世界,他们的愿望就成为调和利益冲突的美的象征。我们应该钦佩的正是他们,而不是一个能把板球打得尽善尽美的人。

曾经有过一个古老的时代,那时候人类发展了一种基于道德理想主义的精神宗教,他们失去了对纯粹破坏力量的敬畏感。今天,我们等待着道德理想和精神生活标准的复兴,这种道德理想和精神生活能把我们从对权力的无上崇拜中拯救出来。

所以我恳求你们,朋友们,请不要因为我已成功就对我述说对我充满敬意的欢迎话语。我不是圣人,即便你们那样做,我也不会接受的。如果你们忠于理想,如果你们认为诗人的使命是在面对着敌对势力也要维护这种信念,如果你们想把你们的爱和尊重献给我这个相信人的这种精神的诗人,那我就应当谦卑和骄傲地接受这种奉献。)

诗人泰戈尔在这次讲话中赞美了东方人的好客,他认为好客就是文明。同时也谴责了"一个一心追求利益和政治权力的日本",批评他们"僵化、排外、多疑、缺乏人性"。他指出,"即使在一个被种族仇恨和民族利己主义所毒害的世界里,在东方纯朴的人民中间,仍然坚守着这种理想信念"。

很多人不喜欢诗人泰戈尔这样谴责西方的机械文明,早在4月14日《北京导报》的社论就批评过诗人泰戈尔谴责西方机械文明的讲话。

《罗宾德罗传记》作者普罗帕特库马尔·穆科巴泰写道:"在上海,还有一天在犹太人联谊会创始人卡杜里先生的家里,诗人泰戈尔受到了欢迎。卡杜里本人就是诗人。他在欢迎泰戈尔时说,几年前他写过一首诗 The Wedding of Death(死亡的婚礼),一些评论者读后说,这首诗里有泰戈尔的思想。卡杜里先生说:'这立刻引起了我极大的兴趣。多亏了泰戈尔博士,才有一个充满灵感的新世界展现在我眼前。'"("This immediately aroused my great interest. Thanks to Dr.Tagore, an inspired vision of a new world was put before my eyes.")

卡杜里先生为帮助国际大学解决用水困难决定捐赠12000卢比。同他的经济援助相类似的事情,在别的地方虽然也提起过,但是在这样的欢迎场面中还有经济方面的援助,在任何地方都是见不到的。

4月18日下午,上海各界举行盛大的欢迎会,欢迎从杭州回来的

上海商务印书馆的图书馆为近代出版家张元济所建

诗人泰戈尔。会场选在位于上海宝山路的商务印书馆新建图书馆会议厅。会场门楣上用松柏树枝粘贴成"欢迎"二字，会场内四壁悬挂着古画和用松柏树枝编织成的带状饰物。主席台后墙上同样粘贴着"欢迎"二字。主席台前摆放着十几盆鲜花。3点的时候，上海各界代表和驻上海的英美和印度人士1200多人陆续走进会场。当身穿黑色长袍、头戴绛红色印度帽的诗人泰戈尔走进会场的时候，乐队奏响了优美的乐曲。3点30分，聂云台①先生宣布欢迎会开始。江苏省教育联合会主席沈信卿②先生致欢迎词，代表中国当地教育和文化团体向诗人泰戈尔表示热烈欢迎。诗人泰戈尔发表了讲话，这是他来中国后的第二次讲话。很遗憾，这次即兴讲话没有被保存下来。中国报刊报道了这次讲话的主要内容。诗人泰戈尔提醒人们说："要晓得幸福便是灵魂势力的伸张，要晓得以一切精神之美的牺牲去换得西方的所谓的物质文明，是万万犯不着的！"诗人认为："物质主义的侵入，我们诚然不能抵抗，可是我们迷信它，甘愿将活的精神埋没了，去换取死的空壳物质，又哪里值得呢？"诗人泰戈尔怀着痛苦的深情讲述了什么是全亚洲的危机，中国问题是何等复杂、何等可怕，他对此表达了他个

张元济（1867—1959），字筱斋，号菊生，浙江海盐人。中国近现代出版家、教育家、爱国实业家、版本目录学家、藏书家。

---

① 聂云台（1880—1953），湖南长沙人，名其杰，字云台。曾国藩外孙。1893年中秀才，后去外国学习英语和电气、化学工程。1917年与黄炎培等人在上海发起成立中华职业教育社，任临时干事。
② 沈信卿（1864—1944），浙江吴兴人。1891年肄业于上海龙门书院，后去日本考察教育，回国后改龙门书院为师范学堂，从事教育事业。曾任中国图书公司总编辑、全国教育联合会主席等职。

人的深切同情，并且指出，贪婪的物质享乐主义必然会招致非自然死亡。作为诗人的泰戈尔并没有谈论诗歌，而是为上海的工业文明和城市化担忧，在他看来，在上海，由于西方物质文明的引入，已经看不到丝毫的中国文化精神。①

泰戈尔讲话后稍事休息，周映湖演奏古筝名曲《普庵咒》，诗人凝神静听，沉醉于优美婉转的乐曲之中。随后徐志摩翻译诗人的讲话，刘湛恩最后发表感谢致辞。欢迎会结束时已经6点多了。

刘海粟在这幅画的右侧题写道：（民国）十五年（1924年）四月十八日写于功德林海粟（此画真迹现由无锡张淳铭先生收藏）

随后诗人泰戈尔一行乘车来到上海四马路的有正书局参观。诗人泰戈尔浏览了该书局出版的美术作品，深为赞叹，并且购买了多种，其中有恽正叔的花卉作品、恽南田的作品、费晓楼的仕女画、改七香的百美嬉春图、戴鹿床的金盏写生、沈石田的精品画作、金冬心的人物画和小画册、八大山人画册、石涛的山水画和陈师曾的遗墨，有正书局赠送诗人一个书箱，为泰戈尔收藏画作之用。

晚上8点，徐志摩、郑振铎、刘海粟、戈公振等上海一些著名人士在著名的功德林素餐馆宴请诗人泰戈尔，席间演奏了中国乐曲。刘海粟现场为诗人泰戈尔画了一幅素描像。晚餐后大家陪同诗人前往剧院观看中国古代京剧表演。午夜12点30分诗人泰戈尔才结束这一天的活动。

① 朱纪华主编：《泰戈尔与上海》，中西书局2012年版，第37页。

乘船北上南京

泰戈尔第一次访华纪实

加尔各答○──仰光○──马来亚○──新加坡○──香港○──上海○──杭州○──南京○──济南○──北京○──太原○──武汉○──上海○

4月19日星期六上午8点,诗人泰戈尔一行离开上海,乘船走水路前往北京。路上诗人泰戈尔与自己同行的伙伴们谈到了亚洲的严峻形势。迦利达斯·纳格在他的日记里记录了这次谈话。诗人泰戈尔说:"很多人都知道,印度人口和中国人口一样多,就其力量基础而言也差不多,可是谁又晓得,俄罗斯可能已经开始对这两个国家进行投机炒作。因此我们也应该有所打算。不过印度的形势与整个亚洲相同。两股势力正在进行争斗,一方面是腐朽旧世界的剥削压榨,而另一方面是新生的布尔什维克——这两者将会以两种方式施展暴力。……我听说,布尔什维克有一个挑战,就是他们要建立新社会、新精神和公平正义。愿望可能是美好的,也可能会成功,通过其内部我们会看到伟大亚洲的重新崛起,但是我看到现在的这种局面,我不能说她就是黄金时代的完美化身。前面说的几句话就作为一点个人的想法。人都希望像人一样长期地活着。共产主义有多少存在的道理,个人主义也就有那么多存在的道理。家庭就是这种个人主义的社会基础,而且经济基础就是财产,去掉这两方面的任何一个方面,真正的共产主义都建不成……不过,我承认这一点,这个新党是真的在努力建设一种社会公平,而且会逐渐建立起来。在这些人中可能会有同情被压迫民族的人物。如果他们能够与中国和印度联合起来,也许,就会开始一场伟大的历史性变革。东方这种巨大的重新崛起被称为国家权力的'革命'。鉴于这种危险,旧势力就会竭力拼命地摧毁它,但是我看见在东方和西方各被压迫民族的痛苦和耻辱中存在的那种真理和正义,任何国家或经济列强都是阻挡不住的——他们一定会成为胜利者,由于这种胜利,全人类就会沿着可能新出现的康庄大道阔步前进。"[1]

那时候了解苏维埃俄国冲破帝国主义包围后的真正形势并不容易,可是清醒的诗人泰戈尔收集了关于国际政治方面如此多的消息,并且对于其他国家的影响方面考虑得很多,看到这种情况,大家都感到惊奇。他就布尔什维克经济政策和政治方面的政策提出了问题,后来的历史证明他的疑虑是正确的。最初是俄罗斯,而后是中国,都采取向其他国家输出革命作为自己的目的,诗人当时已经洞察到这种征兆。

4月20日星期天上午,诗人泰戈尔一行乘坐的客船抵达南京,大家住进江河酒店。徐志摩谈到当前政治话题的时候,诗人泰戈尔插话说:"你可以在中国进行一项重大实验,你们那里人口众多,你们有爱好和平的传统。如果你们不仅能设法努力从被包围的状态中获得解放,而且你们还可以通过这种解放给世人提供很大的教育;如果你们采用非暴力不合作政策,你们看一看:哪些人把你们看作懦夫,对你们进行围困、掠夺、屠杀,如果你们手里已经掌握了这种人作恶的教训,全部世界都会感谢你们的。有两件事你们要记在心里,并且应该脚踏实地去做——对于一切丑陋的坏东西不要麻木不仁地不管,而应

---

[1] কালিদাস নাগ: কবির সঙ্গে একশো দিন (১৩৯৪) ১৮–১৯. 迦利达斯·纳格:《同诗人在一起一百天》1987年,第18—19页。

该对其进行斗争——当然不是用生物武器,聪明的人不是用猛兽的力量,而是用精神的力量,不能以恐怖反对恐怖,而要用宽恕,完全的宽恕——然而,有意义的是实践。在这种战争中最初也会遭受损失,但是你要知道,胜利是属于你们的——巴厘岛上的5000名男人女人自杀后,当地人教训了他们残暴的荷兰主人,他们的反击宛如一部史诗,永远活在人民的心里。你们如果也这样做——成功地采取非暴力手段使亚洲获得成功,全人类都会感激你们的。"

诗人泰戈尔在自己国家没有支持甘地发起的不合作运动,因为他把教育和文化引入了政治领域,否则,他会接受和支持这种非暴力运动的,最有力的证明就是他创作的剧本《赎罪》《摩克多塔拉》,其中在《摩克多塔拉》的人物——摆脱尘世一切责任的苦行者塔南乔耶身上,就体现了诗人泰戈尔所宣传的理想。但是诗人泰戈尔的这种"采取非暴力手段"争取民族解放的主张是不符合中国当时的国情的。

此后诗人会见了江苏、江西、安徽三省的军事领导人(督军)齐燮元[1]。诗人泰戈尔对他说:"我对中国怀有深深的友爱和好奇心,今天有机会表达,我感到特别高兴。中国从很古老的时代起就具有文明的理想,而这一理想是建立在爱好和平的基础上的。这种文明是人类无价的宝贵财富。当今所谓的文明时代的野蛮几乎是在毁灭它。我来这里就是为了向你们提醒关于这种极其可怕危险的存在,因为印度人对中国怀有深厚的亲戚般的情感。印度热切地期待着——中国何时屹立在自由、独立和自己文明之上,在世界面前再一次抬起头来。实现和平愿望的中国将会向世界展现新的理想,中国现在这种同室操戈和互相残杀的一页就会结束。"[2] 齐燮元将军与诗人泰戈尔有相同的

---

[1] 齐燮元(1885—1946),原名齐英,字抚万,直隶省顺天府宁河县(今天津市宁河区)人,中华民国时期直系军阀,后沦为汉奸。1920年,齐燮元继任江苏督军、苏皖赣三省巡阅使,成为直系高层。1924年,齐燮元与浙江督军卢永祥因上海归属问题爆发"江浙战争",齐燮元击败卢永祥。1945年日本投降,齐燮元以汉奸罪被逮捕,1946年在南京被执行枪决。

[2] কালিদাস নাগ কবির সঙ্গে একশো দিন (১৩৯৪). 迦利达斯·纳格:《同诗人在一起一百天》1987年加尔各答出版。

看法，并且说到，他也相信和平，若不遭受侵略，他是不会发动进攻的。

然后诗人泰戈尔会见了江苏省主席韩德勤[①]。韩德勤对他说，读了他在上海的讲话后，他们都受益匪浅。他承诺，他会为中国和印度大学生交流之事尽力的。不过，他还提醒诗人说，诗人泰戈尔的讲话精神，现在中国的一些大学生可能不会接受。

4月20日下午3点，在东南大学体育馆召开欢迎会。与会者达6000多人。东南大学校长郭秉文首先致欢迎词，并向与会者说，泰戈尔先生是印度大教育家，著作闳富，曾以版权所得创立大学，提倡高尚文化，历游美、德、日诸国，备受欢迎。中国人士对先生欢迎之忱尤为热烈，因先生所发表学说，足以阐扬东方文化精神，并于沟通中印及世界文化历程，有伟大之贡献。今因先生过宁之便，请做一度演讲，希望诸君静聆伟伦。

随后，诗人泰戈尔登台发表讲演。由于人太多讲台上面的包厢开始断裂，差点儿塌落，值得庆幸的是，诗人泰戈尔和其他人并没有受到伤害。诗人泰戈尔在拜沙克月初九（4月22日）写给拉奴的信里讲述了当时的情况："……前天我们来到南京。……在这里的大学礼堂为我安排了讲演会。那是很大的礼堂，上面靠墙是一排拱廊。人特别多。在人们的欢呼声中我开始讲演，我刚讲了三四句话，这时候发出咔嚓一声巨响，会场顿时紧张起来，所有人都转脸望着逃往大门的方向。恰恰是我讲演所站在那个讲台的上面，由于拱廊上人多的压力拱廊被撕裂开一个四五英寸宽的裂口，仿佛要塌下来的样子，只有很少的一处还连接着。如果断裂部分掉下来了，我的额头瞬间就会被砸破的，降落在我头上的可不是花雨，而可能是男女生的血肉之雨。恩厚之的脸色吓得煞白，迦利达斯急忙走过来，企图将我拉到外边。我没

---

① 韩德勤（1892—1988），字楚箴，江苏省泗阳县人，陆军中将。曾任江苏省主席、鲁苏战区副总司令，参与徐州会战、策应武汉会战，参加冬季攻势等，又与新四军多次发生冲突。1949年3月逃往台北。曾任台湾地区"战略顾问"。1953年退役。

有动,举手示意让大家安静下来。如果我惊慌失措地看着逃走的路,那么,由于3000人互相拥挤着逃跑,就会发生重大的踩踏灾难事件。我让迦利达斯镇静下来,我继续讲演。因此大家都说,我这次讲演是最好的一次讲演。"①

诗人泰戈尔的这篇讲话由恩厚之记录,题目是 *To Students at Nanking*,收入《在中国的讲演集》,为第三篇。全文如下:

"I feel highly honoured, not so much because your elders have honoured me, but because I feel that silent invitation from the young.

Wherever I have an opportunity of talking to students and the young, I feel the youth within me stirred, and realize the great privilege of the young to claim freedom for its growth. I know that you who are young do not need any props of ready made maxims, or pruning hooks of prohibition, no doctrines from the dead leaves of books, for the guidance of your conscience. Your soul has its natural yearning for the inspiration of the sunlight of joy and spring of life, for all that secretly helps the seed to sprout and the bud to blossom. In this a poet may be of help to you, who fortunately is not your teacher, but who loves you.

You are here with the gift of your life which, like the morning star, shines with hope for the unborn day of your country's future. I am here to sing the hymn of praise to youth, I who am your poet, the poet of youth.

You know that fairy tale—the eternal story of youth which is current, in almost all parts of the world. It is about the beautiful princess taken captive by some cruel giant and the young prince who starts out to free her from his dungeon. When we heard that story in our boyhood, can you not remember how our enthusiasm was stirred, how we felt ourselves setting out in the guise of that prince and rescuing the princess, overcoming all obstacles and

---

① 原信⑩/২৮৮-২৮৫,中国 ১৪২,泰戈尔《书信集》第18卷,第149封信,第284—285页。

dangers, and at last succeeded in bringing her back to freedom? Today the human soul is lying captive in the dungeon of Giant Machine, and I ask you, my young princes, to feel this enthusiasm in your hearts and to be willing to rescue the human soul from the grip of greed which keeps it chained.

We travelled up from Shanghai to this town along your great river, Yang Tse. All through the night I often came out my bed to watch the beautiful scene on the banks, the sleeping cottages with solitary lamps, the silence spreading over the hills, dim with mist. When morning broke what was my delight to find fleets of boats coming down the river—their sails stretching high into the air, a picture of life's activity with its perfect grace of freedom. It moved my heart deeply. I felt that my own sail had caught the wind, and was carrying me from my captivity, from the sleeping past, bringing me out into the great world of man.

It brought to my mind different stages in the history of Man's progress.

In the night each village was self-centred, each cottage stood bound by the chain of unconsciousness. I knew, as I gazed on the scene, that vague dreams were floating about in this atmosphere of sleeping souls, but what struck my mind more forcibly was the fact that when men are asleep they are shut up within the very narrow limits of their own individual lives. The lamps exclusively belonged to the cottages, which in their darkness were in perfect isolation. perhaps, though I could not see them, some prowling bands of thieves were the only persons awake, ready to exploit the weakness of those who were asleep.

When daylight breaks we are free from the enclosure and exclusiveness of our individual life. It is then that we see the light which is all men and for all times. It is then that we come to know each other and come to come to cooperate in the field of life. This was message that was brought in the morning by the swiftly moving boats. It was the freedom of life in their outspread sails that spoke to me and I felt glad. I hoped and prayed that morning had truly come in the human world and that the light had broken forth.

This ago to which we belong, does it not still represent night in the human world, a world asleep, whilst individual races are shut up within their own limits, calling themselves nations, which barricade themselves, as there sleep in cottages were barricaded, with shut doors with bolts and with prohibitions of all kinds? Does not all this represent the dark age of civilization, and have we not begun to realize that it is the robbers who are out and awake? The light of the torches which there men hold high is not the light of civilization, but only points to the sleeping of their good and of the best they possess.

This age, that still persists, must be described darkest age in human civilization. But I do not despair. As the early bird, even while the dawn is yet dark, sings out and proclaims the rising of the sun, so my heart sings to proclaim the coming of a great future which is already close upon us. We must be ready to welcome this new age. There are some people, who are proud and wise and practical, who say that it is not in human nature to be generous, that men will always fight one another, that the strong will conquer the weak, and that there can be no real moral foundation for man's civilization. We cannot deny the facts of their assertion: the strong have their rule in the human world, but I refuse to accept this as a revelation of truth.

I bring to your mind those early days when the creative spirit of life produced huge monsters. Who in those days, could dare to believe that they were doomed? Then happened a miracle. All of a sudden, in the midst of that orgy of bigness and physical strength, appeared Man, without weapons and without protection, naked, small and tender of skin. He discovered the power in his intellect which burned dim among the animals. He stood up against the might of muscle with weapons shaped by his mind, and he held his own and survived.

But the true victory of man's life was not fulfilled even then. For to-day his descendants, half brute and half man, have risen, up all over the world in terrible form, more devastating even that those prehistoric monsters who, at their worst, were frankly physical. This combination of brute and intellect has given rise to a terror which is stupid in its passion and yet cunning in its weapons; it is blindness made efficient and, therefore, more destructive than all other forces in the world.

We in the East had once tried our best to muzzle the brute in man and to control its ferocity. But today the gigantic vision of intellect has overwhelmed our belief in spiritual and power. Power in the animals was, at least, in harmony with life, but not so bombs, poison gases and murderous aeroplanes, the horrible weapons supplied by science.

We should know this, that truth—any truth that man acquires—is for all. Money and property belong to individuals, to each of you, but you must never exploit truth for your personal aggrandizement—that would be selling God's blessing to make profit. Science also is truth. It has its own place, in the healing of the sick, and in the giving of more food, more leisure for life. But when it helps the strong to crush the weaker, to rob those who are asleep, that is using truth for impious ends and those who are so sacrilegious will suffer and be punished, for their own weapons will be turned against them.

But a new time has come, the time to discover another great power, the power that gives us strength suffer and not merely to cause suffering, the immense power of sacrifice. This will help us to defeat the malevolent intellect of brute greed as have of and satanic egotism, as in the pre-historic age intelligence overcame the power of mere muscle.

Let the morning of new age dawn in the East, from which the great streams of idealism have sprung in the past, making the fields of life fertile with their influence. I appeal to you to make trial of this moral power through martyrdom. Prove how, through the heroism of suffering and sacrifice—not weak submission—we can demonstrate our best wealth and strength. Know that no organization however big can help you, no league of prudence or of power, but only the individual with faith in the infinite, the invisible, the incorruptible, the fearless.

The great human societies are the creation not of profiteers, but of dreamers. The millionaires, who produce their bales of merchandise in enormous quantities, have never yet built a great civilization. It is they who are about to destroy what others have built. Come to the rescue and free the human soul from the dungeon of the Machine. Proclaim the Spirit of Man and prove that it lies not in machine-guns and cleverness, but in a simple faith."

（我感到非常荣幸，不是因为你们的长辈给了我荣誉，而是因为我感到来自年轻人的无声邀请。

每当我有机会与学生和年轻人交谈时，我都感到自己内心的青春在激荡，并且意识到，年轻人为自己的成长拥有要求自由的巨大特权。我知道，你们这些年轻人不需要现成的格言作为支柱，不需要禁令的修剪钩，也不需要书本枯页中的教条来引导你们的良心。你们的灵魂自然地渴望快乐阳光和生命春天的鼓舞，渴望一切能够秘密地帮助种子发芽和蓓蕾开花的东西。在这一点上，一位诗人也许会对你们有所帮助，他很幸运，因为他不是你们的老师，但他也爱你们。

你们带着生命的礼物来到这里，就像辰星一样，闪耀着对你们国家未来的希望之光。我是你们的诗人，是青春的诗人，我在这里唱诵赞美青春的诗歌。

你们知道那个童话，那是关于青春永恒的故事，它几乎在世界到处流传。它讲述的是关于美丽的公主被一些残忍的巨人俘虏，年轻的王子开始把她从地牢里解救出来。当我们在孩提时代听到这个故事时，你们当然还记得我们的热情如何被激发出来。我们是如何把自己装扮成王子，去拯救公主，克服一切障碍和危险，最终成功地把她带回来，让她恢复了自由。今天，人类的灵魂被囚禁在巨人机器的地牢里，我请求你们，我年轻的王子们，感受你们心中的这种热情，愿意把人类的灵魂从贪婪的枷锁中解救出来。

我们从上海沿着你们这条大河——扬子江来到这个城市。这一整夜，我常常从床上爬起来，望着河岸上的美景，望着那些点着灯的孤零零的沉睡小屋，望着被薄雾笼罩的山间寂静。天一亮，我高兴地看到一艘艘帆船顺流而下——船帆高高扬起；一幅幅生命活动的画面，生命自由的完美优雅，呈现在我的面前。它深深地打动了我的心。我觉得，我自己的船扬起风帆而来，把我从囚禁中，从过去的沉睡中带出来，带我进入人类的伟大世界。它使我想起了人类进步历史上的不同阶段。

夜晚，每个村庄都以自我为中心，每个小屋都被无意识的锁链束缚着。当我凝视着眼前的景象的时候，我知道在这沉睡的灵魂中飘浮着朦胧之梦，但更令我印象深刻的是，人们在沉睡时都被关在自己个人生活的狭窄范围内。灯光只属于那些在黑暗中完全与世隔绝的小屋。也许，虽然我看不见它们，也许，只有几群鬼鬼祟祟的小偷醒着，准备利用那些沉睡着的人们的弱点。

天一放亮，我们就从个人生活的封闭和排他性中解脱出来。那时，我们才看见光明，那光明就是所有的人和所有时代的光明。正是在那个时候，我们开始相互了解，开始在生活领域合作。这是早晨由快速移动的船只带来的消息。正是它们张开的风帆给我带来生活的自由，我感到很兴奋。我希望并祈祷人类的世界真的迎来了黎明，光明降临到人间。

我们所属于的那个过去，不是仍然代表着人类世界的黑夜一面吗？一个沉睡的世界，而各个种族被关在自己的范围内，自称为民族，他们用各种各样的门闩和各种各样的禁令把自己围起来，就像在茅屋里睡觉一样？这一切不都代表着文明的黑暗时代吗？难道我们还没有开始意识到，在外面的强盗不是还醒着吗？他们高举的火炬所发出的亮光并不是文明之光，而只是亵渎他们的善良和他们所拥有那些最好东西的邪恶之光。

如今仍然存在的那种时代，必然被描述为人类文明史上最黑暗的时代。但我并不绝望。正如早起的鸟儿，在尚存昏黑的黎明时刻，就高声歌唱，宣告太阳即将升起，同样，我的心也在歌唱，宣告伟大未来的时代已经临近。我们必须准备好迎接这个新时代。有一些骄傲的、聪明的和务实的人会说，慷慨大度不是人类的本性，人们总是互相争斗，强者会征服弱者，人类文明不可能有真正的道德基础。我们不能否认他们所断言的事实：强者统治人类世界，但我拒绝接受这种断言，这只是真理的启示。

我使你们想起那些早期的岁月，那时生命的创造精神产生了巨大的怪物。在那个年代，谁敢相信自己注定要失败呢？然后奇迹出现了，突然，在那巨大的体力狂欢中出现了人类，没有武器，没有保护，他们赤裸着身体，他们幼小而皮肤稚嫩。而人发现自己在动物中间燃烧着智慧的力量。他站起来，用自己思想创造的武器去对抗身体的力量，他自己坚持下来，活了下来。

但人类生命的真正胜利甚至在那时也没能实现。因为那时候是半人半兽的时代，在世界各地可怕形式的怪物出现了，甚至比那些史前的怪物更具有破坏性，这些怪物在最坏的情况下是赤裸裸的肉体。这种野蛮和理智的结合产生了一种恐怖，这种恐怖在情感方面是愚蠢的，在武器方面是狡猾的；这种恐怖催生出一种有效的盲目性，因此比世界上所有其他力量都更具有破坏性。

在东方，我们曾经竭尽全力去压制人类的兽性，控制它的残暴。但是今天巨大的智慧愿景已经压倒了我们对精神和力量的信仰。动物身上的力量至少与生命是和谐的，但是炸弹、毒气和杀人飞机这些由科学提供的可怕武器却无和谐可言。

我们应该知道，真理，即人类所获得的任何真理，都是为所有人服务的。金钱和财产属于你们每一个人，但是你们绝不能利用真理来为自己谋取私利，因为那是以出卖上帝的祝福来牟利。科学也是真理，它有其自己的位置，在为病人治疗疾病，在提供更多的食物和更多的闲暇生活。可是当它帮助强者压制弱者，抢夺沉睡之人生命时，那就是将真理用于邪恶的目的，那些如此亵渎真理的人将遭受痛苦和惩罚，因为他们自己的武器将被用来攻击他们自己。

但是一个新的时代已经到来，那是发现另一种伟大力量的时代，这种力量赋予我们力量去忍受痛苦，不是去制造痛苦，而是以牺牲奉献出巨大力量。它将帮助我们打败凶残的贪婪和邪恶的利己主义的恶毒智力，就像在史前时代智力战胜肌肉力量一样。

就让新时代的晨曦在东方绽放曙光吧！过去的理想主义洪流会从东方奔涌而出，它们的影响使生命的田野变得肥沃。我呼吁你们以殉道的方式来考验这种道德力量。可以证明，通过苦难和牺牲的英雄主义，而不是通过软弱的屈服，我们可以展示我们最好的财富和力量。要知道，无论多么强大的组织都不能帮助你们，也没有审慎的联盟或权力能帮助你们，只有那些对无限、无形、坚不可摧而无所畏惧的信念的个人才能帮助你们。

伟大的人类社会不是投机商的产物,而是梦想家的创造。百万富翁们生产了大量的商品,却从来没有建立过伟大的文明。正是他们在摧毁别人的建筑。你们去从机器的地牢中拯救和解放人类灵魂吧。去宣告人类的精神吧,并以此证明,拯救和解放人类灵魂不能靠机关枪和聪明,而要靠一种简单的信仰。)

诗人泰戈尔说,同学生和青年人在一起,使他焕发出新的生命力,让他想起学生时代读过的关于王子从恶魔手中搭救公主的故事,他说:"Today the human soul is lying captive in the dungeon of Great Machine, and I ask you, my young princes, to feel this enthusiasm in your hearts and to be willing to rescue the human soul from the grip of greed which keeps it chained."

(今天,人类的灵魂被囚禁在大机器的地牢里,我请求你们,我年轻的王子们,感受你们心中的这种热情,请把人类的灵魂从贪婪的枷锁中解救出来。)

4月21日(拜沙克月初八星期一)上午,诗人泰戈尔一行乘坐蓝色特快豪华列车,前往北京。南京的军事长官齐燮元为诗人泰戈尔在火车上预订了一间特别的车厢。此前诗人泰戈尔在寄给拉奴的一封信中调侃地写道,他到了中国,强盗们如果把他绑架了,那么,他就能够休息几天。在中国混乱的环境中这种可能性并没有完全排除。去年土匪就从这列火车上绑架了35名美国和欧洲的乘客。所以政府就在火车上设置了武装卫士。

访问济南

泰戈尔第一次访华纪实

加尔各答 ○---- 仰光 ○---- 马来亚 ○---- 新加坡 ○---- 香港 ○---- 上海 ○---- 杭州 ○---- 南京 ○---- 济南 ○ 北京 ○ 太原 ○ 武汉 ○ 上海 ○

在前往北京的中途，诗人泰戈尔在曲阜下了车，前往孔夫子的陵园拜谒。然后前往山东省的省会——中国古代文明的发祥地济南。4月22日清晨5点40分列车抵达济南站。山东省教育厅秘书长张伯秋（即张涛）、女中校长邹少白、一师校长王祝晨、女子职业学校校长秦子明、竞进女小校长张步月以及济南各界代表鞠思敏、王世栋等20多人前往车站欢迎印度客人。诗人泰戈尔走出车厢时众人热烈鼓掌表示欢迎。诗人泰戈尔与众人一一握手，随后乘车前往津浦铁路宾馆下榻。原定计划上午9点在商埠公园举行欢迎会，下午约诗人泰戈尔一行游大明湖，可是，天气不好，风势过大，尘土飞扬，再加上诗人泰戈尔身体疲惫，于是他就休息了。其余人在徐志摩、王统照等人陪同下游览大明湖、图书馆等名胜。下午3点在省议会礼堂开欢迎会，可是还不到2点的时候，各校学生和各报社记者就纷纷来到会场，到3点时，会场的楼上楼下已坐满了人，而且来者仍然络绎不绝。主持人张涛只好宣布，讲演改在会场外面。当时天气炎热，风势依然很大，可听讲者毫不懈怠，仍然聚集在会场耐心地等待诗人。3点40分主持人宣布大会开始。鹤发童颜的泰戈尔登上讲台，会场响起雷鸣般的掌声，诗人开始用英语讲演，徐志摩当场翻译。

诗人泰戈尔讲演的内容是Materialism and the Spiritual Life（"物质主义和精神生活"）。他说，他知道，他关于理想主义的讲话多数人是不喜欢的，但是在这一方面他没有什么可说的，因为他要做的事情就是，努力感悟"真理"并将其揭示出来。他相信，人们有一天会明白的，真理的进步是不存在于物质主义和利己主义之中的，它存在于利他主义和美的创作中。诗人的这番讲话赢得了在场听众的欢呼声。随后他在山东基督教大学发表了讲话。他在这里讲述了圣蒂尼克坦学校和国际大学发展的历史。可惜，这次讲话没有被记录下来。

讲演持续了25分钟，诗人结束讲演后，被请到议长办公室，稍事

图中后排左二为于道泉

休息，就前往齐鲁大学参观，会见了在这里学习的年轻人于道泉，后者后来成为著名的梵语学家。下午6点各校校长在铁路宾馆设晚宴招待诗人泰戈尔一行。

4月23日早晨5点30分诗人一行乘快车经天津前往北京。当时任护路军副司令的王赓[①]是徐志摩的好友，是陆小曼的丈夫，也是十分崇敬和热爱诗人泰戈尔的青年将军。他得知诗人泰戈尔一行已经到达山东济南，于是就派出一支护卫部队去济南专门迎接和护卫诗人一行。

[①] 王赓（1895—1942），江苏无锡人。早年赴美留学，先后入密西根大学、哥伦比亚大学、普林斯顿大学研习哲学，获普林斯顿大学文学学士学位，随即进入西点军校攻读军事，1918年6月毕业，回国后任职于北洋政府陆军部，1922年与陆小曼在北京海军联欢社结婚，1923年任交通部护路军副司令，同年晋升为陆军少将。1942年3月，随熊式辉为团长的军事代表团赴美，先至缅甸腊戌考察。4月，于赴美途中旧病复发，留居埃及首都开罗治疗，同月逝世。

泰戈尔第一次访华纪实

抵达北京

加尔各答○--○仰光○--○马来亚○--○新加坡○--○香港○--○上海○--○杭州○--○南京○--○济南○--○北京○　太原○　武汉○　上海○

4月23日（拜沙克月初十，星期三）晚上7点，诗人泰戈尔一行抵达北京前门火车站。在这之前，北京讲学社社长梁启超前往天津站登上火车车厢欢迎诗人泰戈尔，并且一路上一直同诗人泰戈尔进行交谈。一大群大学生和知识分子燃起了鞭炮，播撒鲜花花瓣，向诗人泰戈尔表示欢迎。几位印度在京的商人给诗人泰戈尔戴上了花环。著名政治家林长民①、北京大学代理校长蒋梦麟②等一大批文化名人也来火车站欢迎诗人，然后陪同印度客人一起前往北京大饭店下榻。4月25日《华北正报》在报道中写道：

No events in the recent years has aroused so much interest in Chinese intellectual circles as the visit of Rabindranath Tagore. Many men have

---

① 林长民（1876—1925），福建闽侯（今福州）人，政治家、外交家、教育家、书法家。林徽因的父亲。曾与梁启超等组建了讲学社。1925年，林长民任奉系将领郭松龄幕僚，参与讨伐张作霖战事，被流弹击中身亡。
② 蒋梦麟（1886—1964），浙江余姚人，中国近现代教育家。参加科举考试并中秀才。后留学美国，获得哲学及教育学博士学位。曾任国民政府第一任教育部部长、行政院秘书长，也是北京大学历史上任职时间最长的校长。1949年随国民党政权去台湾。1964年6月19日因患癌病逝于台湾台北。

come to China and gone yet none of them has been so enthusiastically received. What is the explanation? It is because Dr. Tagore belongs to the East and in honouring him the Chinese intellectuals are honouring the civilization of the East. What is more, Dr. Tagore has come with a message which cannot fail to make a powerful appeal to both Young China and Old China. Young China has often be criticized because of its attempt to transplant Western civilization into Chinese soil, root and branch. The criticism was certainly justified a few years ago; but since then there has been unmistakable evidence that Young China is beginning to turn from the materialism of the West to the culture of their forefathers for spiritual relief. On the other hand, the will of Young China to examine the teachings of their forefathers in the light of the civilization of the West, will be reinforced by the world of Dr. Tagore's visit to this country, he will have rendered a great service to the cause of Chinese civilization.

（近年来，没有一件事像泰戈尔访华那样引起中国知识界如此浓厚的兴趣。许多人来过中国又走了，但没有一个人受到如此热烈的欢迎。如何解释呢？因为泰戈尔博士属于东方，中国的知识分子在赞美他的同时，也是在赞美东方的文明。泰戈尔的讲话，无论对年轻的中国还是年老的中国，都具有强烈的感染力。年轻的中国经常受到批评，因为它试图从根到枝将西方文明移植到中国的土壤中。几年前，这种批评当然是有道理的；但从那以后，有确凿的证据表明，年轻的中国正开始从西方的物质主义转向他们祖先的文化，以寻求精神慰藉。另一方面，年轻的中国想要参照西方文明来研究他们祖先的教诲的愿望，将因泰戈尔博士的访问而得到加强，他将为中国的文明事业作出伟大的贡献。）

诗人泰戈尔也是怀着这种愿望克服犹豫动摇来到了中国，他的期待就是，他要在年轻而又古老的中国和印度这两个亚洲大国的古老文明中间架设起连通的桥梁。

前面已经说过，诗人泰戈尔一行来到北京后起初都住在北京大饭店。基迪莫洪在给妻子姬龙巴拉的信里写道："我们23日来到北京，住在最大的一家饭店里，23日夜里、24日和25日都住那里，26日中午我、侬德拉尔先生和迦利达斯先生三个人离开北京饭店。现在我们三个人住在信德的大商人雷库莫尔先生的家里。28日师尊泰戈尔和恩厚之先生也离开那家饭店，在中国和平饭店内租了一个花园和几个宁静的房间。那里很干净，并且提供西餐。"①

4月24日（拜沙克月十一日，星期四）诗人泰戈尔在饭店里休息。除了一两次会见，他的大部分时间都是在陪同一起来中国的同伴中度过的。诗人对他们所说的话都被迦利达斯·纳格记录下来，主要内容如下：

"今天师尊第一次讲述了他生活中那么多的斗争历史——在如此的逆境中是如何进行创作的——这是何等样的智慧啊！今天我仿佛第一次看到了他是一个人——一位伟大的人——他内心充满大爱。他讲到，最初在童年时代他经历不少痛苦，而且一般人的印象，他是个挥霍无度的诗人。奥寇耶·乔杜里的妻子是第一位否定这种看法的人，因为她了解诗人，不过此人同她兄长普罗达波·马宗达一样，都认为他是一个疯狂的诗人！"

迦利达斯·纳格写道："他喜欢购买和阅读书籍，读过后：卖掉再买。……他家里有一堆困难……债台高筑。他有时便秘，可是他没有钱；装修红房子的50000卢比，被普本·巴苏花掉了。在如此的困境中还要建设圣蒂尼克坦，所有平房里的书籍都给了塞雷斯·马宗达，希望能对静修院有些帮助，可是他一分钱也没有拿到，相反，还

---

① ড প্রণতি খোশাখাঃ: ক্ষিতিমোহন সেন ও অর্শশতাব্দীর শান্তিনিকেতন (১৯৯৯) ২০৬. 普罗诺迪·穆科巴耶：《基迪莫洪·森和150周年的圣蒂尼克坦》，1999年，第206页。

要支付印刷费用——他只好出卖自己的版权,等等。他妻子的首饰几乎都卖掉了,妻子的忍耐令人惊讶,罗廷和米拉得到几件,他们得到更多的是悲伤。"

4月25日(拜沙克月十二日,星期五)中午12点30分,英美协会在格兰特旅社设午宴招待诗人泰戈尔。在这里,诗人泰戈尔做了第一次讲演。英美协会会长弗兰西斯·阿格伦(Francis Aglen)主持了宴会,但是向听众介绍诗人泰戈尔的任务是由诗人以前就认识的Dr. Jocob Gould Schurman(乔科布·古尔德·舒尔曼博士)来承担。在舒尔曼博士做了介绍性的讲话之后,诗人泰戈尔做了发言。他讲述了自己的大学创立以及自己作为诗歌的译者的体会。他谈到,在1912年至1913年旅居英国时了解到几位杰出人物的思想,并且结交了几位极好的朋友。1916年在前往美国的途中又在日本停留。他说:"I realized for the first time…the terrible suffering with which the whole world was afflicted. I saw in Japan the war trophies taken from China publicly exhibited…I felt humiliated in my own mind at this primitive and brutal perpetuation of the defeat of an enemy…Nationalism, therefore, seemed to me to be pure barbarism, based on pride, greed and lust for power, with wealth dominating the disease, and I shuddered when I saw the result."(我第一次意识到整个世界都在遭受着可怕的痛苦。我在日本看到公开展出从中国运来的战争战利品……在我自己的心里,我对敌人失败这种原始和残酷的延续感到羞辱……因此,在我看来,民族主义是纯粹的野蛮行为,它是建立在骄傲、贪婪和对权力的贪欲之上的,财富主宰着疾病。当我看到结果时,我不寒而栗。)

正是处于这种心态的时候他写了一些关于民族主义的文章,他在美国宣读了这些文章。战争结束后诗人泰戈尔去了欧洲,受到广泛的欢迎,因此他就觉得:"The nationalism of the West were looking for some new ideal from the East which would reconstruct their civilization on a better basis."（西方的民族主义正在从东方寻找一些新的理想，以便在更好的基础上重建他们的文明。）正是从这种融合的梦想出发他才创建了国际大学。

泰戈尔第一次访华纪实

出席北海静心斋的欢迎会

加尔各答○----仰光○----马来亚○----新加坡○----香港○----上海○----杭州○----南京○----济南○----北京○----太原○----武汉○----上海○

4月25日下午，有50名著名学者和尊贵的人士在北京的北海静心斋举行茶话会，欢迎诗人泰戈尔，在这里过去是中国皇帝常常接见外国使者的地方。北京讲学社的社长梁启超发表了欢迎诗人泰戈尔的讲话。北京《晨报》1924年4月26日报道了讲学社为招待诗人泰戈尔茶话会的概况，报道的标题为《碧水绿茵之北海与须发皓白之印度诗哲——泰戈尔谓科学为无价宝库》：

前天刮过大风，昨天格外清爽，风和日丽，确是北方春季之模范日。讲学社适于次日招待印度诗哲泰戈尔及其一行诸名人，尤显得天人一致欢迎。……三时前，主人梁任公、汪大燮[1]、熊希龄[2]、

------

[1] 汪大燮（1859—1929），原名尧俞，字伯唐（一作伯棠），浙江钱塘（今杭州）人，晚清至民国时期外交官、政治家、北洋政府国务总理。

[2] 熊希龄（1870—1937），字秉三，湖南湘西凤凰人，祖籍江西丰城石滩。民国时期政治家、教育家和慈善家。曾任北洋政府第四任国务总理。

熊夫人、范源濂①先后莅止。三时二十分诗哲泰戈尔、鲍司、沈②三人同乘一汽车到静心斋。……四时左右,来者益多,胡适、张逢春、张欣海、梁漱溟、林长民、林志钧③、蒋方震④、杨荫榆⑤女士、林女士、王女士、曾女士⑥、威礼贤(德人)、庄士敦(英人)等五十余人。五时开茶会,及半由梁任公起立致欢迎辞,大意约如左述。

中印两国是兄弟之邦,一千三四百年以前,印度伟人来游吾邦者踵相接,故吾国文化上所受印度之影响,深且大。今兹吾人又获与印度现代伟人相接,使数百年中断之沟通,又得一接近之机缘,此实吾人最为荣幸之事。

吾国之哲学、文学、美术、雕刻、小学、音乐,乃至于医学、数学、天文亦莫不受其影响。余将于明日(即26日)及后日(即27日)在师大北大讲演,聊表欢迎泰氏之意。

梁启超演讲毕,由张逢春译成英语。继而由诗人泰戈尔致答词,历三十分钟之久。诗人泰戈尔的答词如下:

"Great men came centuries ago from India to greet your ancestors. That was an epic period of our history when it was possible for India to give birth to great personalities. I have come as a representative of that

---

① 范源濂(1875—1927),字静生,出生于湖南长沙府湘阴县(今湖南省岳阳市湘阴县),中国近代著名教育家。参与创办清华学堂。辛亥革命后,曾任教育部次长、中华书局总编辑部部长、北洋政府教育总长。1923年7月北京国立高等师范正式改为北京师范大学,成为首任校长。中华教育文化基金委员会董事长、南开大学董事会会长、北京图书馆代理馆长。
② 鲍司、沈这里指画家侬德拉尔·巴苏、梵文专家基迪莫洪·森。
③ 林志钧(1878—1961)闽派著名诗人,法学家和哲学巨擘。字宰平,号北云。福建闽县人。林志钧与沈钧儒同为癸卯科举人,辛亥革命前留学日本。曾任北洋政府司法行政部长,后为清华研究院导师,中华人民共和国成立后为国务院参事室参事。
④ 蒋方震(1882—1938),字百里,浙江省杭州府海宁州硖石镇(今海宁市硖石镇)人。中华民国军事教育家,民国时期著名军事理论家和军事教育家,其《国防论》为中国近代国防理论的奠基作品。
⑤ 杨荫榆(1884—1938),小名申官,出生于江苏无锡一个书香门第。中国最早女子高校教育管理人之一。她一生坎坷,早年不幸的婚姻使得她终生不再嫁,致力于学术。她曾留学异乡,颇受现代知识的熏陶,学成归国,成为中国近代史上第一位女大学校长。因抗日被日军杀害。
⑥ 林女士、王女士、曾女士——这里指林徽因及其姑表姐王孟瑜(林徽因大姑的女儿)、曾语儿(林徽因四姑的女儿)女士。

same culture, yet also as a representative of the present age, a mixture which has not yet settled down to anything satisfactory, an age of transition. You can not expect any great person or message to be born in this age. I only want to be acknowledged as one of you, not as a teacher or as a guide.

Since I came to this place I have forgotten that I am in a strange land. You have a wonderful gift of sympathy and I have felt completely natural in my relations with your country. When I parted from those at home, I felt certain pangs of separation, because I never suspected that, out of your generous hospitality, I should even be provided with beautiful grand-daughters in China!

We in India have the privilege of falling in love with our grand-daughters when we reach a safe age, near bout sixty, and I feel that the world is richly great and beautiful when I find that grand-daughters are not lacking in this flowery land, for a guest from across the sea.

I feel somewhat sad when you treat me as a man burdened with a message who has come to you to preach. Deep in my heart I am noting better that a poet, neither a sage nor a saint. Never banish me to the altitude of a lecture platform—away from the immediate neighbourhood of grand daughters and friends. I crave a seat at you side, in your midst, and not to be barricaded off as a philosopher with some reputation on greatness.

I have been asked by my friend, Mr. Hsu, to talk to you of the Institute I have founded. Most of you may not find it possible to be there bodily, but I hope you will accept the ideal represented by this institution and make it you own.

It is a terrible calamity when human being come near to one another and yet to do not recognize the deeper bond of human relationship; when a strong people exploit the weaker, and when some baser passion of men awakens at the meeting of races, obscuring the truth that unites them. This is a shame and should not be allowed to continue. I have felt deeply the pain of this unnatural situation.

You have referred to the golden age when men came from India across desert, mountain and sea to promote a spirit of love among races separated by geographical barriers, almost insurmountable. It was not to injure or to exploit, but to share the best treasure they had with their far distant brothers. I believe that such truth once revealed in human history cannot be dead forever. I have come with a hope that I may be able to remove the obstruction of oblivion from the spring of love that once over-flowed into union of heart between your country and mine, and still lies hidden in the depths of our being.

I had my invitation to America some years ago. On my way I stopped in Japan—Japan, proud with the prosperity of the most newly rich of nations. There it hurt me deeply that the East should not be humble when it had come into sudden good fortune. We ought to know that it is a dangerously critical period in her history when a country is suddenly surprised with a political success that is stupendous. It is a difficult trial, requiring from her all the strength she has in order to save herself from the dust-storm of arrogance that obliterates the path of wisdom.

Pride generates a blind trust in one's exclusive might, causing isolation, sowing its own seed of defeat. It produces continual with our surroundings, gradually wearing out our armour of protection. In Asia we must seek our strength in union, in an unwavering faith in righteousness, and never in the egotistic spirit of separateness and self-assertion. It is from the heart of the East that the utterance has sprung forth:"The meek shall inherit the earth,"for the meek never waste energy in the display of insolence, but are firmly established in true prosperity through harmony with the all.

In Asia we must unite, not through some mechanical method of organization, but through a spirit of true sympathy. The organized power of the machine is ready to smite and devour us, from which we must be rescued by that living power of spirit which grows into strength, not through, addition, but through assimilation that is organic. That we should borrow science from the West is right. We have a great thing to accept from the people of the West—their treasure of intellect, which is immense and whose superiority we must acknowledge. But it would be degradation on our part, and an insult to our ancestors, if we forgot our own moral wealth of wisdom, which is of far greater value that a system that produces endless material and physical power that is always on the warpath.

I have keenly felt this great degradation and disaster that has overcome the world. Men's soul have become hypnotized and their knees are bent before idols—the idols of money and power. I have found in my travels that in a campaign against this organized cultivation of egoism, mere preaching is of no use. I came to conclusion that what was needed was to develop and give form to some ideal of education, so that we might bring up our children, in the atmosphere of a higher life.

For some time past education has lacked idealism in its mere exercise of an intellect which has no depth of sentiment. The one desire produced in the heart of the students has ben an ambition to win wealth and power,—not to reach some inner standard of perfection, not to obtain self-emancipation. Such an ideal is not worthy of human being.

For the last century and a half, the cultured nations of the earth have given up their faith in a spiritual perfection on life. Their doom is upon them, and when we in the East become enamoured of the glamour of their success, we must know that the terrific glow we see upon the western horizon is not the glow of sunrise, or of a new birth fire, but of a conflagration of passion. that only those who have lost their mind, gazing at the sudden eruption of a flaming success, can be enamoured, as the victim is enamoured of the glittering serpent's eyes.

I say again that we must accept truth when it comes from the West and not hesitate to render it our tribute of admiration. Unless we accept it our civilization will be one-sided, it will remain stagnant. Science gives us the power of reason, enabling us be actively conscious the worth of our own ideals.

We have been in need of this discovery to lead us out of the obscurity of dead habit, and for that we must turn to the living mind of the West with gratefulness, never encouraging the cultivation of hatred against her. More over the western people also need our help, for our destinies are now intertwined.

No one nation today can progress, if the others are left outside its boundaries. Let us try to win the heart of the West with all that is best and not bases in us, and think of her and deal with her, not in revenge or contempt, but with goodwill and understanding, in a spirit of mutual respect.

Our institution of Visva-Bharati represents this of cooperation, of the spiritual unity of man. And I ask you, my brothers and sisters, to take part in building it, you who still have men among you mindful of the bond of love once established between our two peoples of the olden days."

（几个世纪前，一些伟大的人物从印度来到你们伟大祖先的身边。那是我们历史上一个史诗般的时期，那时候印度有可能诞生伟大的人物。我是作为同一种文化的代表而来到这里，同时也是作为当今时代的代表而来到贵国，这是一个尚未稳定到令人满意的混合文化的过渡时代。你们不能期望在这个时代诞生伟大人物或带来重大福音。我只希望你们大家承认我是你们中的一员，而不是老师或指导者。

自从我来到这个地方，我就忘了我是处在一个陌生的地方。你们有一种奇妙的同情心，我在与贵国的交往中感到十分自然。当我和家里亲人分别时我感到别离的痛苦，因为我从来没有想到，由于你们的盛情款待，我在中国竟然会有你们这些美丽的孙女们！

我们印度人到了六十岁左右的安全年龄，就有特权慈爱我们的孙女。当我发现这片花海般的彼岸土地上并不缺少孙女的时候，我作为一个远渡重洋的客人，感到这个世界是多么的伟大和美丽啊。

当你们把我看作是担着重担到你们这里来传播福音之人的时候，我就感到有些忧愁。在我的内心深处，我并不比别的诗人高明，我既不是贤哲，也不是圣人。请不要把我撑到讲坛上去——让我远离我的孙女们和朋友们。我渴望在你们身边，在你们中间有一个座位，而不是像一个有伟大名声的哲学家那样被隔离开来。

我的朋友，徐志摩先生要求我向你们谈一谈我创立的那所大学。你们中的大多数人可能无法亲自到那里去，但我希望你们能接受这所学校所代表的理想，并把它变成自己的理想。

人类彼此走近，却认识不到人类关系的深层中有一种纽带，这是一种可怕的灾难；当一个强大的民族剥削弱小民族的时候，当人们一些卑鄙的激情在种族集会上觉醒并掩盖他们不团结真相的时候，我就觉得这是一种耻辱，不应该允许其继续存在下去。我为这种不自然情况的存在而深感痛苦。

你们提到了黄金时代，一些人从印度穿越沙漠、高山和海洋，来为在被几乎不可逾越的地理障碍所隔开的种族之间传播促进友爱的精神。他们不是为了伤害或剥削别人的目的，而是为了与远方的兄弟们分享他们最好的财富。我相信，这样的真理一旦在人类历史上被揭示出来，就永远不会消失。我就是怀着这样的希望而来的，这就是我也许能够消除被忘却的障碍。那种友爱之泉曾经在你们和我们两国的心灵中涌动，至今仍深藏在我们心灵的深处。

几年前我收到了去美国的邀请。在我的旅途中，我在日本停了下来——我曾经为日本，为那个新兴而富裕的国家的繁荣而自豪。在那里，我深深感到痛心的是，东方这个国家在突然获得好运后竟然不知道应该谦逊。我们应该知道，当一个国家突然获得惊人的政治成功时，这也许就是她历史上一个关键的危险时期。这是对她的一场艰难的考验，需要她倾尽所有的力量，才能把自己从傲慢的沙尘暴中拯救出来，傲慢的沙尘暴会摧毁理智之路的。

骄傲使人盲目相信自己的排他性力量，造成自我孤立，播下失败的种子。它不断地与我们的环境发生冲突，逐渐磨损我们的保护盔甲。在亚洲，我们应该在团结中寻求力量，在对正义的坚定信念中寻求力量，而不是在分裂和自我肯定的傲慢精神中寻求力量。这是从东方人的心中发出的声音："温顺的人将继承大地。"因为温顺的人从不在展示傲慢上浪费精力，而是在真理中，通过与万物的和谐，稳固地发展自己的繁荣。

在亚洲，我们必须团结起来，不是通过组织某种机械力量的方法，而是通过一种真正的同情精神。有组织的机械力量随时准备打击和吞噬我们，我们必须用精神的生命力量来拯救我们，这种生命力量不是通过补充，而是通过有机的同化而形成。我们应该借鉴西方科学，这是对的。我们要从西方人民那里接受一件伟大的东西，那就是他们的智慧宝藏，那种智慧宝藏是巨大的，我们必须承认它的优越性。但是，如果我们忘记我们自己的智慧道德财富，那将是我们的堕落，也是对我们祖先的亵渎，道德财富比一个不断生产无尽物质和物质力量的体系更有价值。

我已经敏锐地感受到，一种巨大的堕落和灾难已经征服了这个世界。人们的灵魂被催眠了，他们在金钱和权力的偶像面前卑躬屈膝。我在旅行中发现，在一场反对这种有组织的培养利己主义的运动中，仅仅进行说教是没有用的。我得出的结论是，我们所需要的是发展和形成一种理想的教育，这样我们就可以在更高的生活氛围中培育我们的孩子。

在过去的一段时间里，教育缺乏理想主义，仅仅是对孩子们进行毫无深厚感情的智力训练。学生们心中萌生的唯一愿望就是追求财富和权力，而不是追求达到某种内在的完美，也不是获得自我解放。这样的理想是不值得人类追求的。

在过去的一个半世纪里，地球上有文化的民族已经放弃他们对精神完美生活的信仰。当我们在东方迷恋上他们成功的魅力时，我们必须知道，我们在西方地平线上看到的可怕的光芒不是日出的光芒，也不是新生的火焰，而是激情的燃烧。只有那些失去理智的人，在凝视着突然爆发的火焰般的成功才会迷恋其中，就像受害者迷恋着闪闪发光的毒蛇眼睛一样。

我再说一遍，科学真理来自西方，我们必须接受它，毫不犹豫地对它表示钦佩。除非我们接受它，否则我们的文明将是片面的，还会继续停滞不前。科学赋予我们理性的力量，使我们能够积极地意识到自己理想的价值。

我们一直需要这一发现来引导我们走出死气沉沉的习惯，为此，我们必须怀着感激之情转向西方的鲜活思想,绝不鼓励培养对她的仇恨。更重要的是,西方人民也需要我们的帮助,因为我们的命运已经交织在一起了。

今天,如果把其他国家拒之门外,就没有一个国家能够进步。让我们努力用我们最好的而不是用我们自己的一切来赢得西方的心,我们用善意和理解,本着相互尊重的精神,而不是报复或蔑视的方式来思考西方、与之打交道。

我们的国际大学代表了这种合作和人类的团结精神。我请求你们,我的兄弟姐妹们,参与建设国际大学,你们中间还有人记得我们两国人民过去建立起来的大爱的纽带。)

诗人泰戈尔在北京北海静心斋的这篇讲话,深情地回顾了中印两国思想文化交往的历史,然后讲述了自己在日本的感受,并对日本提出了批评,他说:"几年前我收到了去美国的邀请。在我的旅途中,我在日本停了下来——我曾经为日本,为那个新兴而富裕的国家的繁荣而自豪。在那里,我深深感到痛心的是,东方这个国家在突然获得好运后竟然不知道应该谦逊。……当一个国家突然获得惊人的政治成功时,这也许就是她历史上一个关键的危险时期。"

在谈到西方时他说:"科学真理来自西方,我们必须接受它,毫不犹豫地对它表示钦佩。除非我们接受它,否则我们的文明将是片面的,还会继续停滞不前。科学赋予我们理性的力量,使我们能够积极地意识到自己理想的价值。……我们必须怀着感激之情转向西方的鲜活思想,绝不鼓励培养对她的仇恨。更重要的是,西方人民也需要我们的帮助,因为我们的命运已经交织在一起了。今天,如果把其他国家拒之门外,就没有一个国家能够进步。让我们努力用我们最好的而不是用我们自己的一切来赢得西方的心,我们用善意和理解,本着相互尊重的精神,而不是报复或蔑视的方式来思考西方、与之打交道。"

最后，诗人讲述自己所创办的国际大学："我们的国际大学代表了这种合作和人类的团结精神。我请求你们，我的兄弟姐妹们，参与建设国际大学，你们中间还有人记得我们两国人民过去建立起来的大爱的纽带。"

我们从诗人为国际大学所启用的名称中就能够体会到它的办学理想，国际大学的孟加拉文为বিশ্বভারতি（bishvabaarati），其中的বিশ্ব词义为"全世界"，ভারতি（baarati）的词义为"文化"，两个词语合起来，其含义就是"全世界文化"，我们就可以理解为"全世界文化的聚集场所"。我觉得，将বিশ্বভারতি翻译成"国际文化大学"，更贴近诗人的思想。

泰戈尔第一次访华纪实

为欢迎泰戈尔,梁启超在北师大的讲演

加尔各答〇——仰光〇——马来亚〇——新加坡〇——香港〇——上海〇——杭卅〇——南京〇——济南〇——北京〇——太原〇——武汉〇——上海〇

1924年4月26日，梁启超为欢迎泰戈尔在北京师范大学发表讲演，标题是《印度与中国文化之亲属的关系》。

诸君：印度诗哲泰谷尔先生来了，不久便要和我们学界几万青年相见。我今天和明天两次公开讲演，要把我们欢迎他的意思先说说。

讲演之前，要先声明几句话，凡伟大人，方面总是很多的，所谓"七色摩尼，各人有各人看法"。诸君总知道，我是好历史的人，我是对于佛教有信仰的人，俗语说得好，"三句离不了本行"，我今天所说，只是历史家或佛学家的个人感想，原不能算是忠实介绍泰谷尔，尤不能代表全国各部分人的欢迎心理，但我想一定有很多人和我同感的。

泰谷尔也曾几次到过欧洲、美国、日本，到处受很盛大的欢迎，这回到中国，恐怕是他全生涯中游历外国的最末一次了。看前天在前门车站下车时景况，我敢说我们欢迎外宾从来没有过这样子热烈而诚恳的。我要问问，我们是把他当一位偶像来崇拜他不是？不，不，无意识地崇拜偶像,是欧美社会最普通现象,我们却还没有这种时髦的习惯。我想,欢迎他的人,一定各有各的意义,各种意义中,也许有一部分和欧美人相同,内中却有一个特殊的意义,是因为他从我们最亲爱的兄弟之邦——印度来。

"兄弟之邦"这句话,并不是我对于来宾敷衍门面,这是历史告诉我们的。我们中国在几千年前,不能够像地中海周围各民族享有交通的天惠,我们躲在东亚一隅,和世界各文化民族不相闻问。东南大海,海岛上都是狉狉獉獉的人——对岸的美洲,五百年前也是如此。西北是一帮一帮的犷悍蛮族,只会威吓我们,踩躏我们,却不能帮助一点。可怜我们这点小小文化,都是我们祖宗在重门深闭中铢积寸累地创造出来,所以我们文化的本质,非常之单调的,非常之保守的,也是吃了这种环境的大亏。

我们西南方却有一个极伟大的文化民族,是印度,他和我从地位上看,从性格上看,正是孪生的弟兄两个。咱们哥儿俩,在现在许多文化民族没有开始活动以前,已经对于全人类应解决的问题着实研究,已经替全人类做了许多应做的事业,印度尤其走在我们前头,他的确是我们的老哥哥,我们是他的小弟弟。最可恨上帝不做美,把一片无情的大沙漠和两重冷酷的雪山隔断我们往来,令我们几千年不得见面,一直到距今二千年前光景,我们才渐渐地知道有恁么一位好哥哥在世界上头。

印度和中国什么时候开始交通呢?据他们的历史,阿育王曾派许多人到这东方传佛教,也许其中有一队曾到过中国。我们的传说,秦始皇时已经有十几位印度人到过长安,被始皇下狱处死了(王子年《拾遗记》说的)。始皇和阿育同时,这事也许是真,但这种半神话的故事,我们且搁在一边,我们这历史家敢保证的,是基督教纪元第一个世纪,咱们哥儿俩确已开始往来。自从汉永平十年至唐贞元五年——西纪六七至七八九,约七百年间,印度大学者到中国的共二十四人，加上罽宾（即北印度之Kashmir，今译克什米尔，唐译迦湿弥罗，从前不认为印度之一部分），来的十三人，合共三十七人，此外从葱岭东西的西域各国来者还不计。我们的先辈到印度留学者，从西晋为贡品到唐——二六五至七九〇——共一百八十七人，有姓名可考的一百零五人。双方往来人物中最著名者，他们来的有鸠摩罗什，有佛陀跋陀罗，即觉贤，有拘那陀罗，即真谛；我们去的有法显，有玄奘，有义浮。在那七八百年中梵夹经间，咱们哥儿俩事实上真成一家人，保持我们极甜蜜的爱情。

诸君呵，我们近年来不是又和许多"所谓文化民族"往来吗？他们为什么来，他们为看上了我们的土地来，他们为看上了我们的钱来，他们拿染着鲜血的炮弹来做见面礼，他们拿机器——夺了他们良民职业的机器——工厂所出的货物来吸我膏血。我们哥儿俩从前的往来却不是如此，我们为的是宇宙真理，我们为的是人类应做的事业。我们感觉着有合作的必要，我们中国人尤其感觉有受老哥哥印度人指导的必要，我们彼此都没有一毫自私自利的动机。

当我们往来最亲密的时候，可惜小兄弟年纪幼稚，不曾有多少礼物孝敬哥哥，却是老哥哥给我们那份贵重礼物，真叫我们永世不能忘记。他给我们什么呢？

一、教给我们知道有绝对的自由——脱离一切遗传习惯及时代思潮所束缚的根本心灵自由，不为物质生活奴隶的精神自由，总括一句，不是对他人的压制束缚而得解放的自由，乃是自己解放自己"得大解脱""得大自在""得大无畏"的绝对自由。

二、教给我们知道有绝对的爱——对于一切众生不妒、不恚、不厌、不憎、不诤的纯爱，对于愚人或恶人悲悯同情的挚爱，体认出众生和我不可分离"冤亲平等""物我一如"的绝对爱。

这份大礼的结晶体，就是一部《大藏经》。《大藏经》七千卷，一言以蔽之曰"悲智双修"，教我们从智慧上求得绝对的自由，教我们从悲悯上求得绝对的爱。

这份大礼物已经够我们享用了,我们慈爱的老哥哥犹以为未足,还把许多副礼物文学、美术等等送给我们。

我们得着这些副礼物的方法,约有以下几个来源:

一、从西域——即葱岭内外各国间接传来。

二、印度人来中国的随带着来,如各梵僧大率都带有雕刻、绘画等物作为贡品。

三、中国人游历印度的归赆,例如《玄奘传》详记他带回来的东西、除梵夹经卷外,各种美术品都有。

四、从翻译经典上附带得来的知识和技术。

这些副礼物,屈指数来,最重要者有十二件:

一、音乐。音乐大抵从西域间接传来的居多。中国古乐,我们想来是很好的,但南北朝以后,逐渐散失,在江南或者还存一部分,中原地方,却全受西方传来的新音乐影响。隋唐承北朝之统,混一区宇,故此后音乐全衍北方系统。最盛行的音乐,是"甘州""伊州""凉州""梁州"诸调,这些调都是从现在甘肃、新疆等地方输进来,而那时候这些地方的文化,全属印度系。后来又有所谓龟兹部乐、天竺部乐等,都是一条线上衍出来。这些音乐,现在除了日本皇室或者留得一部分外,可惜都声沉响绝了,但我们据《唐书·乐志》及唐人诗文集、笔记里头所描写记载,知道那时的音乐确是美妙无伦,所以美妙之故,大约由中国系音乐和印度系音乐结婚产出来。

二、建筑。中国建筑受印度影响是显而易见的。《洛阳伽蓝记》里的遗迹,我们虽不得见,水平寺、同泰寺、慈恩寺……诸名区的庄严美丽,我们虽仅能在前人诗歌上或记录上歆歙凭吊,但其他胜迹留传至今的还不少,就中窣堵坡(塔)一项,尤为我们从前所无。自从这项建筑输入之后,增饰我们风景的美观真不少,你看,西湖上的

"雷峰""宝俶"两塔,增他多少妩媚,汴梁城上若没有"铁塔"和"繁台",还有什么意趣?北京城最古的建筑物,不是彰仪门外隋开皇间——六世纪末的"天宁寺塔"吗?北海的琼华岛,岛上"白塔"和岛下长廊相映,正表示中印两系建筑调和之美。我想,这些地方,随处可以窥见中印文化连锁的秘密来。

三、绘画。中国最古的画,我们看不见了。从石刻上——嘉祥县之武梁祠堂等留下几十张汉画,大概可想见那时素朴的画风。历史上最有名的画家,首推陆探微、顾虎头,他们却都以画佛像得名。又如慧远在庐山的佛影画壁,我猜是中国最初的油画。但这些名迹都已失传,且不论他,至如唐代的王维、吴道子所画佛像,人间许尚有存留。依我看来,从东晋至唐,中印人士往来不绝,印度绘画流入中国很多,我们画风,实生莫大影响,或者可以说我们画的艺术在那个时代才确立基础。这种画风,一直到北宋的"画苑",依然存在,成为我国画史上的正统派。啊啊!真是中印结婚产生的"宁馨儿"①。

四、雕刻。中国从前雕刻品,像只有平面的,立体雕刻,我猜度是随着佛教输入。晋朝有位名士戴安道②(王羲之的儿子王子猷剡溪雪夜访戴的故事,访的便是他),后人都知道他会作诗画画,我们从《高僧传》上才知道他和他的兄弟都是大雕刻家,他们哥儿俩曾合雕一佛像,雕时还留下许多美谈。此后六朝隋唐间所刻有名工妙的佛像,见于历史者不计其数,可惜中间经过"三武毁法"(北魏孝武、北周武帝、唐武宗)的厄运,和历代的兵燹,百不存一。但毁不掉的尚有洛阳龙门山壁上三四千尊的魏齐造像,我们现在除亲往游览外,还可以随处看见拓片,其尤为世界环宝的,莫如大同府云冈石窟中大大小小几百尊石像,据说是"犍陀罗美术"

---

① 宁馨儿——意指"这样的孩子",是赞美孩子健康英俊的用语。
② 戴安道(326—396),名逵,安徽省濉溪县临涣镇人,终身不仕。东晋时期隐士、美术家、雕塑家,博学多才,善于鼓琴,工于绘画人物和山水。

（犍陀罗为今阿富汗地，他的美术，是印度和希腊所产）的结晶作品，全世界找不出第二处。就只这票宝贝，也足令我们中华民族在人类文化史上留下历劫不磨的荣誉，但倘非多谢老哥哥提拔，何能得此？

还有一种艺术要附带说说，我们的缂丝画，全世界都公认他的价值，但我敢说也是从印度学来的，玄奘归赆的清单，便列有这种珍贵作品。

五、戏曲。中国最古的戏曲，所谓"鱼龙曼衍之戏"，大概是变戏法的玩意儿。歌和舞自然是各有很古的历史，但歌舞并行的戏剧，魏晋以前却无可考见，最初的歌舞剧，当推"拨头"一曲，亦名"钵头"。据近人考证，像是从那离代京（大同）三万一千里南天竺附近的拔豆国传来，那戏是演一个人。他的老子被虎吃掉，他入山杀虎报仇，演时且舞且歌，声情激越，后来著名的"兰陵王""踏摇娘"等等戏本，都是从"拨头"变化出来。这种考证若不错，那么，印度又是我们戏剧界恩人了。

六、诗歌和小说。说中国诗歌和印度有关系，这句话很骇人听闻——连我也未敢自信为定论。但我总感觉，东晋时候所译出印度大诗人马鸣菩萨的《佛本行赞》和《大乘庄严经》这两部名著，在我文学界像有相当的影响。我们古诗，后三百篇到汉魏的五言，大率情感主于温柔敦厚，而资料都是现实的，像《孔雀东南飞》和《木兰诗》一类的作品，都起自六朝，前此却无有。（《孔雀东南飞》向来都认为汉诗，但我疑心是六朝的，我别有考。）《佛本行赞》现在译成四本，原来只是一首诗，把佛一生事迹添上许多诗的趣味谱为长歌，在印度佛教史上，力量之伟大固不待言，译成华文以后，也是风靡一时，六朝名士几于人人共读，那种热烈的情感和丰富的想象力，输入我们诗人的心灵中当不少，只怕《孔雀东南飞》一路的长篇叙事抒情诗，也间接受着影响罢。（但此说别无其他证据，我未敢自信，我要再三声明。)

小说受《大乘庄严经》影响，我十有九相信，《庄严经》是把"四阿含"里头所记佛弟子的故事加上文学的风趣搬演出来，全书用几十段故事组成，体裁绝类我们的《今古奇观》。我国小说，从晋人《搜神记》等类作品，渐渐发展到唐代丛书所收之唐人小说，依我看，大半从《庄严经》的模子里镕铸出来。这还是就初期的小说而言，若宋元以后章回体的长篇小说，依我看，受《华严经》《宝积经》等影响一定不少，这些经典都是佛灭后六七百年间，由印度文学家的想象力构造，这是治佛学史的人公认的。然而这些经典，中国文学家大半爱读他，又是事实。

中国文学本来因时代变迁自由发展，所受外来影响或比较的仅少，但既有这类新文学作品输入，不管当时诗家或小说家曾否有意模仿他，然而间接受他熏染，我想总不能免的。

七、天文历法。这门学问，中国原来发达很早，但既和印度交通后，当然得他补助，唐朝的"九执术"，便纯从印度传来，僧一行的历学，在我们历学史上是有位置的。

八、医学。这亦是我们固有的，和印度交通后，亦有补助增益，观《隋书·经籍志》《唐书·艺文志》所载婆罗门医药书之多可知。

九、字母。中国文字是衍形的，不能有跟着言语变化的弹力性，这是我们最感不便的一件大事。自从佛教输入，梵文也跟着来，于是许多高僧想仿造字母来救济这个问题。神珙、守温等辈先后尝试，现存"见溪群疑"等三十六字母，虽然形式拙劣，发音漏略，不能产出什么良果，但总算把这问题提出，给我们以极有益的动机和资料。

十、著述体裁。中国从前书籍，除文学作品及注释古典的训诂书不计外，虽然称"体大思精"的经书子书，大都是囫囵统括的体裁，没有什么组织，不容易厘清眉目，看出他的条理。自从佛典输入之后，每一部经论都有他首尾一贯盛水不漏的主义，里头却条分缕析，秩序谨严，这种体裁，求诸中国汉魏以前是没有的。（《荀子》和《论衡》算是最谨严的，但还比不上。）这种译书既盛行，于是发生"科判"的专门学——把全部书脉络厘清，令人从极复杂的学说中看出他要点所在，乃至如天台贤首诸师将几千卷藏经判为"三时五教"之类，是都用分析综合的观察，开一研究新途径。不但此也，当六七世纪时，印度的新因明学正从佛教徒手里发挥光大起来，研究佛学的人，都要靠他做主要工具。我们的玄奘大师，正是最深造此学之人，他自己和他们门下的人的著述，一立一破（立是自己提出主张，破是反驳别人），都严守因明轨范，应用得极圆滑而致密。这种学风，虽后来因禅宗盛行，一时消歇，然而已经在学界上播下良种，历久终会发新芽的。

十一、教育方法。中国教育，不能不说发达得很早，但教育方法怎么样，共有若干种，我们不容易调查清楚。即如聚许多人在一堂讲演，孔子、孟子书中像没有看见这种痕迹，汉朝伏生、申公诸大师，也不见得是如此，我很疑心这种讲演式的教育，是佛教输入后从印度人学来。不唯如此，即在一个固定的校舍中，聚起许多人专研究一门学术，立一定课程，中国前此虽或有之，但像是从佛教团成立以后，这种制度越发完密而巩固。老实说，唐以后的书院，实从佛教团的教育机关脱胎而来，这种机关和方法善良与否，另一问题，但在中国教育史上不能不特笔重记。

十二、团体组织。中国团体组织，纯家族为单位，别的团体，都是由家族扩大或加减而成，佛教输入，才于家族以外别有宗教或学术的团体发生，当其盛时，势力很大，政治上权威，一点也不能干涉到他。即以今日论，试到普陀山一游，便可见我们国里头有许多享有"治外法权"的地方。不必租界，他们里头，有点像共产的组织，又有点像"生产事业国有"的组织。这种组织对不对，另一问题，但不能不说是在中国全社会单调组织中添些新颖的色彩。

以上十二项，都是佛教传来的副产物，也是老哥哥——印度人赠给我们的随帖隆仪，好在我们当小弟弟的也很争气，受了哥哥提携便力求长进。我们从印度得来的学问完全消化了来荣卫自己，把自己特性充分发展出来，文学、美术等等方面，自己建设的成绩固不用说，即专就"纯印度系的哲学"——即佛教论，天台宗、贤首宗、禅宗、净土宗这几个大宗派，都是我们自创，乃至法相宗虽全出印度，然而成唯识论乃由玄奘集合十大论师学说抉择而成，实是玄奘一家之学。其门下窥基、圆测两大派，各个发挥尽致，剖析入微，恐怕无著世亲一派学问，到中国才算真成熟哩。所以我们对着老哥哥，自问尚可以无惭色。

哎，自唐末到今日，咱们哥儿俩又一别千年了。这一千多年里头，咱们两家里都碰着千灾百难，山上的豺狼虎豹，水里的龙蛇蚌鳖，人间的魑魅魍魉，不断地恐吓咱们，揶揄咱们，践踏咱们。咱们也像有点老态龙钟，英气消减，不独别人瞧不起咱们，连咱们自己也有点瞧不起自己了。虽然，我深信"业力不灭"的真理——凡已经种在人心上的灵苗，虽一期间偶尔衰萎，终究要发新芽，别开一番更美丽的境界。不信，你看曲阜孔林里的汉楷唐柏，皱瘦到像一根积锈的铁柱，却是阳春三月，从他那秃顶上发出几节"孙枝"，比"鹅黄柳条"的生机还充盛。咱们哥儿俩年纪虽老，"犹有童心"，不信，你看哥哥家里头现成的两位现代人物——泰谷尔和甘地。

哈哈！一千多年"爱而不见"的老哥哥，又来访问小弟弟来了。咱们哥儿俩都是饱经忧患，鬓发苍然，揩眼相看，如梦如寐。我们看见老哥哥，蓦地把多少年前联床夜雨的苦辛兜上心来。啊啊！我们要紧紧握着他的手不肯放，我们要搂着他亲了又亲，亲了又亲……我们要把从娘胎里带来的一副热泪，浸透了他托腮上那可爱的大白胡子。

我们用一千多年前洛阳人士欢迎摄摩腾①的情绪来欢迎泰谷尔哥哥，用长安人士欢迎鸠摩罗什的情绪来欢迎泰谷尔哥哥，用庐山人士欢迎真谛②的情绪来欢迎泰谷尔哥哥。

泰谷尔对我们说："他并不是什么宗教家、教育家、哲学家……他只是一个诗人。"这话是我们绝对承认的。他又说："他万不敢比千年前来过的印度人，因为那时是印度全盛时代，能产出许多伟大人物，现在是过渡时代，不会产出很伟大人物。"这话我们也相对地承认，但我们以为凡成就一位大诗人，不但在乎有优美的技术，而尤在乎有崇高的理想。泰谷尔这个人和泰谷尔的诗，都是"绝对自由"与"绝对爱"的权化，我们不能知道印度从前的诗人如何，不敢妄下比较，但我想泰谷尔最少也可比二千年前做《佛本行赞》的马鸣菩萨。我盼望他这回访问中国所发生的好影响，不在鸠摩罗什和真谛之下。

泰谷尔又说："他这回不能有什么礼物送给我们，只是代表印度人向我们中国致十二分的亲爱。"我说，就只这一点，已经比什么礼物都隆重了。我们打开胸臆欢喜承受老哥哥的亲爱，我们还有加倍的亲爱奉献老哥哥，请他带回家去。

我最后还有几句话很郑重地告诉青年诸君们，老哥哥这回是先施的访问我们了。记得从前哥哥家里来过三十七个人，我们却也有一百八十七个人，往哥家里去，我盼望咱们两家久断复续的爱情，并不是泰谷尔一两个月游历昙花一现便了，咱们老弟兄对于全人类的

---

① 摄摩腾——天竺高僧。公元68年，汉明帝从西域请来印度僧人摄摩腾和竺法兰，在京都洛阳建白马寺，是中国建佛寺的开端。同年摄摩腾和竺法兰来到五台山，看中五台山的风水，并奏明汉明帝在这里破土建庙，揭开了五台佛国历史的第一页。

② 真谛(499—569)，印度优禅尼国人，精通佛教经典。在南北朝梁武帝时真谛携带大量梵文经典，乘船来到梁都建康，在准备开始译经之时爆发了"侯景之乱"，于是他辗转到富春，才开始译经。之后真谛又多次迁移，在兵荒马乱的年代坚持译经，与鸠摩罗什、玄奘、不空并称为中国佛教四大译经师。

责任大着哩，咱们应该合作互助的日子长着呢。泰谷尔这次来游，不过替我们起一个头。倘若因此能认真恢复中印从前的甜蜜交谊和有价值的共同工作，那么，泰谷尔此游才真有意义啊！那么，我们欢迎泰古尔才真有意义啊！①

(The great sage and poet–philosopher, Rabindranath Tagore, will arrive very soon and will meet our students to the number of several thousands. I take this opportunity, therefore, of preparing a welcome for him.

First of all, I want you understand that all great personalities are many-sided. They are like the seven-coloured Mani, which presents different aspects of brilliance to different observers. You all know too that I am fond of treating things from a historical point of view; you know too that I have deep faith in Buddhism. As the proverb says: "No man can speak three words without disclosing his own craft." So what I am going to tell you today is but my own impression as a historian and a Buddhist. I cannot give a proper introduction to Rabindranath Tagore, still less can I pretend to give adequate expression to the enthusiastic welcome of all sections of our people.

Rabindranath Tagore has visited Europe, America and Japan. Wherever he goes he receives a tremendous welcome. You will recall that outburst of enthusiasm in the Chien Men Station, on the day he arrived, such as has never been accorded to any other foreign guest, so warm it was, and so sincere.

The meaningless idolatry of hero-worship is common amongst the people of Europe and America. We, Chinese, have not yet acquired this fashionable habit. We, who welcome Rabindranath Tagore, may each have our several

---

① 《梁启超全集》第十六集　演说二，中国人民大学出版社1918年版，第89—96页。

reasons—it may even be that, like the Europeans and Americans, some of us are merely hero-worshiping him; but we must all recognize the one great central idea, that he comes to us from the country which is our nearest and dearest brother—India.

To say that the country of India is our brother is not a mere matter of courtesy to our guest. It has its foundation in history.

In ancient times China did not enjoy that facility of communication which was the privilege of the races bordering the Mediterranean Sea. We suffered from the disadvantage of being shut up in one corner of eastern Asia without any means of communicating with other great races and cultures. The islands in the eastern and southern oceans were populated by savages. America, on the far side the Pacific, gave no civilization. Beyond our western and northern frontiers there were those barbarous and ferocious races, whose business is ever was to threaten and devastate, but never to help us.

It is well for us to remember that this little privilege of culture, which we possess today, has been handed down to us by our ancestors, who labored long within secluded boundaries, unaided and single-handed. It is also due to this seclusion of its environment that our culture gives the impression of being monotonous and conservative to an extraordinary degree.

About across our south-west boundary, there was a great had cultured country, India. Both in character had geography, India and China are like twin brothers. Before most of the civilized races became active, we two brothers had already begun to study the great problems which concern the whole of mankind. We had already accomplished much in the interests of humanity. India was ahead of us and we, the little brother, followed behind. But nature had not been kind. She had placed between us a vast area of unfeeling desert and two great ranges of cruel snowy peaks, which separated us for thousands of years. It was not till two thousand years ago that we were given gradually to know that we had a very good elder brother on the earth.

When did these two great countries begin to communicate with each other?

According to Indian history, King Asoka sent a number of missionaries to propagate Buddhist ideas. Probably some of them had travelled as far as China. Our own tradition says that in the time of the famous Chin Sze Huang (who built the Great Wall), there were already more than ten Hindus, who had been to Chang-an and who were imprisoned had killed by him. Asoka and Chin Sze Huang were contemporaries and therefore this might have been true. But we need not worry over half fairy tales.

When we as historians are able to vouch for is that the first communication between us as brothers occurred in the first century of the era of Christ. From the tenth year of Han Yung Tsin to the fifth year of Tang Chen Yuan (67-789 A.D.), roughly during eight hundred years, the Hindu scholars, who came to China, numbered twenty-four, do which may be added thirteen from Kashmir (which in Tang times was not recognized as part of India) thus making thirty-seven in all, not counting those who came from other countries on the eastern and western side of Chung Lin (Turkestan). Our scholars, who went to India to study, during the period from the western Tsin to the tang dynasties (265-790 A.D.) numbered 187, the names of 105 of whom we can ascertain. Among the most famous from India were Tamolosa (Dharma-raksha), Chu Shien (Buddha-bhadra) and Chen Ti (Jina-bhadra) and from China, Fa Hien, Yuan Chuang and I Tsing.

During the period of 700 or 800 year, we lived like affectionate brothers, loving and respecting one another.

And now we are told that, within recent years, we have at last come into contact with civilized races. Why have they come to us? They have come coveting our land and our wealth; they have offered us as presents cannon balls dyed in human blood; their factories manufacture goods and machines which daily deprive our people of their crafts. But we two brothers were not like that in the days gone by. We were both devoted to the cause of the universal truth, we set out to fulfil the destiny of mankind, we felt the necessity for cooperation. We Chinese specially felt the need for leadership and direction from our elder brothers, the people of India. Neither of us were stained in the least by any motive of self-interest—of that we had none.

During the period when we were most close and affectionate to one another, it is a pity that this little brother had no special gift to offer to its elder brother, whilst our elder brother had given to us gifts of singular and precious worth, which we can never forget.

Now what have we so received?

1. India taught us to embrace the idea of absolute freedom—that fundamental freedom of mind, which enables us to shake off all the fetters of past traditions and habits as well as the present customs of a particular age—that spiritual freedom which casts off the enslaving forces of material existence. It was not merely that negative aspect of freedom. Which consists in ridding ourselves of outward oppression and slavery, but that emancipation of the individual from his own self, through which men attain great liberation, great ease and great fearlessness.

2. India also taught us the idea of absolute love, that pure love towards all living beings which eliminates all obsessions of jealousy, anger,

impatience and disgust, which expresses itself in deep pity and sympathy for the foolish, the wicked and the sinful—that absolute love, which recognizes the inseparability between all beings, "The equality of friend and enemy", "The oneness of myself and all things". This great gift is contained in the Ta Tsang Jen (Buddhist classics). The teachings in these seven thousand volumes can be summed up in one phrase: To cultivate sympathy and intellect, in order to attain absolute freedom through wisdom, and absolute love through pity.

3. But our elder brother had still something more to give. He brought us invaluable assistance in the field of literature and art. In the first place, these came indirectly through Si Yu, and then directly from the Indian sages who came to China bringing with them as gifts for presentation to our Emperor, their pictures, sculptures and books. Thirdly, they were brought by the Chinese scholars on their return from India, for instance in the biography of Tuan Chuang, besides his observations on the classics, there was a list of articles in which were included all kinds of works of art. Lastly we learnt from the translated classics not only of India's wisdom, but also of its art.

4. Of minor gifts, I will enumerate only the following:

Music—This came indirectly through Si Yu. We have no idea what our ancient music, for after the Southern and Northern Dynasties, it had degenerated and had almost disappeared. It is possible that something was left in the south of the Yang Tze river, but in the North our own music gave way before the Indian influence, which were brought in by Si Yu. The Suei and the Tang dynasties succeeded the Northern Dynasties and united the empire and thereafter this northern music predominated. The most popular tunes were "Kan Chou", "Yi Chou" and "Liang Chou", all names of districts in the Sin Chang and Kan-Su provinces. But at that time these provinces were almost wholly under the influence of India. Today we have no record of the music of this era, except what has been preserved by the Japanese Royal House. But from what is recorded in *Tang Shu: the Book of Music* as well as in the appreciations of music found in our general literature, we can be certain that that music must have been beautiful and exquisite. The cause of such excellence is probably due to the union of Chinese and Indian modes.

Architecture—That China has been influenced by India in her architecture is an obvious fact although we have lost sight of the great work in the Cha Lan Temple in Lo Yang, and although we have to rely upon accounts met with literature and poetry to obtain any idea of the beauty and grandeur of the Temples of Yung Pin (Perpetual Peace) and Tsze (Material Grace). But we have still standing a number of ruins which tell us of the glory of those olden days. The pagoda is purely India in origin; we never had anything like it before the days of Indian influence. We do not always realize how much this particular form of architecture adds to the natural beauty of our landscape. We cannot imagine the West Lake in Hangchou without its two pagodas, the grand Luei Fong (Thunder Peak) and the graceful Pan Su. What charm would be in the City of Pien Liang, if it were not for the presence of the iron pagoda and the pagoda Tan Tai (House of Abundance) ? The oldest piece of architecture in Peking is the pagoda in front of the temple Tien Nien (Heavenly Peace) built at the end of the 6th century A.D. What beauty of harmony does the island of Chung Hua (Fairy Flower) in Pei Hei, reveal with the white pagoda on its peak and the long verandah below, which the combination of Chinese and India architecture alone could have achieved! There as elsewhere we see the wonderful interplay of these two cultures.

Painting—The paintings of the most ancient period of our history have disappeared. Only from the stone tablets and stone inscriptions, such as the Famous Han paintings Wu Liang Tsze and Joh Siang Shien, do we obtain a glimpse of the fine simplicity of style in the paintings of that period. The most renowned painters in our early history were Kuo Tan Wei and Kuo Hu To. they were famous for their paintings of Buddha. Another interesting relic is still to be found in Lo San, the famous shadow of Buddha, which I suspect to be the first piece oil painting in China. A few of the works of Wang Wei and Wu Tao Tsze are still preserved and for the most part they are Buddhistic pictures. It seems obvious that, from the East Chin Dynasty to that of Tang, there was continuous communication between India and China and this, with its introduction of numerous Indian pictures, had a shaping influence upon Chinese art; in fact we might go further and say that we probably owe the very foundation of our Chinese painting to Indian influence. A great school continued to flourish till the North Sung Dynasty, when it was superseded by the artists of our Royal Academy. It is till regarded as embodying the classical style of Chinese painting.

Sculpture—In olden times we had engravings upon stone, but never I think, sculpture in three dimensions before the introduction of Buddhism. From *the Book of Famous Monks*, we learn that Tai An Tao (Tsin Dynasty), who was well know as a painter and a literary man, was also sculptor. He and his brother worked together upon a large image of Buddha, which enjoyed great fame in its day. Then there are records of famous sculptures executed during the six dynasties and the Sui and

Tang. Unfortunately all these were destroyed during the Civil Wars as by the deliberate vandalism of three emperors, who were bitterly opposed to Buddhism. We still possess today the great rock sculptures and reliefs, three or four thousand in number, at Lo Yang and Lung Men executed during the Wei and the Tsi dynasties. But the greatest treasure we have is the group of figures at Yung Kuang, Ta Tung and Shensi, large and small, not less than a thousand in number. It is said that the style is of Gandhara in Afghanistan, the result of the meeting between the Greek and the India cultures. This is indeed a priceless possession of which, if it had not been for our elder brother, we should have been deprived. Incidentally, we might also mention the art of the kakemono, whose origin we also owe to India. In fact in the inventory of Yeun Tsang, there is a record of a number of kakemono, which he brought back with him from India.

Drama—We can trace, the art of drama back to the play of first and Dragon, which was probably a species of magic or trickery, rather than drama in the modern sense. Dancing and singing had their respective origin in ancient days, but the combination of the two does not seem to appear till after the Tsin Dynasty. The earliest operatic play we know of was called Pu Tou. The story of the play centres round a man who went into the mountains to avenge his father and was killed by a tiger. The hero expresses his feelings in passionate songs and dances. Later plays such as *Lian Ling Wang, the King of Lian Ling* and the *Tao Yao Niang* were all patterned on Pu Tou. If this is true, then we are again in debt to India in the field of drama.

Poetry and Fiction—To say that India influenced us even in poetry and fiction would perhaps seem astonishing. But we have reason to believe that the cerebrated translation of the two great books, *Fun Pen Shen Tsai* (*The Life of Sakuamuni* by Asvaghosha) and *Ta Shen Chung Yen Tsin* (*Mahayana Sutra*) by the great Indian poet Ma Ming (Indian name unknown) did exert a decided influence upon our literature. Our original poetry from *The Book of Odes* to the five syllable lines of Han and Wei included only short personal lyrics. Narrative poetry never made its appearance until the six dynasties when such poems as *Kung Chou Tung Nan Fe* and *Mou Lan, Fun Pen Shin Tsai*, originally a long biographical poem, but now rendered into Chinese prose in four books, were composed. They not only introduced the great influence of Hindu literature but remained actively influential among literary circles in China during the six dynasties. The vast imagination and rich emotional appeal of Hindu literature opened new vistas for the Chinese poets. There is clear evidence that our novel writing originated under the direct the influence of Mahayana translations. It seems to me that our tales from the Tsin to the Tang period, were modelled on them. Our novels, properly speaking, did not appear till the Sung period and were largely the product of our study of Hua Yuan and Pan Chi.

Astronomy and Calendar—This special branch of science was early cultivated in China, but received further development in the Tang period, when the publication of Ju Tchu Sie showed the distinct influence of India.

Medicine—This was an original art in China but it received great encouragement from our contact with India. What is recorded in the History of Suey and the Books on Art and Literature in the History of Tang is sufficient proof of my assertion.

Alphabet—The Chinese language is by nature pictorial, and that is a great disadvantage. With the introduction of Buddhism and Sanskrit a number of Indian scholars attempted to invent an alphabetical system to solve our difficulties. Although it was rather crude and did not yield very satisfactory results, it furnished us with valuable material for further experimentation.

Literary style—Ancient Chinese written books do not show sufficient effort at organization and therefore lack clarity of presentation. With the coming in of Buddhist classics, it began to more systematic and consequently more lucid and logical in the exposition of ideas. Indian logic (Hetuvidya) and methodology opened a new era in China in the art of writing. Yuan Chuang was one of most painstaking students of this new science and he and his followers created a new school of thought famous for its rigorous analytical and critical method, which stood in direct opposition to the contemplative and introspective method of the Dhyana (Chha or Zen) school of Buddhists.

Educational method—Exactly how education was conducted in ancient China no one is able to say, but we are quite certain that Confucius and Mencius did not resort to the method of addressing large audiences for the propagation of their teachings, and it is quite likely, therefore, that the system of formal lecturing, with which we are so familiar today, came from India. Furthermore the academies which flourished since the Tang Dynasty cannot be other than Buddhist in origin. Whether this setting apart of particular institutions for the investigation of specialized problems, has great educational value or not is another question, but we must acknowledge the important position which this method occupies in Chinese educational history.

Social organization—The unit of Chinese society is the family. The different forms of social organization are only the family in its various modifications. Since Buddhism became popular in China, public bodies with religious and scholarly purposes, independent of the family, began to appear. And these flourished in such extraordinary degree that the power of government could have no control over them. The Pu To islands, up to the present day, enjoy exclusive judicial privileges and are administered on a peculiar social basis of a more or less communistic nature.

What I have referred to above comprise the main elements of our Buddhistic heritage and I am proud to say that we have made use it to good purpose. Indian thought has been entirely assimilated into our own world of experience and has become an inalienable part of our consciousness. It has helped us to develop our faculties and has enabled us to achieve notable results in various fields of literary and artistic endeavor. Even if we confine our case to Buddhism itself, we find that we have made some worthy contributions to its many metaphysical systems, forming ever new schools of thought upon the foundation of the old, though the energy and application of men like Yuan Chuang; so that we may take just pride in sayig that Buddhism has become as distinctly Chinese as it is Indian.

We have unfortunately been separated from one another now for at least one thousand years and have each pursued our respective lines of development. We have had calamities during these years of separation. What have we not experienced? We have been threatened, mocked, trampled upon and have suffered all possible mortifications, so much so indeed that not only have we been looked upon with contemptuous eyes but we ourselves have begun to lose our sense of self-respect.

But we have faith in the imperishability of human endeavor and the seeds we have sown, in spite of the many vicissitudes and in clemencies which we are passing through, will eventually bring us a harvest in the fullness of time. Do not we find an inspiring symbol in the ancient trees of the sacred wood round Confucius' tomb, reputed to have been planted by himself and his chief disciples, which though shrunk with senility and almost in a petrified state, are yet capable of manifesting their hidden vitality by shooting forth new branches of tender green, when the earth is awakened to the call of spring? Both the civilization represented by India and China are hoary with ancient traditions and yet I feel there is in them the vigour of eternal youth, which shows itself today in India in the two great personalities of Tagore and Gandhi.

After a thousand years of separation during which period, however, we two continued to cherish thought of love for one another, this elder of ours has once more come to us animated with fraternal sentiments. Both of us bear lines of sorrow on our face, our hair is grey with age, we stare with a blank and vacant look as if we are just awakened from a dream; but, as we gaze on each other, what recollections and fond memories of our early youth rose in our mind—of those, when we shared our joys and sorrows together! Now that we have once more the happiness of embracing each other we shall not allow ourselves to be separated again.

We would welcome Rabindranath Tagore in the same spirit as when more than one thousand years ago the people of Lu San welcome Chang Ti. Rabindranath Tagore wishes to make it known that he is not a religious teacher or an educationist or a philosopher, he says that he is only a poet. This we fully acknowledge. And he says also that he cannot under any circumstances place himself on the same level as his predecessors, who came in our early dynasties, because India at that time was in a period of great epic preeminence; it was an epoch which capable of giving birth to great ideals and noble personalities, and therefore totally different in its spirit to the present era of transition, when human thoughts and ideals are in state of turmoil and confusion and therefore offer no encouragement to the development of genuine and worthy personalities. This sentiment we can also, I think, indorse.

And yet, to be a great poet needs more than an exquisite sense of what is artistic—one must also be inspired by serious and magnanimous thoughts. In the personality Rabindranath Tagore, as well as in his poetry, we find that exemplification of those principles of absolute love and absolute freedom, which form the basis of Hindu culture and civilization. I have no adequate idea Hindu poetry in great classical period and cannot, therefore, compare that with the work of our distinguished guest. But I am perfectly sure that Rabindranath Tagore is as important to us as Asvaghosha who wrote the life of Buddha was in ancient days, and we hope the influence he is going to exert on China will not in any way be inferior to that of Kumarajiva and Chang Ti.

Rabindranath Tagore says also that he has nothing to offer as a gift from India, but he wishes to express the sentiments of love of the entire people of India from which he has come as representative. I wish to say in reply that the sentiments of love are more worthy than all the gifts that he can possibly offer us, We are more than overjoyed to receive them and we wish that he would take back with him our love and sympathy, which are, I can assure him, even more intense than his own.

I wish, in concluding, to say something of great practical importance to you. Rabindranath Tagore has come to visit us; and we ought to remember that when of old thirty-seven representatives came from India there were actually some hundred and eighty-seven people to return the visit. We hope that on this occasion the love between China and India will not terminate with the one or two months which Rabindranath Tagore is able to spend in this country. The responsibility that we bear to the whole of mankind is great indeed, and there should be I think, a warm spirit of co-operation between India and China. The coming of Rabindranath Tagore will, I hope, mark the beginning of an important period of history.

If we can avail of this occasion to renew the intimate relationship which we had with India and to establish a really constructive scheme of cooperation, then our welcome to Rabindranath Tagore will have real significance.)[①]

在这篇讲演中，梁启超从历史学家和佛学家的角度比较详细地介绍了一千多年前印度与中国大量文化交流历史以及中国文化受到印度佛教文化的影响，后来中断了。通篇讲话情真意切，充满对诗人泰戈尔真挚的友爱。梁先生动情地说："一千多年'爱而不见'的老哥哥，又来访问小弟弟来了。咱们哥儿俩都是饱经忧患，鬓发苍然，揩眼相看，如梦如寐。我们看见老哥哥，蓦地把多少年前联床夜雨的苦辛兜上心来。啊啊！我们要紧紧握着他的手不肯放，我们要搂着他亲了又亲，亲了又亲……我们要把从娘胎里带来的一副热泪，浸透了他托腮上那可爱的大白胡子。"

最后他深情地对年轻的同学们说："我盼望咱们两家久断复续的爱情，并不是泰谷尔一两个月游历昙花一现便了，咱们老弟兄对于全人类的责任大着哩，咱们应该合作互助的日子长着呢。泰谷尔这次来

---

① The English Writings of Tagore.《泰戈尔英文作品集》第2卷，第572—579页。

游,不过替我们起一个头。倘若因此能认真恢复中印从前的甜蜜交谊和有价值的共同工作,那么,泰谷尔此游才真有意义啊!那么,我们欢迎泰谷尔才真有意义啊!"

泰戈尔第一次访华纪实

在法源寺观赏丁香花

加尔各答〇----仰光〇----马来亚〇----新加坡〇----香港〇----上海〇----杭州〇----南京〇----济南〇----北京〇----太原〇----武汉〇----上海〇

4月26日，北京佛化新青年会邀请诗人一行来北京古老佛教寺庙法源寺观赏丁香花，以此表示对诗人泰戈尔的欢迎。当天早晨，该会同仁释道阶、葛文园、刘灵华、庄蕴宽、释佛慈、陈源湘、邵秀夫、宁达蕴、杨蝶父和空也法师等齐聚法源寺内恭候。一辆汽车驶来，停在庙门。车门打开，下车的是三位印度学者、葛玲女士、恩厚之先生和徐志摩6人，却不见诗人泰戈尔。徐志摩解释说，诗人泰戈尔早晨应卡尔浩文夫人邀请去赴早餐，回来感到身体不适，所以没有来。众人对徐志摩说，大家都心怀诚意欢迎泰戈尔先生，如果诗人不能来，大家会感到很失望的。若诗人病体不甚要紧，盼望诗人能来欣赏丁香花。诗人秘书恩厚之于是返回住所，劝诗人前往。诗人泰戈尔深觉盛情难却，于是在林徽因、梁思成的陪同下前往法源寺。众人在门外合掌致意，欢迎诗人的莅临。泰戈尔先生双手合十含笑作答。

　　张宗载致欢迎词，陈源湘将其翻译成英语。随后葛文园女技师率领女生高唱欢迎歌曲，歌声和雅幽妙。诗人泰戈尔听罢欢迎词和优美歌声，面带喜色，口发微笑，站起身过来，发表了即兴讲话。他说：

There are many things in India, belonging to the far-distant centuries, which seem to be continuing, but are really now dead. In this place there is something of the old yet living. I feel a touch of that great stream of life that sprang from the heart of India and flowed across mountain and desert until at last it came to this land and fertilized the heart of your people. That water of everlasting life is still flowing: its wisdom defies time and fills my mind with reverence.

I feel here the touch of our ancestors and a blessing comes on us who are their descendants. Their spirits must be happy because we have followed their footsteps to this land which they loved and helped so mach. We also have come on the same errand, the errand of peace and love. I feel in this present age, when the human races are fighting and robbing one another, that this same spirit of India is urging us on to try and bring peace into the heart of their turmoil and conflict. I hope this spirit of India will give us strength in our mission.

When I had lunch at our meeting of foreigners and Europeans resident in this land, I had for my neighbor one who had lived in this place a long time. When he heard me talk of the mission of cooperation and conciliation which I had in my heart, this man said that China was the one place where I would find good soil for the seed of ideals I had come to sow. And I also now feel certain that there must be in this country an innate love of peace, of order and of beauty which made it possible for China to accept the message of infinite love for all creatures that came here from India.

I have not the same voice that my ancestors had. I have not the wisdom they possessed. My life has never attained that consciousness of fulfilment needed to make this message fruitful. Nevertheless, unworthy through I be,

I still try to carry on this mission of my ancestors, knowing that, as their children, it is our bounden duty to take it up and bring it the door of all mankind.

I am overjoyed when I realize with what a kind welcome you have received me—not the personal me, but the bearer of the same message that came to you thousands of years ago. I can see no difficulty in the way of my work being fruitful in this land and, with that glad expectation, I stand by you and claim your help, your sympathy and your understanding.

Some have come to China to gain profit some to take away commodities of value—they have crowded into your markets everywhere. We, who have come from India, we also need to take away something from your land, which however is not a market commodity, but the fruit of the seed which was sown centuries ago, the fruit of love and peace and friendship.

The harvest is carried away and distributed to the famine-stricken world which needs it so much. It is for you not merely to enjoy these ideals but to accept the responsibility of offering them to the world, the peace that you have attained in your soul and the love that is growing mature every day. The whole world claims it.[①]

（印度有许多东西，属于遥远过去的世纪，似乎现在还继续存在，但实际上已经死亡。在这个地方有一种古老而又鲜活的东西。我感到一股生命激流从印度的中心地带奔流而过，越过高山和沙漠，最后来到你们这片土地，滋润了你们人民的心灵。那种永恒的生命之水仍在流动：它的智慧超越了时间，使我心中充满了敬畏。

我在这里感受到我们祖先的触摸，祝福降临在我们这些后代的身上。我们的祖先一定很高兴，因为我们跟随他们的脚步来到了这片他

---

① The English Writings of Rabindranath Tagore, 2/650-51. 《泰戈尔英文作品集》第2卷, 第650—651页。

们如此热爱和帮助过的土地。我们也是为了同样的使命而来,那就是为了和平与大爱的使命。我感到,在这个人类相互争斗、相互掠夺的时代,同样的印度精神正在敦促我们努力把和平带入混乱和冲突的中心。我希望印度的这种精神能给予我们的使命以力量。

当我在这里出席午餐会时遇到了居住在这片土地上的一些外国人和欧洲人,其中一位是与我相邻而坐,他在这里生活了很长时间。当他听我说到我心中的合作与和平使命的时候,他说中国是我播下这种理想种子的一处沃土。我现在也确信,在这个国家一定有一种天生的对和平、秩序和美好的热爱,这使得中国有可能接受从印度传来的、对所有生物都持有无限关爱的理念。

我没有我祖先那样的声音,也没有他们那样的智慧。我的生活也从来没有达到使这种信息结出果实所需的那种满足感。然而,尽管我不配,但我仍然试图继承我祖先的这个使命,因为我知道,作为他们的后裔,我们应该义不容辞地接过这一使命,把它带到全人类的门前。

当我意识到你们如此热情地欢迎我的时候,我欣喜若狂,不是欢迎我个人,而是欢迎我作为传递的信使。这些思想理念在几千年前曾由我的先辈向你们传递。我不认为我的工作在这片土地上取得成果有什么困难,我就是怀着这种愉快的期望站在你们身边,请求你们的帮助、同情和理解。

有人来中国谋利,有人来抢夺有价值的商品,他们到处涌入你们的市场。我们这些来自印度的人,也需要从你们的土地上拿走一些东西,但这不是市场上的某一种商品,而是几个世纪前播撒的种子所结出的果实——关爱、和平与友谊。

收获的粮食被运走,分发给饥荒肆虐的世界,那里非常需要粮食。你们不仅要享受这些理想,而且要承担起向世界奉献这些理想的责任——这就是你们灵魂中所获得的平静和日益成熟的大爱。全世界都这样断言。）

诗人泰戈尔对青年佛教徒说，在这里受到如此热情欢迎时，他欣喜若狂。他看不出他的工作在这片土地上取得成果有什么困难，他就是怀着这种愉快的期望站在中国朋友的身边，请求在座朋友们的帮助、同情和理解。有人来中国谋利，有人来抢夺有价值的商品，他们到处涌入中国的市场。而这一次他们这些来自印度的人，也需要从中国的土地上拿走一些东西，但这不是市场上的某一种商品，而是几个世纪前播撒的种子所结出的果实——关爱、和平与友谊。

听众围绕着诗人，聆听其讲话，不时鼓掌，树影婆娑，香气袭人。诗人讲完，四座立即响起热烈的掌声，随后女生又唱起歌来，然后摄影拍照。诗人泰戈尔拾起桌上绿糖两块，将其中一块递给一位小女生。美术学校的游少彬女士向诗人泰戈尔赠送一幅牡丹画。

迦利达斯·纳格在《泰戈尔国际大学的使命》（*Rabindranath Tagore's Visva-Bharati Mission*）一文中描述了这次聚会的场景："The poet and his party were welcomed by the priests of Fa Yuan-ssi, one of the oldest temples of Peking. Here under the lilac trees Tagore addressed the priests and the members of the young men's Buddhist Association. The temple bell souded its rich music and the poet also in his wonderfully musical voice expatiated on the deathless doctrine of main—universal love, like a Buddhist Saritri of yore."①

（诗人及其一行人受到了北京最古老的寺庙之一法源寺僧侣们的欢迎。在这里，在紫丁香树下，泰戈尔向僧侣和青年佛教协会的成员们发表演说。寺庙响起了宛如乐音的悠扬钟声，诗人就像一个古老的佛教圣人，也用他美妙的音乐般的声音阐述了佛祖永恒教义中的大爱。）

---

① The modern Review, sep. 1924,/293. 《现代评论》，1924年9月号，第293页。

泰戈尔第一次访华纪实

游览紫禁城和在海军俱乐部的讲话

加尔各答〇──仰光〇──马来亚〇──新加坡〇──香港〇──上海〇──杭卅〇──南京〇──济南〇──北京〇──太原〇──武汉〇──上海〇

1912年中华民国成立，当时只有6岁的清朝小皇帝溥仪失去了皇权，被囚禁在自己的皇宫里。一位名叫雷堪奈尔德·约翰·弗莱明·庄士敦的英国学者被指定为溥仪的家庭教师。这位英国教师给溥仪取名为"亨利"，因此这个退位皇帝就以"溥仪亨利"而著称。诗人泰戈尔应邀去西方访问的时候，这位英国学者庄士敦一直在关注着他。

4月27日（拜沙克月十四号星期天）上午10点，应清朝退位皇帝溥仪的邀请，诗人泰戈尔一行前往皇宫紫禁城会见溥仪和郑孝胥。

从紫禁城城门到皇宫大约有1英里的距离。诗人泰戈尔和与他同行的2位女士——葛玲和林徽因女士乘坐轿子，其余3位印度学者和徐志摩等人，步行前往皇宫。溥仪身着布衣，在御花园里等候诗人泰戈尔的到来，并召原内务府大臣郑孝胥作陪。诗人进入御花园时溥仪甚为高兴，以左手示意向诗人泰戈尔让座，以右手按郑孝胥，令其入座，随后对诗人泰戈尔说："先生为印度大诗人，郑孝胥则为我国大诗人，今日相遇于此，实为不易得之机会。我先为两大诗人留影以为纪念。"说完离座，他为两人合拍一照。随后又坐于两人之间，请摄影师又拍一合影。诗人泰戈尔对郑孝胥说："您为中国大诗人，是否懂英文？"

郑回答道："我所知者甚浅。"继而溥仪与诗人泰戈尔用流利的英语进行交谈。然后，溥仪陪同诗人泰戈尔参观御花园各处景点。

诗人泰戈尔赠送给2位皇后的礼物是象征着幸福吉祥的贝壳手镯，其他人也向皇帝赠送了各种礼品。溥仪送给诗人泰戈尔一尊珍贵的佛像和一幅织锦。随后诗人泰戈尔及其一行人与退位皇帝溥仪及其后妃告辞，步行至神武门，乘车离去。

这一天的晚上（4月27日），爱好文学的各界人士在金鱼胡同海军俱乐部举行宴会，招待诗人泰戈尔一行。来宾有诗人泰戈尔、农德拉尔·巴苏、迦利达斯·纳格、基迪莫洪·森、葛玲小姐和恩厚之6人，还有德国人威礼贤、英国人庄士敦作陪；主人方面有梁启超、林长民、冯玉祥、李晔、胡适、傅铜、陈源、张歆海、张彭春、蒋百里、林宰平、徐志摩等30多位政坛名人、学者出席。

本来茶话会并没安排长篇讲演，不料林长民在席间站起来，首先致欢迎词。他说："泰戈尔博士一行抵达中国后，到处受到了热烈的欢迎：在上海、南京、北京都受到欢迎。然而，这种欢迎确实不足以表达我们内心的感受。今晚，在这个小小的聚会上，我很荣幸能表达我们的一些感情，并说几句欢迎的话语。我们欢迎泰戈尔博士，不是将他看作为一位圣人或形而上学家，不是将其作为一位宗教改革家，甚至不是将其看作为一位普通的教育家，而是把他看作是一位诗人，一位非常伟大的诗人，一位世界诗人，一位将对我们自己诗歌产生重大影响的诗人。很遗憾，我们在座的所有人都不能阅读这位伟大诗人作品的原文。我们中有几个人拜读过英文版的，中文译本更是阅读得不充分。如果我们能阅读诗人的原著，我们会受到比现在更大的影响。

中国是一个古老的国家,我们可以说,她是一个文学的国度。我们有各种各样的文学作品,表达着不同类型的人类情感,其中有庄严的,也有悲伤的,有美好的,也有温馨的,也许,我们可以通过阅读我们过去一千年来的作品来获得对文学的最宏大的感受。但是我们的诗歌有其局限性。诗歌的伟大使命就在于,表现人类从某种精神根源中迸发出来的最崇高、最细腻的情感。诗歌给予我们一种精神世界的感受,并激励我们走向更高尚的人性之路。

我们的第一个缺陷是我们的语言,因为它太复杂,无法表达人类思想的微妙变化,所以它是不够丰富的。它不允许我们有足够的自由来表达我们最私密的想法。它不是发自内心的声音,因此不能给予人们充分的机会来最好地表达自己的灵魂。

我们的另一个不利条件是音乐已成为一门失传的艺术。今天的音乐只能让人粗略地了解它过去的样子。虽然音乐和语言上的这两种缺陷都不属于诗歌的范畴,但这两种缺陷造成了诗歌目前令人不满意的状况。

第三个不利条件在于我们的诗歌风格。我们的诗歌受到最严格的格律束缚,它阻碍了对灵魂的自然表达。此外,我们的诗歌本应塑造时代精神,却成为它的附庸,而且常常受到它的限制。

自唐代以来,我们的诗人就非常胆小和传统。他们几乎都在盲目地效仿以前的诗人,以致他们的诗歌都被束缚了手脚,在形式和行动上都受到禁锢。现在已经到了进步的时代,我们需要的是更好的东西,我们需要具有革命气质的、不墨守成规的诗人,他们敢于尝试创作符合新要求的新形式。

年轻时我曾经尝试着写诗,可是,我无论走哪一条路,巨大的规则之墙都阻碍着我。我没有自由。现在革命已经到来,我愿意和我的同伴们一起领引这场革命。

不过，即便如此，我们的新时代仍然缺乏勇气，因此，我们感到特别幸运的是，我们有一位伟大的革命家，一位伟大的革命诗人，我们希望从他那里得到伟大的灵感，创造新的东西。

去年，当传来消息说，我们期待着的一位诗人可能会到来，我们的期待和热情被激发起来了。他现在就坐在这里。我们无法告诉他，他的出现使我们多么感动。他的眼睛，他的举止，他的美髯，他的衣服——他的一切都富有诗意。他本身的体魄实际上就是诗。我们希望我们的这位诗人能给我们力量、勇气和胆识。

我们希望他能向我们揭示真理的现实、道德的勇气和奉献的壮美。我也愿意在人群后面挥舞着我的小旗，跟随他环游世界。"

(Dr. Tagore and his party since their arrival in China have received a very enthusiastic reception. They have been welcomed in Shanghai, in Nanking and in Peking. This welcome however is really quite an inadequate expression of what we feel at heart. Tonight in this small gathering it is my privilege to try and express some our of our sentiments and to present a few words of welcome.

We welcome Dr. Tagore, not as a sage or as a metaphysician, not as a religious reformer or even as an ordinary educator, but as a poet, a very great poet, a world poet, and as one who will expert a great influence on our own poetry.

It is unfortunate that all of us here cannot read this great poet's works in the original. A few of us have read them in English, and the Chinese translations are even more inadequate. If we could read the poet in the original, we would have received a much greater influence than we are able to do now.

China is an old nation; we might say she is a literary nation. We have all kinds of literature expressing different types of human sentiments containing grandeur and tragedy, beauty and sweetness, and probably the grandest view of that literature is to be obtained by reading our poets of the last 1000 years. But our poetry has its limitations. It is the great mission of poetry to give expression to the highest, the most exquisite feelings that spring from some spiritual source, in mankind. It gives us a view of the spiritual world and urges us on to a nobler humanity.

The first defect with us is our language which, because it is too sophisticated to express the subtly varying shades of human thought, it inadequate. It does not allow the necessary freedom for the expression of our most intimate ideas. It is not the heart's own voice and has not, therefore given the fullest opportunity to the people's soul to manifest itself at best .

Another disadvantage with us is that music has become a lost art. The music of today gives but a poor idea of what it used to be. Though these two drawbacks in regard to music and language, lie outside the proper domain of poetry, yet both have been responsible for its present unsatisfactory condition.

A third disadvantage lies in our poetic style. Our poetry has suffered from metrical laws of the strictest kind, which encumber the spontaneous expression of our poetic soul and besides instead of shaping the thought of the age, our poetry has been satisfied with following it and is very frequently circumscribed by it.

Since the Tang Dynasty our poets have been very timid and traditional. They have almost slavishly followed the example of former poets, so that their poetry may be compared to bound feet, imprisoned in form as well as in action. Now has come the age of evolution. We want something better, we want poets of revolutionary temper, who are not content to abide by conventions, and who have the audacity to experiment in new forms suited to our new requirements.

When I was young I tried to write poetry, but, whichever way I turned, huge walls of law encumbered me. I had no freedom. Now the revolution has come and I am willing to join my companions here in leading it.

But even yet our new age is not courageous enough; that is why we deem it specially fortunate in having with us an arch-revolutionary, a great poet of revolution, and we hope to derive great inspiration from him and to build something new.

Last year when news came that we might expect a rival of our own poets, our expectation and enthusiasm were aroused. He is now here. We cannot tell him how moved and touched we are by his presence. His eyes, his deportment, his beard, his clothes—everything about him is poetic. He is in fact poetry itself. We hope our poet will give us strength, courage and audacity.

We hope that he will reveal to us the reality of truth, the beauty of moral courage and sacrifice. I also am willing to wave my little banner behind the crowd and follow him round the whole world.)[1]

林长民先生的这一番长篇讲话,触动了诗人泰戈尔的心扉,于是诗人泰戈尔起身,发表了如下即席长篇讲话:

Even when we come to a foreign land we seek for our own. And that we only find in something which comes from the abundance in the heart of its people, representing their surplus which can be offered to and appropriated by their hearts and homes. Only those who are rich in love can afford to give shelter.

The soil on which has flourished an ancient forest with innumerable generations of trees, becomes deep, rich and fruitful by the shedding of

---

[1] *The English Writings of Rabindranath Tagore*, 2/656-58. 《泰戈尔英文作品集》第2卷,第656—658页。

leaves and flowers. Your old civilization has enriched the soil of the heart. Its constant human touch has a vitalizing effect upon everything belonging to it. This civilization could not have lasted so long, if it had not been eminently human, if it had not been full of the life of the spirit.

There have been other civilizations which have produced their harvest of thought and ideals and beauty, but these have not persisted and after a while they have become barren. But yours, because of its depth of soil, has nourished the great tree of life producing hospitable shade and fruit for travelers who come from a far off land. I have felt it and I cannot but believe that your literature and all your other forms of self-expression are deeply instinct with this spirit of hospitality. For the best and highest form of self-expression is society itself, and I feel that I have already drunk from its cup some drought of amrita, of deathlessness, because of which we who come from other land feel at home in this land of ancient civilization.

I have read this afternoon in a paper that you have been described as human. I find its evidence everywhere. I have received a wonderful welcome which has made me feel that you are eminently human.

I have been reading translations from some of your books of poetry and I have been fascinated by something in the quality of your literature. It is characteristically your own, and I have not seen anything like it in any other literature that I know of.

But it is not my intention to talk of your literature before those who know it so well.

What I want to tell you of is the problem of literature in my own country. We also have been dominated by a classical form that was rigid, a classical perfection that had not the movement of life. But the influence of the Sanskrit classics was limited only to learned communities and had no real sway over the literature of the people themselves. We have lost all traces of our ancient folk literature, which however must at one time have had a separate existence of its own. In the classic literature of India we find indications of a parallel stream flowing in the heart of the people which must have found expression in their own spoken language and from which the Sanskrit poets often received their inspiration. But because dialects had continually changed and had not been recorded in writing, many of them became obsolete and disappeared.

Some of our modern vernaculars however developed permanent forms and Produced a very rich harvest of literature. Our friend here, Professor Kshitimohan Sen, who has studied the poetry of mediaeval India, can tell you of the great mystic poets who flourished in India from the 13th to the 16th and the 17th centuries. I became acquainted with their writings through him, and I was amzed to discover how modern they were, how full of genuine and earnest feeling of life and of beauty. All true things are ever modern and can never become obsolete.

We find in India that a deep mystic and religious sentiment has kept the mind of the people alive. In fact, it has always been the mission of our sages to give consolation to those living outside the pale of respectability and belonging to the castes which are looked down upon. They were inspired with some thing that was divine in their own being, which made the heart of the people vocal. The poems that have come out of such contact have marvelous depth of wisdom and beauty of form. We have in Bengal a wealth of such old lyrics inspired by the Vaishnava movement.

When I began my life as a poet, the writers among our educated community however took their inspiration from English literature. I suppose it was fortunate for me that I never in my life had what is called an education, that is to say, the kind of school and college training which is considered proper for a boy of respectable family. Though I cannot say I was altogether free from the influence that ruled the young minds of those days, the course of my writings was nevertheless saved from the groove of imitative forms. I believe it was chiefly because I had the good fortune to escape the school training which could set up for me an artificial standard based upon the prescription of the school master. In my versification, vocabulary and ideas I yielded myself to the vagaries of an untutored fancy which brought castigation upon me from critics who were learned and uproarious laughter from the witty. My ignorance combined with my heresy turned me into a literary outlaw.

When I began my career I was ridiculously young; in fact, I was the youngest of the writers of that time who had made themselves articulate. I had neither the protective armour of mature age, nor that of a respectable English education. So in my seclusion of contempt and qualified encouragement I had my freedom. Gradually I cut my way through derision and occasional patronage into recognition in which the proportion of praise and blame was very much like that of land and water on our earth.

If you ask me what gave me boldness, when I was young, I should say that one thing was my earth acquaintance with the old Vaishnava poems of Bengal, full of the freedom of metre and courage of expression. I think I was only twelve when these poems first began to be re-printed. I surreptitiously got hold of copies from the desks of my elders. For the edification of the young I must confess that this was not right for a boy of my age. I should have been passing my examinations and not following a path that would lead to failure. I must also admit that the greater part of these lyrics was erotic and not quite suited to a boy just about to reach his teens. But my imagination was fully occupied with the beauty of their forms and the music of their words; and their breath, heavily laden with voluptuousness, passed over my mind without distracting it.

My vagabondage in the path of my literary career had another reason. My father was the leader of a new religious movement, a strict monotheism based upon the teaching of the *Upanishads*. My countrymen in Bengal thought him almost as bad as a Christian, if not worse. So we were completely ostracized which probably saved me from another disaster, that of imitating our own past.

Most of the members of my family had some gift, some were artists, some poets, some musicians and the whole atmosphere of our home was permeated with the spirit of creation. I had a deep sense, almost from infancy of the beauty of nature, an intimate feeling of companionship with the trees and the clouds, and felt in tune with the musical touch of the seasons in the air. At the same time I had a peculiar susceptibility to human kindness. All these craved expression, and naturally I wanted to be true to give them my own expression. The very earnestness of my emotions yearned to be true to themselves though I was too immature to give their expression any perfection of form.

Since then I have gained a reputation in my country but a strong current of antagonism in a large section of my countrymen still persists. Some say that my poems do not spring from the heart of the national traditions; some complain that they are incomprehensible, others that they are unwholesome. In fact, I have never had complete acceptance from my own people, and that too has been a blessing; for nothing is so demoralizing as unqualified success.

This is the history of my career. I wish I could reveal it to you more clearly through the narration of my own work in my own language. I hope that will be possible some day or other. Languages are jealous. They do not give up their best treasures to those who try to deal with them through an intermediary belonging to an alien rival. You have to court them in person and dance attendance on them. Poems are not like gold or other substantial things that are transferable. You cannot receive the smiles and glances of your sweetheart through an attorney, however diligent and dutiful he may be.

I myself have tried to get at the wealth of beauty in the literature of the European language. When I was young I tried to approach Dante, unfortunately through a translation. I failed utterly, and felt it my pious duty to desist. Dante remained a closed book to me.

I also wanted to know German literature and, by reading Heine in translation, I thought I had caught a glimpse of the beauty there. Fortunately I met a missionary lady from Germany and asked her help. I worked hard for some months, but being rather quick-witted, which is not a good quality, I was not persevering. I had the dangerous facility which helps one to guess the meaning too easily. My teacher thought I had almost mastered the language, which was not true. I succeeded, however, in getting through Heine, like a man walking in sleep crossing unknown paths with ease, and I found immense pleasure.

Then I tried Goethe. But that was too ambitious. With the help of the little German I had learnt, I did do through *Faust*. I believe I found my entrance to the palace, not like one who has keys for all the doors, but as a casual visitor who is tolerated in some general guest room, comfortable but not intimate. Properly speaking, I do not know my Goethe, and in the same way many other great luminaries are dark to me.

This is it should be. Man cannot reach the shrine, it he does not make the pilgrimage. So, you must not hope to find anything true from my own language in translation. You must come in person to woo her, win her heart and discover her beauty. You are trying to believe upon inadequate evidence that I am a poet. You faith is therefore dim, and you are collecting easy and external proofs to give it strength. I am gratified to hear from you that you are convinced that I am a poet because I have a beautiful grey beard. But my vanity will remain unsatisfied until you know me from my voice that is in my poems.

I hope that this may make you want to learn Bengal some day. I hope yonder rival poet, taking notes opposite me, will consider this seriously. I will admit him into my class and help him so far as I am able. Now I must also let you know something of our art movement.

It was started by my nephew Abanindranath, and is full of promise. If my frend, Nandalal, over there, who is a great artist, would deign to speak he would let you know it is growing in vitality and how its influence is spreading far and wide.

In regard to music, I claim to be something of a musician myself. I have composed many songs which have defied the canons of respectable orthodoxy and good people are disgusted at the impudence of a man who is audacious only because he is untrained. But I persist, and God forgives me because I do not know what I do. Possibly that is best way of doing things in the sphere of art. For I find that people blame me, but also sing my songs, even if not always correctly.

Please do not think I am vain. I can judge myself objectively and can openly express admiration for my own work, because I am modest. I do not hesitate to say that my songs have found their place in the heart of my land, along with her flowers that are never exhausted, and that the folk of the future, in days of joy or sorrow or festival, will have to sing them. This too is the work of a revolutionist.

I say unequivocally that my songs, along with those flowers that never blossom, are deeply rooted in our country. And the people of the future will sing my songs in times of joy, sorrow and rejoicing. This, too, is the work of a revolutionary."

（我们即使来到他乡异国，也依然苦苦地追寻自我精神。而我们只有从贵国人民丰富的内心世界中才能找到自我精神，因为它体现了他们心灵和家庭的富有，足以奉献给他们的宾客享用。那些内心精神贫乏的人是不会邀请异国人进入他们的心灵和居所的。只有那些富有爱心的人才能提供庇护所。

一片土地上世世代代生长着数不清的树木，久而久之，便形成了繁茂蓊郁的古老森林。这片土地因为长年累月的落花落叶而变得深厚、肥沃、丰饶。你们古老的文明滋养了心灵的沃土。它那种富有人性的不断的轻轻触摸，生机盎然地影响了一切附属于它的事物。假如这一文明不是特别地富有人性，假如它不是充满精神的活力，它就不会延续得如此长久。

曾经有过其他文明，它们也曾产生过思想的收获，产生过理想和壮美，但是那些文明却没能坚持下来，最终变成了一片荒芜。然而，你们的文明，由于其深厚的土壤，却培育出伟大的生命之树，它产生殷勤好客的树荫与果实，供远道而来的异邦游子享用。有感于此，我不能不相信你们的文学和你们用以自我表现的其他一切艺术形式都深深浸透着这种兼收并蓄的文明精神。因为自我表现的最佳和最高形式就是社会本身，我感到我已从它的杯中饮到了甘露，我深深地陶醉了。因此，我们这些来自另一国度的人在这一具有古老文明的国土上才会有宾至如归的感觉。

今天下午我在一张报纸上读到，你们被描绘为富于人性的人。我发现对于这一点的证明比比皆是。我受到了极为热烈的欢迎，这使我感受到你们特别富有人情味。

我一直在读你们的一些诗集的译文，你们文学中的品位令我着迷。它具有你们自己的特色，在我所知道的所有其他文学中，我从未见过与之相似的文学。

但是，我并不打算在你们这些行家面前谈论你们的文学。

我想给你们讲述的是我们自己国家的文学问题。我们也曾被一种僵化的古典形式所支配，被一种没有生动气韵的古典完美所主宰。然而，梵文古典作品的影响仅仅限于知识界，它并没有能够真正左右人民自己的文学。我们古代民间文学的一切遗迹都已荡然无存，不过，它在某一时期肯定有过其自身的独立存在。在印度的古典文学中，我们发现有不少迹象，还有一条与之平行的溪流在人民的心中流淌。它肯定是在他们自己的口头语言中找到了表达的方式，而梵语诗人们也常常从这条溪流中获得灵感。但是，由于方言总是在不断地变化，却没有以书面的方式记录下来，因此它们中的许多作品都已经过时或者失传了。

然而，我们的一些现代方言逐步形成固定的形式，并获得了文学上的一个极大的丰收。这里我的一个朋友基迪莫洪·森教授是研究中古印度诗歌的，他会告诉你们活跃于印度第十三到第十六、十七世纪的伟大神秘派诗人的情况。我就是通过他而开始了解他们的作品的。我惊奇地发现，他们是多么的现代性，对于生活和壮美充满了多么真实而真挚的情感啊！一切真实的事物永远是现代性的，永远不会过时。

我们发现，在印度，一种深厚的神秘主义和宗教的情感，使人民的心灵保持着活力。实际上，我们圣贤们的使命一直是安慰那些生活在体面之外的人，被人看不起的低种姓的人。他们受到存在于他们自身中某种神圣东西的鼓舞，从而唱出了人民的心声。与此相关联的诗歌便蕴含着极为深邃的智慧和美妙的形式。在孟加拉邦，我们就拥有大量的受毗湿奴教派①运动的激发而创作出的这种古老的抒情诗。

然而，当我开始我的诗人生涯时，在我们知识界中的作家们却从英国文学中获取灵感。我想，我是幸运的，因为在我的一生中，从未接受过所谓的教育，即没有受到过那种中小学和大学阶段的训练。而对于一个有身份的家庭男孩子来说，这种教育被认为是天经地义的。虽然我不能说我完全没有受到主宰着那一时期青年人思想的影响，但是我的写作课程却幸免于那种老一套的仿效别人的形式。我认为，这主要是因为我有幸避免了学校的训练，而这种训练会根据校长的规定而为我建立起一个人为的标准。在我的诗体、词汇和思想中，我总是异想天开，沉浸于原始质朴的想象中，从而招致博学的批评家们对我的严厉批评，引得智者们哄然大笑。我的无知再加上我的异端倾向，使我在文学上被打入另册。

当我开始我的文学生涯时，我年轻得令人发笑。事实上，我是当时有发言权的作家中最为年轻的一个。我既无成熟的年龄作为保护色，又无高雅的英语教育作为挡箭牌。因此，在遭人白眼的孤立中与被保留的鼓励中，我有着我的自由。渐渐地，我年岁大了，不过，对此我并不要求赞誉。渐渐地，我从嘲笑和偶尔的庇护中解脱出来，我达到了这样的认识：人们对我的褒贬之比，同我们地球上的陆地与水面十分相似。

如果你们问我年轻时是什么给了我勇气，我会说，一件事是我对孟加拉古老的毗湿奴派诗歌的实地了解，这些诗歌充满了韵律的自由和表达的勇气。这些诗歌第一次被重印的时候我才十二岁。我偷偷地从长辈的桌子上拿了几本。我必须承认，为了教育年轻人，这种诗歌

---

① 毗湿奴教派，印度教一个教派的名称。该教派的成员以一种特殊的方式崇信毗湿奴，即印度教三大神中的第二大神。某些毗湿奴派诗歌的艳情倾向，特别是与虔信罗陀和黑天有关的诗歌，在头脑更为清醒的印度教徒中唤起了反抗意识。

对我这个年龄的男孩来说是不合适阅读的。我应该通过我的考试，而不是走一条会导致失败的道路。我也必须承认，这些歌词的大部分都是色情的，不太适合一个即将迈入青春期的男孩子。但我的想象力却完全被她们优美的体态和动听的语言所占据；她们的气息，充满了淫荡的色彩，掠过我的脑海，没有分散我的注意力。

我在我的文学生涯中踏上流浪者的道路，还有另外一个原因。我的父亲是深谙《奥义书》①学说的，他是当时发生的严肃一神教新兴运动的一位领导人。我的孟加拉同胞们认为，他简直就像基督教徒一样坏。因此，我们完全被社会所排斥，这大概又使得我幸免于另一场灾难，即仿效我们自己的过去文学传统。

我家的大多数成员都有一些天赋，有些是艺术家，有些是诗人，有些是音乐家，我们家的整个氛围都洋溢着创造精神。几乎从孩提时代起，我就对大自然之美有着深刻的感受，对于树木和云彩有一种发自内心的情感，感觉自己与空气中六季的音乐旋律很合拍。与此同时，我对人类的友善有一种特殊的敏感性。我对于所有这些都渴望表达，于是我自然想要真实地对其做出我自己的表达。虽然我还不太成熟，无法以完美的形式表达情感，但我的情感却渴望真实地表达自己。

从那时起，我在我们国家赢得了声誉，但是在我们国家大部分同胞仍然对我存在强烈的敌对情绪。有人说，我的诗歌不是出自民族传统的情感；一些人抱怨，它们难以理解，另一些人则认为，它们不健康。事实上，我从来没有被自己的国人完全接受，这也是一种福气，因为没有什么比不合格的成功更令人沮丧的了。

这就是我的文学生涯历史。我真希望能够通过运用我自己的语言描述我自己的工作，使它更清楚地展现在你们的面前。但愿有一天这个愿望能够实现。语言是有嫉妒性的，它不会将自己最珍贵的财富

---

① 这里指的是若干含有印度先哲们的哲学思索的梵文论文或对话录，其年代约始于公元前1000年。

拱手让给那些企图通过属于某一异国对手的中介而交给与之做交易的人。你们必须亲自向它求爱,向它献殷勤。诗歌不像黄金或者其他物体那样可以随意传递。你们不可能通过一个代理人来得到你们情人的笑靥和秋波,不管这个代理人是多么的勤奋和尽职。

我自己也曾试图从欧洲语言文学中汲取丰富的美善。我年轻的时候我试图接近但丁,不幸的,是通过翻译。我彻底失败了,我觉得我有虔诚的责任停下来,因此但丁对我来说仍然是个谜。

我还想了解德国文学,通过阅读海涅作品的译本,我想我已瞥见那里的瑰宝隐隐闪现的微光。我有幸遇到了一位来自德国的女传教士,便请求她的帮助。我勤奋地学习了几个月,但是由于我的头脑相当灵活,这并非是什么好品质,我不能持之以恒。我具有一种危机感的敏捷头脑,它只能助长我过于轻易地猜测意思。我的老师认为,我几乎已经掌握了这种语言,但这并不是真的。不过,我成功地达到了目的,了解了海涅。我犹如一个在梦中漫步的人,轻松地穿越了一条未知的道路。我感受到极大的满足。

然后我又尝试读歌德,但那未免有些过于野心勃勃了。借助于我所学的一点点德文,我确实在通读《浮士德》。我相信我找到了这座宫殿的入口,但不像一个配有所有房门钥匙的人,却如同一个偶然来造访的宾客,被允许在某一普通客房中逗留,虽然舒适,却感到生疏。严格说来,我还不懂得歌德。同样,许多其他伟大的杰出人物,对我来说,也是如同雾里看花。

这也是很自然的。如果人们不去朝圣,就到达不了圣地。所以,你们不要指望通过翻译而从我自己的语言中发现什么真实的东西。你们必须亲自前来向她(这里指孟加拉语——作者注)求爱,赢得她的芳心并发现她的美丽。你们都试图根据并不充足的证据来相信我是个诗人。因而你们之所信是模糊不清的,你们正在搜集表面的、易得的证据以支持你们的结论。我很高兴听到你们说,你们之所以确信我是位诗人,是因为我生有一副灰白的美髯。不过,直到你们能从我的诗歌中了解我,我的虚荣心才会获得满足。

我希望,你们将来有一天想要学习孟加拉语。我希望在那边的那位诗人,就是正在我对面做笔记的人,他会认真地考虑一下这个问题。我将会接受他来我校就读,并尽我所能帮助他。现在我还必须让你们了解一些我们的绘画艺术运动的情况。

这一运动是由我的侄子奥波宁德罗纳特发起的,前景可观。如果我的朋友侬德拉尔,愿意屈尊讲话的话,他就坐在那边,是一位伟大的画家。他会让你们了解这个运动是如何生气勃勃地发展着的,以及它的影响是如何的深远。

关于音乐,我自己在某种程度上可以称作是音乐家。我谱写了许多首公然蔑视可敬的正统派经典的歌曲,而守规矩的人都厌恶我的这种放肆—— 一个仅仅因为缺乏教养而胆大妄为之人的放肆。我可以毫不含糊地说,我的歌曲与那些永远开不败的花朵一起,已深深植根于我国的国土之中。而未来的人们,无论在欢乐、悲哀还是在喜庆的日子里,都必将会唱起我的那些歌曲。这也是一个革命者的劳动成果。然而我依然坚持着,天神会宽恕我的,因为我不知道我在做什么。这也许就是在艺术领域中创作的最佳方法。因为我发现虽然人们责备我,却仍在唱我的歌,尽管唱得并非总是那么正确。

请不要认为我自视过高。我能够客观地评价自己,并且能够直率地表达对我自己的作品的赞美,因为我是一个谦虚的人。)

1924年4月27日晚,诗人泰戈尔在海军俱乐部的这次长篇讲话,系统叙述了自己年轻时的学习经历和文学创作,也可以说,这是他个人在文学艺术领域成长的历史。诗人特别讲到,他自己诗歌创作的源泉是毗湿奴教派的抒情诗歌。这种诗歌给予了他创作灵感,让他感受到其韵律的自然壮美;诗人尝试学习西方文学,企图从但丁的作品中获取养分,但是失败了,而后又学习德国文学,在一位德国女传教士的帮助下,他学会了德语。并且能够阅读,开始翻译海涅、歌德的原文作品,通读了《浮士德》。他诙谐地对听众说:"我很高兴听到你们说,你们之所以确信我是位诗人,是因为我有一副灰白的美髯。不过,直到你们能从寓于我的诗歌中和我的声音里了解我,我的虚荣心才会获得满足。"

诗人泰戈尔还认为,自己在歌曲创作方面是个革命者,并且取得了成就。最后他对中国听众说:"我毫不含糊地说,我的歌曲与那些永远开不败的花朵一起,已深深植根于我国的国土之中。而未来的人们,无论在欢乐、悲哀还是在喜庆的日子里,都必将会唱起我的那些歌曲。这也是一个革命者的劳动成果。"诗人真诚地希望,听众中有人去他的国际大学学习孟加拉语,他许诺他会尽自己的所能给予帮助的,因为他认为,只有阅读他的孟加拉原文诗歌,才能够真正体会到他诗歌的优美。

泰戈尔第一次访华纪实

在北京先农坛的讲演

加尔各答○──仰光○──马来亚○──新加坡○──香港○──上海○──杭州○──南京○──济南○──北京○──太原○──武汉○──上海○

1924年4月28日星期一下午3点，诗人泰戈尔应邀前来北京先农坛内的雩坛草坪上，向近万听众发表讲演，林徽因搀扶诗人泰戈尔走上讲坛，徐志摩为诗人做翻译。听众中的大部分是北京各高等院校的大学生和青年知识分子。诗人的讲话全文如下：

"I am deeply moved at the sight of your faces turned towards me. You came to listen to me, but I know it is not to me, the personal man who comes from India, but you want to hear someone speak who is of Asia. You are glad that I have come to you as in a sense, representing Asia. I feel myself that Asia has been waiting long and is still waiting to find her voice.

There was time when Asia saved the world from barbarism. Then came the night, I do know how. And when we were aroused from our stupor by the knocking at our gate, we were not prepared to receive Europe who came to us in her pride of strength and intellect. The West came, not to give of its best, or to seek for our best, but to exploit us for the sake of material gain.

It even came into our homes robbing us of our own. That is how Europe overcame Asia.

We did Europe injustice because we did not meet her on equal term. The result was the relation of superior to inferior; of insult on the one side and humiliation on the other. We have accepting things like beggars. We have been imagining that we have nothing of our own. We are still suffering from want of confidence in ourselves. We are not aware of our own treasures.

We must rise from our stupor, and prove that we are not beggars. This is our responsibility. Search in your own homes for things that are of undying worth. Then you will be saved and will be able to save all humanity. Some of us, of the East, think that we should copy and imitate the West. I do not believe it. What the West has produced is for the West, being native to it, but we of the East cannot borrow the Western mind nor the Western temperament. The West is becoming demoralized through being the exploiter, through tasting of the fruits of exploitation. We want to find our own birthright.

We must fight with our faith in the moral and spiritual power of men. We of East have never reverenced death-dealing generals, nor lie-dealing diplomats, but spiritual leaders. Through them we shall be saved, or not at all. Physical power is not the strongest in the end. That power destroys itself. Machine-guns and bomb-dropping aeroplanes crush living men under them, and the West is sinking to its dust. We are not going to follow the West in competition, in selfishness, in brutality.

Think of evolution. First the earth, then the animals. It was dark, then it was light. Then there came intellect and physical life found its highest strength through mind. It extended its arms into weapons, enlarging the domain of physical power and man became master over the other animals, but evolution did not stop here. There is another instinct also evolution in human beings, which is not to gain, but to give up—the spirit of sacrifice.

The chicken within the egg has rudimentary wings, rudimentary eyesight and legs, there are of no use while the chick is still in the shell. But some chicks let us suppose, even while there, might feel that there must be a realm beyond where they can make full use of their potential faculties. Other chicks, again, being rationalists or logicians, might argue that there was no life beyond the shell. Human beings are likewise divided into those who have faith in the life beyond the shell, and those who have not; those who believe that we have faculties which are not to be accounted for by the intellect alone, and those who do not.

We live in a dusk. We cannot fully understand the outer world. We are within the shell. The loss entailed in breaking the shell, in selfe-sacrifice, is not an absolute loss—the gain is greater. All religions have dwelt upon this point of gaining by sacrifice. It has been the faith of great-hearted men. It is the faith in humanity, dependent upon faith in the soul. When we give ourselfves, we gain ourselves.

The bees do nothing except accumulate honey, but man having soul is always searching into the beyond. He follows his instinct for ultimate truth, for ultimate, not ulterior values. Our faith is in the infinite and in the region of the will be touch the infinite.

Truth is not to be confounded with fact. Evil instincts are mere facts which stand for negation, but facts have not the power to contradict truth, for truth is the everlasting light of the spirit and overcomes them all. The final voice is not the voice of skepticism or of negation, but of faith, of love. Truth has the heart of man. Otherwise the world would have long ago sunk into utter darkness. The thing to do is to serve the supreme truth of goodness, of beauty and of love.

Your civilization has been nurtured in its social life upon faith in the soul. You are the most long-lived race, because you have centuries of wisdom nourished by your faith in goodness, not in the merely strong. This has given you your great past. You have come to listen to me because I speak of Asia, because I am proud of our continent, and I thank you for the welcome you have accorded me."

（看到你们与我面对面，我很感动。你们是来听我讲话的，但我知道，你们不是来听我这个印度人讲话的，你们是想听一个亚洲的人讲话。我来了，你们很高兴，因为在某种意义上我是代表亚洲而来。我自己觉得，亚洲已经等待了很长时间，现在仍在等待着寻找到自己的声音。

曾几何时，亚洲将世界从野蛮状态中拯救出来。然后黑暗降临了，我不知道这是怎么造成的。当有人敲打我们的大门，把我们从昏迷中唤醒时，我们还没有做好迎接欧洲人的准备，他们因为有力量和智慧而傲慢地来到我们的面前。西方人的到来，不是为了给我们最好的东西，也不是为了寻求我们最好的东西，而是为了物质利益来剥削我们。他们甚至闯进我们的家园，抢走我们自己的东西。这就是欧洲战胜亚洲的方式。

有人说我们与欧洲相处不公平，因为我们没有以平等的地位同他们相见。结果形成优势对劣势的关系；一边是侮辱，另一边是蒙羞。我们像乞丐一样被接受。我们一直以为自己一无所有。我们仍然因缺乏自信而痛苦。我们没有意识到自己拥有财富。

我们必须从沉睡麻木中醒来，证明我们不是乞丐。这是我们的责任。在你们自己的家中寻找具有永恒价值的东西，这样你们就能得救，也能拯救全人类。我们东方的一些人认为，我们应该复制和模仿西方的做法，可是我不相信。西方生产的东西是为西方人生产的，是属于西方的东西。但是我们是东方人,不能借用西方的思想和气质。西方成为剥削者,我们通过品尝剥削的苦果就会变得士气低落。我们想找到我们自己与生俱来的权利。

我们必须带着对人类道德和精神力量的信念去战斗。我们东方人从来不尊敬杀人的将军,也不尊敬说谎的外交官,我们只敬重精神领袖。通过他们,我们要么得救,要么根本不能得救。体力终究不是最强的。这种力量会自我毁灭。机关枪和投掷炸弹的飞机把活人炸得粉碎,西方正在沉沦为尘土。我们不会在竞争、自私和残暴方面追随西方。

想一想进化吧。首先是地球,然后是动物。天黑了,尔后就天亮了。然后是智力和物质生活通过思想找到了最高强的力量。这种力量把手臂延伸成武器,扩大了体力的范围,人类成为其他动物的主人,但是进化并没有止步于此。在人类进化过程中还有另一种本能,那就是不求收获,只愿放弃,那就是牺牲精神。

在蛋壳里的鸡有初始翅膀,初始视力和腿脚,当小鸡还在蛋壳里的时候,这些都是无用的。不过,让我们猜想一下,有些雏鸟即使在蛋壳里,也可能觉得一定有一个领域,在那里它们可以充分利用自己的潜能。作为理性主义者或逻辑学家,可能会争辩说,小鸡在蛋壳之内是没有生命的。人类也同样分为两类:一类是相信壳内有生命的人,另一类人是不相信壳内有生命,这后一种人相信,我们不能单靠智力来解释能力,另一种人则不这样认为。

我们生活在暮色中,我们无法完全了解外部世界。我们在蛋壳里。打破蛋壳,自我牺牲所带来的损失并不是绝对的损失,而是更大的收获。所有的宗教都重视通过牺牲来求得收获。这是伟大人们的信仰。这是对人性的信仰,出自对灵魂的信仰。当我们奉献自己时我们就获得了自我。

蜜蜂除了采集蜂蜜,什么也不做,但有灵魂的人总是在寻索彼岸的世界。他们遵循着爱好终极真理的天性——追求对终极真理的爱好,而不是对隐蔽价值的爱好。我们的信仰是追求"无限",在意志的领域里我们接触到了"无限"。

真理不应与事实相混淆。邪恶的本能仅仅是代表否定的事实,但事实却无力反驳真理,因为真理是永恒的精神之光,并能战胜一切。最后的声音不是怀疑或否定,而是信仰的声音,大爱的声音。真理赢得了人心。否则,世界早就陷入彻底的黑暗之中了。我们要做的就是,服务于善、美、爱等最高真理。

你们的文明是在具有精神信仰的社会生活中哺育出来的。你们是最长寿的种族,因为你们有长达许多世纪的智慧,这些智慧来自于你们对善良的信仰,而不仅仅是对强者的信仰。这赋予了你们辉煌的过去。你们来听我讲话,是因为我谈到亚洲,因为我为我们的大陆而感到骄傲,我感谢你们给予我的欢迎。)

在演讲的时候,诗人泰戈尔当然注意到了,有几个年轻人在听众中间散发反对他的传单。诗人泰戈尔在南京发表讲话的时候也发生过类似的情况。

恩厚之早在4月24日写给罗廷德罗纳特的信里就提到过这种情况:"There was an organized opposition at Nanking which produced pamphlets criticizing Gurudebv's attitude on pacifism, to militarism, industrialism and the spiritual life."(在南京有一个有组织的反对派,他们印制小册子批评师尊对和平主义、军国主义、工业主义和精神生活的态度。)当然,诗人泰戈尔对于这种反对他的声音并没有特别的在意。

当时在北京大学教授梵语的教授巴龙·斯塔尔·霍斯坦因,是基迪莫洪在迦尸读书时的同学。4月29日上午,诗人一行前往霍斯坦因教授的家里做客,参观他的藏书室和他珍藏的绘画和雕塑作品。

当日傍晚，溥仪的英语教师庄士敦先生在位于景山他的家里举行茶话会，诗人泰戈尔一行应邀前往参加。在那里，诗人泰戈尔也看到了很多书籍、画作和雕刻作品。

　　这一天北京讲学社安排诗人泰戈尔住进了另一处住所，就是在北京城西北10英里远的一个美丽小湖的岸边——清华大学的客舍休息了几天。他的同行伙伴们前往各处游览参观名胜古迹了。

泰戈尔第一次访华纪实

参观贵州会馆的画展

加尔各答〇——仰光〇——马来亚〇——新加坡〇——香港〇——上海〇——杭州〇——南京〇——济南〇——北京〇——太原〇——武汉〇——上海〇

4月29日上午11点。诗人泰戈尔在恩厚之和徐志摩的陪同下，前往樱桃斜街参观中国画家同志会举办的绘画作品展览。中国画家同志会的会员姚茫父、陈半丁、凌文渊等预先得知此消息，早早到会准备茶点，招待泰戈尔等人。闻讯来者100余人。凌文渊致欢迎词，他说，今日本会同志，以画人资格，欢迎泰戈尔先生，皆具有特别感想。吾国前贤评诗与画者，有言"诗中有画、画中有诗"此二语，世界上凡诗画名家，无不承认，盖诗画在艺术上有一致之精神也。本会今日欢迎泰戈尔先生，意即在斯。唯今之艺术趋势，如徒墨守成规，而无一种创造思想寄寓其间，则所谓诗，无不为格律所拘；所谓画，无不为稿本所陷，其真正美感，绝难自由发挥。故诗画在今日，均有改革之必要，泰戈尔先生于诗之革命，已着有大功绩。本会同志甚盼泰戈尔先生，就其革命于诗者，导我同志于画，俾令东方艺术上开一新纪元，本会同志愿闻教言。

诗人泰戈尔随后发言，他说，凌先生所举"诗中有画，画中有诗"二语，他很赞同。诗人与画人在艺术上有一致之精神，他亦有同感。盖艺术无国界，最称高尚。中国艺术源流，在历史上最为悠久而深奥，西方人不了解中国文化，往往误谓中国艺术将有断绝之虞，其实不然。他说："我曾游历过日本，看到那里某收藏家所收藏的中国画，我早已赞叹不止。"他这次来中国，觉得中华民族爱美之实现，有自己的理想，甚是相合。他深信，爱美之精神不易磨灭，唯有暂时消沉，但是就像泉水之流于地下，不久又能涌出地上，继续流淌或者反而更加活泼。"今天观看诸君作品，已入此境矣。不过，我对中国画上有两层意思：一须将历史的遗传与现在的关系合一进行研究；二要使印度与中国美术得到融洽的机会，如百川合流，越流越大，于美术前途大有希望。"诗人泰戈尔又说，他也曾经游历过西方，但其见闻所及，有如旅行沙漠，干燥无味。一到中国，如睹绿洲。今观诸君

在庄士敦景山居所门前合影：前排诗人泰戈尔、颜惠庆；后二排葛玲、林徽因；后二排左1徐志摩，左3恩厚之，其左右及后排右1为印度三位学者，最后排中间者为庄士敦

参观贵州会馆的画展　　177

作品，咸有趋于新的反战之倾向，此等愉快，岂可言宣？诗人泰戈尔讲完，大家热烈鼓掌。

诗人泰戈尔离开贵州会所，就前往庄士敦的居所，参加茶话会。参加茶话会者以英美人士居多。出席茶话会的华人有颜惠庆、陈源、胡适、张彭春、徐志摩、王统照、林徽因等，中外来宾共有30多人。席间没有长篇演说，拍照甚多。诗人泰戈尔参加此会，很是开心，与庄士敦先生交谈良久。会后徐志摩、恩厚之陪同诗人泰戈尔去清华园休息，小住3日。

印度画家依德拉尔·巴苏、学者基迪莫洪·森、迦利达斯·纳格本来计划于4月29日前往山西大同参观游览，可是没有买到火车票，所以没有能成行。4月30日上午10点，他们3人来到樱桃斜街的贵州会馆参观绘画展览，在这里会见了凌文渊、齐白石、姚茫父、陈半丁、王梦白、凌宴池。黄子美为其做翻译。3位印度客人仔细观看了展出的绘画展品，随后与中国画家进行坦诚的交谈。巴苏就中国绘画提出了一些问题，姚茫父和凌文渊2人做了认真回答。

《大公报》1924年5月8日第3版做了如下报道：

问：中国画派别如何？

答：中国画简单分类，可因时代、地域、家数几种不同，分出派别极多。时代则自上古以迄近代，几各朝各有特点。地域则有南派北派之分。今因时间仓促，不及详谈。家数可分为文人画、画家画、匠人画三种。文人画大都高人逸士，偶然寄兴，不求其工，自然超妙。画家画则法度井然，功诣甚深，其画法可以教人，可以力学。匠人画则临摹而已。文人画不易多观，画家画较为流行。至匠人画则以供社会绘画物件等之实用，不能列入美术界内。唯有一种人，专以临摹翻写古人及今人之画家为事，其术固优于匠人，而其品则下于画家。此类应列入画家及匠人之间，无以名之，名之曰画之贼。不独吾国如是，想各国画界亦均有此类人焉也。鲍斯（今译"巴苏"，即依德拉尔·巴苏——作者注）

谓，此种分派，与印度大略相同。（按：泰戈尔之画系文人画，鲍斯画系画家画。凡匠人画用手，画家画用脑，文人画用精神。）

问：在何朝何派最盛？

答：朝代相连，不能显分界限。今约略言之，匠人画发源最古，吾国六书象形一种即有画之雏形。降至秦汉六朝石刻，均可谓之匠人之画。至唐五代北宋时，画学进步，画家迭出，可谓画家画兴盛时期。至宋元以迄近代，文人学士往往寄兴于丹青，文人画遂多。此时代可算文人画兴盛时期。唯文人之画，初本无法，后人效之者众，以其笔法为师，推为画宗。斯时文人画与画家画无异，故其界限亦难以显然画清之也。

问：此数种画最古者，刻下可有真本见示否？

答：六朝之画，仅有石印。唐宋画真者几等凤毛麟角。以唐宋古画，均用绢，不易保存。元以后始用纸画，纸质较绢经久。故元画今尚有存者，但赝鼎极多，真者亦不易得。近来古画之著名者，如吴道子画人物等数幅，均已盗卖于西人，殊为可惜。余曾在伦敦、巴黎，见中国古画数幅。

问：元代纸画此时能仿造否？

答：亦可仿造，唯有识者，总能辨识。

问：辨识古画之真伪，有何简单之方法否？

答：辨识古画，可以其绢底颜色、笔法之不同而加判断，唯各有心得，大约经验既多，自有眼力，难以言语形容也。

问：中国习用颜色，古今有何区别？

答：画之颜料，大约可分矿物、草料两种，元以前用矿物居多，元以后始用草料及墨。

问：中国画书画相通，究于何时书法融入画内？

答：吾国书与画相通，始于上古篆文象形，几乎书即是画，画即是书。以后画逐渐于书中分出。故呼吸相通，大凡不善书者，对于画亦难于登峰造绝也。

问：中国画由数多笔数集成，其画法有分别否？

答：画法分类极多，人物、花草、山水各有画法，山水尤多，另有专书，非力谈所能尽。

问：各种画法何人发明？

答：人数极多，难以一一指出，亦有不易查究者。大约创造此法者，往往无意出之，后人守其法度，又经考古家收藏品评，加以名称，遂成各种名目。（鲍斯谓：收藏家、考古家在画界可算功臣矣。）

（答：然。古画之宣扬流传及优劣之指导，全凭此类人也。）

问：学中国画，如何学法？从学校中学，抑系各人自学？并用何法？

答：匠人画由师传授，等于学徒。画人画个人自学，后由学校学习均可。文人画，须胸襟高超、学问渊博者方能为之。非学校教师之所能教授。即闭门自学，亦非人人所能也。

问：学中国画者，心中着想，应从何处入手，并用何种方法入门呢？

答：学者各有方法，各有会心之处，难以言传，匠画不论。愚见以为画家画应从法度入手，文人画应从文学、诗歌、哲学等入手，并须于人品上注意。

问：画家写出天然境物有何书本方法可学否？

答：书少善本，尽信书不如无书，唯有《芥子园》一书，尚可备参考。唯少精刻本。（鲍斯谓，印度画亦有六法，大约与中国画有相同之处，后当对于论画书籍，寄奉数种，以备参考。）

问：三种人如何生活？

答：文人画作者，大抵生前负重名而不愿为人画者。亦有为社会轻视而没，其后声名大著者。画家画作者大都另有职业，以此为附属业务而已。唯匠人画，则其人均专以此为生耳。

以上问答，历二时半之久。后有凌、姚等导观各种陈列画品回去。

泰戈尔第一次访华纪实

在清华大学的讲演

加尔各答〇──仰光〇──马来亚〇──新加坡〇──香港〇──上海〇──杭卅〇──南京〇──济南〇──北京〇 太原〇 武汉〇 上海〇

4月29日下午，清华大学举行欢迎会，诗人泰戈尔向清华大学的学生们发表了讲话。这个讲话被记录下来，收录到《在中国的演讲集》①。全文如下：

　　"My young friends, I gaze at your young faces, beaming with intelligence and eager interest across the distance of age. I have come to the shore of the sunset land. You stand over there in the land of the rising sun. My heart reaches out to your hearts and blesses them.

　　I envy you. When I was a boy, in the dusk of the waning night, we did not fully know to what a great age wen had been born. The meaning and message of that great age has become clear to-day. I believe there are individuals all over the world this moment who have heard its call.

　　What a delight it may be for you, and what a responsibility, this belonging

---

① The English writings of Rabindranath Tagore, 2/ 653-656.《泰戈尔英文作品集》第2卷，第653—656页。

to a period which is one of the greatest in the whole history of man! We realize the greatness of this age dimly, in the light of this glowing fire of pain, in that suffering that has come upon us, a suffering that is worldwide; we do not even know fully what form it is going to take.

The seed, in which life remains selfe-contained, does not know its complete truth. Even when the sheath bursts, it is not known in what shape its life will manifest itself, what fruit the branches will bear.

In human history, through the forces of creation work oftenest in the dark, it is the privilege of human beings to give them direction, and thus to take part in the development of their own destiny. The sheath of the present age has burst. It lies in you, in each one of you, to give this new born life the impulse of growth.

What is the great fact of this age? It is that the messenger of an immense future has come; he has knocked at our gate and all the bars have given way. Our doors have burst open. The human races have come out of their enclosures. They have gathered together.

We had been engaged in cultivating each his own individual life, in the seclusion of our own national workshops. We did not know what was happening outside the walls. We had neither the wisdom nor the opportunity to harmonize our growth with world tendencies. But there are no longer walls to hide us. We have, at length, to prove our worth to the whole world, not merely to admiring groups of our own people. We must justify our own existence. We must show, each in our own civilization, that which is universal.

Now I am in China, I ask you, I ask myself, what have got, what out of your own house can you bring in homage to this age? You must answer this question. Do you know your own mind? Your own culture? What is best and most permanent in your own history? You must know at least that, if you are to save yourselves from the greatest of insults, the insult of obscurity, of rejection. Bring out your light, add it to this great festival of lamps of world culture.

I have heard it saidsome among your own people say it—that you are pragmatic and materialistic; that you cling to this life and this world; that you do not send out your dreams into the air, searching the distant heavens for a far away life beyond. If it be true, we must accept this fact and not try to fight against it. We must realize that this gift has been given to you and that out of it you can make your own contribution.

I cannot, however, bring myself to believe that any nation in this world can be great and yet be materialistic.

I have my own idea, superstition if you like, that no people in Asia can be wholly given to materialism. There is something in the blue vault of its sky, in the golden rays of its sun, in the wide expanse of its starlit night, in the procession of its seasons, each bring its own basket of flowers, which somehow gives to us an understanding of the inner music of existence, and I can see that you are not deaf to it.

Materialism is exclusive, and those who are materialistic claim their individual rights of enjoyment, of storing and possessing. You are not individualists in China. Your society is itself the creation of your communal soul. It is not out some of a materialistic, of an egoistic mind—a medley of unrestricted competition, which refuses to recognize its obligations to others.

I see that you in China have not developed the pre-vailing malady of world, the lunacy of an unmeaning multiplications, the production of those strange creatures called multimillionaires. I have heard that, unlike others, you do not give great value to brute power of militarism. All this could not be possible if you were really materialists.

It is true that you love this world and the material things about you with an intensity of attachment, but not by enclosing your possessions within walls of exclusiveness. You share your wealth, you make of your distant relatives your guests and you are not inordinately rich. This is only possible because you are not materialistic.

I have travelled through your country and I have seen with what immense care you have made the earth fruitful, what a wondrous perfection you have endowed the tings of every day use. How could this have been possible through a greedy attachment to material things?

If you had acknowledged greed as your patron, then, at touch, mere utility would have withered away all the beauty and grace of your environment. Have you not seen this? In Shanghai, Tientsin, huge demons of ugliness that stalk all over the world—in New York, London, Calcutta, Singapore and Hongkong, all big ugliness? Everything that they touch becomes dead, denuded of grace as if god's blessing had been withdrawn. Of this your Peking shows no sign, but rather reveals a marvelous beauty of human association. Even the most ordinary shops here have their simple decoration. This shows that you have loved your life. Love gives beauty to everything it touches. Not greed and utility: they produce offices, but not dwelling houses.

To be able to love material things, to clothe them with tender grace, and yet not be attached to them, this is a great service. Providence that we should make this world our own, and not live in it as through it were a rented tenement. We can only make it our own by some service, and that service is to lend it love and beauty from your own experience you can see the difference bet ween the beautiful, the tender, hospitable; and the mechanically neat and monotonously useful.

Cross utility kills beauty. We have now all over the world a huge production of things, huge organizations, huge administrations of empire, obstructing the path of life. Civilization is waiting great consummation, for an expression of its soul in beauty. This must be your contribution to the world.

What is it that you have done by making things beautiful? You have made, for me who come from a distant country, even your things hospitable by touching them with beauty. I acknowledge them as my own, instead of finding in the too obvious fact of your things an obstacle in my way, because my soul delights in their beauty. With their mere piles of things, life in other countries, has become like some royal grave of ancient Egypt. Those things darkly shout "keep away". When I find in your country this attractiveness in the things of every day use, they offer no repulse, but send out their invitation: "Come and accept us."

Are you going forget the obligations of your great gift, to let this genius for turning everything to beauty go to waste, to kill it by letting in a flood of maleficence?

Deformity has already made its bed in your markets, it is fast encroaching upon the region of your heart, and of your admiration. Supposing you accept it as your permanent guest, supposing you succeed in doing this violence to yourselves; then indeed, in a generation or two, you will kill this great gift. What will remain? What will you offer humanity in return for your privilege to exist?

But you have not the temperament will enable you to maintain ugliness. It is impossible for me to believe that.

You may say: "We want progress." Well, you did make wonderful progress in your past age, you devised great inventions, inventions that were borrowed and copied by other people. You did not lie idle and supine. And yet all that progress never encumbered your life with non-essentials.

Why should there remain forever this gulf between progress and perfection? If you can bridge this gulf with your gift of beauty you will do a great service to human.

It is your mission to prove that love for the earth, and for the things of the earth, is possible without materialism—love without the strain of greed. The man of greed is tied to his possessions with the rope of passion. That you are not so tied is shown by the trouble you take to brings to their perfection.

You have instinctively grasped the secret of the rhythm of things—not the secret of power which is in science, but the secret of expression. This is a great fact, for God alone knows this secret. Look at the miracle of expression in all the things of creation, the flowers, the stars, the blade of grass. You cannot analyse this elusive beauty in your laboratory and pocket it. How fortunate you are! You who have this instinct. It cannot easily be taught, but you can allow us to share it with you.

Things that possess this quality of perfection belong to all humanity. Being beautiful they cannot be secured within closed doors—that is a desecration which providence does not permit. If you have been successful in making beauty, that in itself is hospitality, and I, a stranger, can find my home here in the heart of beauty.

I am tired and old. This is perhaps my last meeting with you. With all my heart I take this occasion to entreat you not to be turned away by the call of vulgar strength, of stupendous size, by the spirit of storage, by the multiplication of millions, without meaning and without end.

Cherish the ideal of perfection, and to that relate all your work, all your movements, Then, though you love the material things earth, they will not hurt you and you shall bring heaven to earth and soul into things.

（我年轻的朋友们，我跨越年龄的距离，凝视着你们洋溢着智慧和热切希望的年轻面孔。我正走近日落之地的海岸。你们站在太阳升起的地方。我的心触及到你们的心，我祝福你们。

我真羡慕你们。当我还是个孩子的时候，在夕阳的黄昏里，我们完全不知道，我们生在一个多么伟大的时代。那个伟大时代的意义和信息今天已经变得清晰起来。我相信此刻全世界都有人听到了那个时代的呼唤。

你们将会拥有多么美好的前景，又将肩负多么重要的责任，因为这属于整个人类历史上一个最伟大的时代！因为处在熊熊燃烧的痛苦之光中，处在突然向我们袭来的这场世界性的苦难之中，我们隐约地认识到这个时代的伟大；我们甚至不完全知道，它将采取什么形式。

那粒将生命整个包容在内的种子，并不了解自己生命的全部真谛。即使当其鞘裂开的时候，也不知道它的生命将以什么形式表现出来，它的枝干将结出什么果实。

在人类历史上，创造的力量往往总是在黑暗中工作，人类有特权给它们指明方向，从而参与自己命运的发展。当今时代的外鞘已经破裂。促进这一新生命的成长要靠你们，要靠你们当中的每一个人。

这个时代最伟大的事实是什么？那就是带领伟大未来的使者已经到来；他敲响了我们的门，所有的铁栏都已塌陷。我们的门突然打开了。人类已经走出了他们的围栏。他们聚集在一起。

我们一直隐居生活在各自国家的作坊中，致力于培养自己的个人生活。我们不知道墙外发生了什么。我们既没有智慧也没有机会使我们的成长与世界趋势相互协调，但再也没有围墙能把我们藏起来了。最终，我们必须向全世界证明我们自己的价值，而不仅仅是向那些仰慕我们的人民证明我们自己的价值。我们必须证明自己的存在。我们每个人都必须在自己的文明中表现出被世人都接受的东西。

现在我在中国，我问你们，我也问我自己，我得到了什么，你能从自己的房子里拿出什么来向这个时代致敬？你们必须回答这个问题。你们知道你们自己的想法吗？知道你们自己的文化吗？在你们自己的历史中，什么是最好的、最悠久的？如果你们要使自己免遭最大的侮辱，不想默默无闻、不想遭受被唾弃的侮辱，你们至少必须知道这一点。亮出你们的光辉，加入到这个世界文化之灯的盛大节日。

我听人说——你们自己人中也有人这么说——你们是务实的唯物主义者；你们要坚持今生今世不会把你们的梦想放飞到空中去，不会到遥远的天上去寻找遥远的来世。如果这是真的，那我们必须接受这个事实，而不是试图与之抗争。我们必须认识到，这个礼物是给予你们的，你们可以用它做出你们自己的贡献。

不过，我自己无法相信，世界上还有哪个国家既是伟大的，同时又是追求物质主义的。

我有我自己的理想，如果你们喜欢迷信，那么，亚洲人也不可能都完全沉溺于物质主义之中。在蔚蓝色的天空中，在金色的阳光下，在星光灿烂的夜空里，在四季更替中，都有某种东西存在，每一种都有自己的花篮，它们以某种方式让我们明白了内在音乐的存在，我能看到，你们并不是听不见这种音乐。

物质主义是排他性的，物质主义者主张享受、储存和占有个人权利。在中国，你们不是个人主义者。你们的社会本身就是你们共同灵魂的创造。它不是源于某种物质主义的、利己主义的思想——不是一种不受限制的竞争混合体，不是拒绝承认自己对他人承担义务。

我看，你们在中国没有发展出世界上普遍存在的弊病，没有发展毫无意义的疯狂增殖，没有发展出那些被称为百万富翁的奇怪生物。我听说你们不像别人，不重视军国主义的野蛮力量。如果你们是真正的物质主义者，这一切弊端都是无法避免的。

的确，你们爱这个世界，爱你们身边的物质，爱得很强烈，但不是把你们的财产封闭在排他性的围墙里。你们分享你们的财富，你们把你们的远房亲戚当作你们的客人，你们不是特别富有。如果你们真的是追求物质主义者，这一切都是不可能做到的。

我走过你们国家的一些地方，我看到你们是多么细心地使这片土地硕果累累，你们赋予日常生活用品多么奇妙的完美。你们又怎么可能通过对物质的贪婪依恋而实现这一切呢？

如果你们承认贪婪是你们的赞助者，那么，一接触到功利，就会使你们周围的一切美丽和优雅变得黯然失色。你们难道没看到吗？在上海、天津，在纽约、伦敦、加尔各答、新加坡和中国香港——这些潜伏在世界各地的巨大丑陋恶魔，不都是巨大的丑陋吗？他们所接触到那里的每一样东西都变成了死气沉沉的，失去了优雅，仿佛上帝的祝福被收回去了。你们的北京没有表现出这一点，反而显示出人类交往的一种奇妙的美。这里即使是最普通的商店，其装饰也很简单。这表明你们热爱你们自己的生活。这种热爱赋予人们所接触到的一切都是美丽的。贪婪和功利却是这样：它们只建造办公室，而不是住宅。

能热爱物质的东西，给它们披上温柔的外衣，而不去贪恋它们，这是一种伟大的奉献服务。上帝让我们把这个世界变成我们自己的家园，而不是像住在租来的房子里那样生活。我们只有通过一些服务才能使它成为我们自己的家园，而这种服务就是从我们的灵魂中赋予它关爱和美丽。从你们自己的经历中你们就能看到美丽、温柔、好客以及与机械的整齐划一和单调的使用之间的区别。

单纯的享用会抹杀美。现在我们在世界各地都在生产大量产品，有庞大的组织和庞大的帝国管理，这一切都在阻碍生活之路。文明在期待伟大的成就，在期待其灵魂的美丽表达。在这一方面你们一定会对世界做出贡献。

你们做了什么让事物变得美丽？对于我这个从远方来的人，你们使你们的东西变得美丽，变得好客。我不但没有感到它们妨碍我，相反我认作它们是我自己的东西，因为我的内心灵魂喜欢这些东西的美丽。在其他国家，人们的生活就像古埃及王室的坟墓一样，只有成堆的东西。那些东西黑暗地喊着"走开"。当我在你们国家的日常用品中发现这种吸引力时，他们没有拒绝我，而是向我发出邀请："来接受我们吧。"

难道你们要忘记你们伟大天赋所承担的义务，让这个把一切都变得美丽的天才白白地浪费掉，让一股邪恶的洪流将其扼杀吗？

畸形已经在你们的市场上搭起了床铺，它正在迅速地侵占你们的心灵和你们的爱慕。假如你们接受它作为你们永久的客人，假如你们成功地对自己施加这种暴力，那么，再过一两代人，你们就必会毁灭这种大恩赐。剩下的会是什么呢？你们会用什么来换取你们生存的权利？

可是，你们若没有气质，你们就会显得丑陋——我不可能相信这一点。

你们可能会说："我们想要进步。"嗯，你们在过去的时代确实取得了惊人的进步，你们有过伟大的发明，这些发明被别人借鉴和复制。你们没有懒散地躺着。然而，所有这些进步从来没有让那些不需要的东西妨碍你们的生活。

为什么进步和完美之间的鸿沟会永远存在？如果你们能用你们的美貌弥合这种鸿沟，你们将会为人类做出巨大的服务。

你们的使命就已证明，对地球的爱和对地球上诸事的爱是可能的，那是没有物质主义、没有贪婪的爱。贪婪的人被激情的绳索绑在他们的财产上。你们没有被束缚，这可以从你们为使他们臻于完美而付出的努力中看得出来。

你们本能地掌握了事物节奏的秘密——不是科学中力量的秘密，

而是表达的秘密。这是一个伟大的事实,因为只有上帝知道这个秘密。看看万物中表达的奇迹,花朵、星星、草叶。你们不能在实验室里分析这种难以捉摸到的美,然后把其装进口袋。你们真幸运!你们有这种本能。这种本能是不容易被教会的,但你们可以允许我们与你们分享。

拥有这种完美品质的事物属于全人类。它们是美丽的,不能将其关在紧闭的房门里,那样做是上帝不允许的亵渎。如果你成功地创造这种美,这本身就是好客的表现,而我,一个陌生人,可以在这种美丽的心中找到我的家园。

我感到很疲惫,而且年事已高。这可能是我和你们最后一次见面了。借此机会,我衷心地恳求你们,不要被庸俗的势力、巨大的阵势、一味储物的精神所吓倒,不要被无数财富不断地增加引入歧途。

请珍惜完美的理想,把你们所有的工作和行动都与之联系起来,这样,尽管你们热爱大地上的物品,它们也不会伤害你们,你们可以使天堂降临到大地上,并赋予物品以灵魂。)

诗人泰戈尔的这篇讲话表达了他自己的理想,并且希望中国青年人也要怀有理想,不要一味地追求物质享受,要珍惜自己的理想,要把理想与自己从事的实际工作联系起来。最后诗人语重心长地说:"我感到很疲惫,而且年事已高。这可能是我和你们最后一次见面了。借此机会,我衷心地恳求你们,不要被庸俗的势力、巨大的阵势、一味储物的精神所吓倒,不要被无数财富不断地增加引入歧途。"

清华大学是美国人用中国支付的战争赔款建造的,因此清华大学的教学大纲在很多方面都是追随美国的教育模式,所以清华大学的学生们都掌握了英语。诗人泰戈尔讲述了一段之后,当徐志摩进行翻译的时候,很多学生都离开报告厅。后来一些学生又私下同诗人泰戈尔进行亲切交谈。

泰戈尔第一次访华纪实

同清华大学同学座谈并宣读《文明与进步》

上海 ○
武汉 ○
太原 ○
北京 ○
济南 ○
南京 ○
杭州 ○
上海 ○
香港 ○
新加坡 ○
马来亚 ○
仰光 ○
加尔各答 ○

有一天，一群清华学生陪同诗人泰戈尔出去散步，诗人看到了遭到战争破坏的一座佛塔和各种古代艺术，他就向学生们讲述了艺术的价值。清华大学的学生们向诗人提出各种问题，例如，学生们问他："您对神灵的概念是什么，您与神灵是什么关系，人生的幸福是什么，何为罪过？"等等。诗人耐心地一一做了回答，同时向同学们宣读了一篇自己的文章 Civizationg and Progress（《文明与进步》）。在这篇长篇文章中诗人阐述了关于文明与宗教的观点。全文如下：

A Chinese author writes: "The terribly tragic aspect of the situation in China is that, while the Chinese nation is called upon to throw away its won civilization and adopt the civilization of modern Europe, thereis not one single education man in the whole empire who has the remotest idea of what this modern Europan civilization really is."

I have read elsewhere an observation made by a Frenchman, quoted in a magazine, in which he says that China is not a country but a civilization. Not having read the full discussion, I cannot be certain what he means. But it seems to me that, according to the writer, China represents an ideal and not the production and collection of certain things, or of information of a particular character about the nature of things; that is to say, it stands for not merely progress in wealth and knowledge and power but a philosophy of life and the art of living.

The word *"civilization"* being a European word we have hardly yet taken the trouble to find out its real meaning. For over a century we have accepted it, as we may accept a gift horse, with perfect trust, never caring to count its teeth. Only very lately we have begun to wonder if we realize in its truth what the western people mean when they speak of civilization. We ask ourselves, "has it the same meaning as some word in our own language which denotes, for us the idea of human perfection?"

Civilization cannot merely be a growing totality of happenings that by chance have assumed a particular shape and tendency which we consider to be excellent. It must be the expression of come guiding moral farce which we have evolved in our society for the object of attaining perfection. The word "perfection" has simple and definite meaning when applied to an inanimate thing, or even to a creature whose life has principally a biological significance. But man being complex and always on the path of transcending himself, the meaning of the word "perfection" as applied to him, cannot be crystallized into an inflexible idea. The has made it possible for different races to have different shades of definition for this term.

The Sanskrit word *Dharma* is the nearest synonym in our own language, that occurs to me, for the word civilization. In fact, we have no other word except perhaps some newly coined one, lifeless and devoid of atmosphere. The specific meaning of *Dharma* is that principle which holds us firm together and leads us to our best welfare. The general meaning of this word is the essential quality of thing.

Dharma for man is the best expression of what he is in truth. He may reject *Dharma* and may choose to be an animal or a machine and thereby may not injure himself, may even gain strength and wealth from an external and material point view; yet this will be worse than death for him as a man. It has been said in our *Scriptures:* 'Through Adharma (the negation of dharma) man prosper, gains what appears, desirable, conquers enemies, but perishes at the root.'

One who is merely a comfortable money-making machine does not carry in himself the perfect manifestations of man. He is like a gaudily embroidered purse which is empty. He raises a rich alter in his life to the blind and deaf image of a yawning negation and all the costly sacrifices continually offered to is are poured into the mouth of an ever hungry abyss. And according to our scriptures, even while he swells and shouts and violently gesticulates, he perishes.

The same idea has been expressed by the great Chinese sage, Lao-tze, in a different manner, where he says: 'One who may die, but will not perish, has life everlasting.' In his he also suggests that when a man reveals his truth he lives, and that truth itself is dharma. Civilization according to this ideal, should be the expression of man's dharma in his corporate life.

We have for over a century been dragged by the prosperous West behind its chariot, choked by the dust, deafened by the noise, humbled by our own helplessness, and overwhelmed by the speed. We agreed to acknowledge that this chariotdrive was progress, and that progress was civilization. If we ever ventured to ask, "progress towards what, and progress for whom—it was considered to be peculiarly and ridiculously oriental such doubts about the absoluteness of progress. Of late, a voice has to us bidding us to take count not only of the scientific perfection of the chariot but of the depth of the ditches lying its path.

Lately I read a paragraph in *American Weekly* which is more frank than prudent in its espousal of truth discussing the bobbing of the Mahsud villages in Afghanistan by some British airmen. The incident commented upon by this paper happened when "one of the bombing planes made a forced landing in the middle of a Mahsud village", and when "the airmen emerged unhurt from the wreckage only to face a committee of five or six old women, who had happened to escape the bombs brandishing dangerous looking knives." The editor quotes from *London Times* which runs thus:

"A delightful damsel took the airmen under her wing and led them to a cave close by, and a *malik* (chieftain) took up his position at the entrance, keeping off the crowd of forty who had gathered round, shouting and waving knives. Bobs were still being dropped from the air, so the crowd, envious of the security of the cane, pressed in stiflingly, and the airmen pushed their way out in the teeth of the hostile demonstration...They were fed and were visited by neighbouring *maliks*, who were most friendly, and by a *mullah* (priest), who was equally pleasant. Women looked after the feeding arrangements, and supplies from Ladha and Razmak arrived safely... On the evening of the twenty-fourth they were escorted to Ladha, where they arrived at daybreak the next day. The escort disguised their captives as Mahsuds as a precaution against attack...It is significant that the airmen's defenders were first found in the younger generation of both sexes.

In the above narrative the fact comes out strongly that the West has made wonderful progress. She has opened her path across the ethereal region of earth; the explosive forces of the bobs has developed its mechanical power of wolesale destruction to a degree that could be represented in the past only by the personal valour of a large number of men. But such enormous progress has made Man diminutive. He proudly imagines that he expresses himself when he displays the things that he produces and the power that he holds in hands. The bigness of the results and the mechanical perfection of the apparatus hide from him the fact that Man in him has been smothered.

When I was a child I had the freedom to make my own toys out of trifles and create my own games from imagination. In my happiness my playmates had their full share; in fact the complete enjoyment of my games depended upon their taking part in them. One day, in this paradise of our childhood, entered a temptation from the market world of the adult.

A toy bought from an English shop was given to one of our companions; it was perfect, it was big, wonderfully lifelike. He became proud of the toy and less mindful of the game; he kept that expensive thing carefully away from us, glorying in his exclusive possession of it, feeling himself superior to his playmates wholes toys were cheap. I am sure if he could use the modern language of history he would say that he was more civilized than ourselves to the extent of his owing that ridiculously perfect toy.

One thing he failed to realize in his excitement—a fact which at the moment seemed to him insignificant—that this temptation obscured something a great deal more perfect than his toy, the revolution of the perfect child. The toy merely expressed his wealth, but not the child's creative spirit, not the child's generous joy in his play, his open invitation to all who were his compeers to his playworld.

Those people who went to bomb the Mahsud villages measured their civilization by the perfect effectiveness of their instruments which were their latest scientific. So strongly do they realize the value of these things that they are ready to tax to the utmost limit of endurance their own people, as well as those others who may occasionally have the chance to taste in their own persons the deadly perfection of these machines. This tax does not merely consist in money but in humanity. These people put the birth rate of the toy against the death rate of man; and they seem happy. Their science makes their prodigious success so utterly cheap on the material side, that they do not care to count the cost which their spirit has to bear.

On the other hand, those Mahsuds that protected the airmen, who had come to kill them wholesale, men, women and children.—were primitively crude in their possession of life's toys. But they showed the utmost carefulness in proving the human truth through which they could express their personality. From the so-called *Nordic* point of view of the would be rulers of men, this was foolish.

According to a Mahsud, hospitality is a quality by which he is known as a man and therefore he cannot afford to miss his opportunity, even when dealing with someone who can be systematically relentless in enmity. From the practical point of view, the Mahsud pays for this very dearly, as we must always pay for that which we hold most valuable. It is the mission of civilization to set for us the right standard of valuation. The Mahsud may have many faults for which he should be held accountable; but that, which has imparted for him more value to hospitality than to revenge, may not be called progress, but is certainly civilization.

The ruthlessness, which at time of crisis disdained to be too scrupulous in extirpating some cause of trouble, and uses its indiscriminate weapon against the guilty and the innocent, the combatant and the non-combatant, is certainly useful. Through such thoroughly unfeeling methods men prosper, they find what they consider desirable, they conquer their enemies—but there they stop, incomplete.

We can imagine some awful experiment in creation that began at tail end abruptly stopped when the stomach was finished. The creature's power of digestion is perfect, so it goes on growing stout, but the result is not beautiful. At the beginning of the war, when monstrosities of this description appeared in various form, West humanity shrank for a moment at the sight. But now she seems to admire them, for they are fondly added to other broods of ugliness in her nursery. Terrific movements produced by such abnormalities of truncated life, may widen the path of what is called progress for those who want to be rulers of men, but certainly they do not belong to civilization.

Once there was an occasion for me to motor down to Calcuttu from a place a hundred miles away. Something wrong with the mechanism made it necessary for us have a repeated supply of water almost every half an hour. At the first village where we were compelled to stop, we asked the help of a man to find water for us. It proved quite a task for him, but when we offered him his reward, poor though he was, he refused to accept it. In fifteen other villages the same thing happened. In a hot country where travellers constantly need water, and where the water supply grows scanty in summer, the villagers consider it their duty to offer water to those who need it. They could easily make a business out of it, following the inexorable law of demand and supply. But the ideal which they consider to be their *dharma* has become one with their life. To ask them to sell it is like asking them to sell their life. They do not claim any personal merit for possessing it.

Lao-tze speaking about the man who is truly good says: 'He quickens, but owns not. He acts, but claims not. Merit he accomplishes, but dwells not it. Since he does not dwell on it, it will never leave him.' That which is outside ourselves we can sell, but that which is one with our life we cannot. This complete assimilation of truth belongs to the paradise of perfection; it lies beyond the purgatory of self-consciousness. To have reached it proves a long process of civilization.

To be able to take a considerable amount of trouble in order to supply water to a passing stranger and yet never to claim merit or reward for it seems absurdly and negligibly simple compared with the capacity to produce an amazing number of things per minute. A millionaire tourist ready to corner the food market and grow rich by driving the whole world to the brink of starvation is sure to feel too superior to notice this simple thing while rushing through our villages at sixty miles an hour. For it is not aggressive like a telegraphic pole that pokes our attention with its hugely long finger, or resounding like his own motor engine that shouts its discourtesy to the silent music of the spheres.

Yes, it is simple; but that simplicity is product of centuries of culture; that simplicity is difficult of imitation. In a few years time it might be possible for me to learn how to make holes in thousands of needles instantaneously by turning a wheel, but to be absolutely simple in one's hospitality to one's enemy or to a stranger requires generations of training. Simplicity takes no account of its own value, claims no wages, and there those who are enamoured of power do not realize that simplicity of spiritual expression is the highest product of civilization.

A process of disintegration, can kill this rare fruit of a higher life, as a whole race of birds of possessing some rare beauty can be made extinct, by the vulgar power of avarice which has civilized weapons. This fact was clearly proved to me when I found that the only place where a price was expected for the water given to us, was when we reached a suburb of Calcutta, where life was richer, the water supply easier and more abundant, and where progress flowed in numerous channels in all directions. We must get to know this force of disintegration, and how it works.

Creation is the revelation of truth through the Rhythm of form, its dualism consisting of the expression and the material. Of these the material must offer itself as a sacrifice in absolute loyalty to the expression. It must know that it can be no end in itself and therefore by the pressure of its volume nousness it should not carry men away from their creative activities.

In India we have a species of Sanskrit poem in which all the complex grammatical rules are deliberately illustrated. This produces continual sparks of delight in the minds of some readers, who, even in a work of art, seek some tangible proof of power, almost physical in its manifestation. This shows that by special cultivation a kind of mentality can be produced which is capable of taking delight in the mere spectacle of power, manipulating materials, forgetting that materials have no value of their own. We see the same thing in the modern western world where progress is measured by the speed with which materials are multiplying. Their measure by horse-power is one before which spirit-power has made itself humble. Horse-power drives, spirit-power that sustains. That which drives is called the principle of progress, that which sustains we call *dharma*; and this word *dharma* I believe should be translated as civilization.

We have heard from the scientist that an atom consists of a nucleus drawing its companions round it in a rhythm of dance and thus forms a perfect unit. A civilization remains healthy and strong as long as it contains in its centre some creative ideal that binds its members in a rhythm of relationship. It is a relationship which is beautiful and not merely utilitarian. When this creative ideal which is *dharma* gives place to some overmastering passion, then this civilization bursts into conflagration like a star that has lighted its own funeral pyre. From its modest moderation of light this civilization flares up into a blaze of the first magnitude, only for its boisterous brilliancy to end in violent extinction.

Western society, for some ages, had for its central motive force a greatspiritual ideal and not merely an impetus to progress. It had its religious faith which was actively busy in bringing about reconciliation among the conflicting forces of society. What it held to be of immense value was the perfection of human relationship, to be obtained by controlling the egoistic instincts of man, and by giving him a philosophy of his fundamental unity. In the course of the last two centuries, however, the West found access to Nature's store-house of power, and ever since all its attention has rresistibly been drawn in that direction. Its inner ideal of civilization has thus been pushed aside by the love of power.

Man's ideal has for its field of activity the whole human nature from its depth to its height. The light of this ideal is gentle because diffused, its life is subdued because all embracing. It is serene because it is great; it is meek because it is comprehensive. But our passion is narrow; its limited field gives it an intensity of impulse. Such an aggressive force of greed has of late possessed the western mind. This has happened within a very short period, and has created a sudden deluge of things smothering all time and space over the earth. All that was human is being broken into fragments.

In trying to maintain some semblance of unity among such a chaos of fractions, organizations are established for manufacturing, in a wholesale quantity, peace, or piety, or social welfare. But such organizations can never have the character of perfect unit. Surely they are needed as we need our drinking vessels, but more for the water than for themselves. They are mere, burdens by themselves as they are; and if we take pleasure in multiplying them indefinitely the result may be astoundingly clever, but crushingly fatal to life.

I have read somewhere an observation of Plato in which he says: "An intelligent and socialized community will continue to grow only as long asit can remain a unit; beyond that point growth must cease, or the community will disintegrate and cease to be an organic being." That spirit of the unit is only maintained when its nucleus is some living sentiment of *dharma*, leading to cooperation and to a common sharing of life's gifts.

Lao-tze has said: Not knowing the eternal causes passions to rise; and that is evil. Comforts and conveniences are pursued, things are multiplied, the eternal is obscured, the passions are roused, and the evil marches triumphant from continent to continent mutilating man and crushing under its callous tread life's bloom—the product of the Mother-heart that dwells in the sanctuary of human nature. And we are asked to build triumphal arches for this march of death. Let us at least refuse to acknowledge its victory, even if we cannot retard its progress. Let us die, as your Lao-tze has said, and yet not perish.

It is said in our *Scriptures*:' In greed is sin, in sin death.' Your philosopher has said: 'No greater calamity than greed.' These sentences carry the wisdom of ages. When greed becomes the dominant character of a people it ebodes destruction for them and no mere organization like the League of Nations a never save them. To let the flood of self-seeking flow unchecked from the heart of the Nation and at the same time try to build an outer dam across its path can never succeed. The deluge will burst forth with a greater force because of the resistance. Lao-tze says: "Not self-seeking, he gains the life." Life's principle is in this and therefore in a society all the trainings and teachings that make for life are those that help us in our control of selfish greed.

When civilization was living, that is to say, when most of its movementswere related to an inner ideal and not to an external compulsion, then money had not the same value as it has now. Do you not realize what an immense difference that fact has made in our life, and how barbarously it has cheapened those things which are invaluable in our inheritance? We have grown so used to this calamitous change that we do not fully realize the indignity it imposes upon us.

I ask you to imagine a day, if it does ever come, when in a meeting everybody will leave his chair and stand up in awe if a man enters there who has a greater number of human skulls strung in his necklace than have his fellow beings. We can have no hesitation today in admitting that this would be pure barbarism. Are there no other tokens of a similar degradation for man, are there no other forms of human skulls than those which the savages so proudly wear?

In olden times the mere hoarding of millions was never considered as wealth unless it had some crown of glory with which to proclaim its ideal greatness. In the East as well as in the West, man, in order to save his inherent dignity, positively despised money that represented merely a right to possession and no moral responsibility. Money-making as a profession was everywhere contemptuously treated, and men, who made big profits the sole end of their life, were looked down upon.

There was a time in India when our Brahmins were held in reverence, not only for their learning and purity of life, but for their utter indifference to material wealth. This only shows that our society was fully conscious that its very life depended upon its ideals, which were never to be insulted by anything that belonged to a passion for self-seeking. But because today progress is considered to be characteristic of civilization, and because this progress goes on gathering an unending material extension, money has established its niversal sovereignty. For in this world of ambition money is the central power-house sending impulsions in all directions.

In former days, the monarchs of men were not ashamed humbly to pay their respect to men of intellect or those who had spiritual or creative gifts. For the qualities of the higher life were the motive force of the civilization of those times. But doday, men, whatever their position, never think that they are humiliating themselves when they offer their homage to men of corpulent cash, not always because they expect any benefit therefrom, but because of the bare fact of its possession. This denotes a defeat of the complete man by the material man. This huge degradation, like a slimy reptile, has spread its coils round the whole human world. Before we can rescue humanity from the bondage of its interminable tail, we must free our mind from the bondage of its terminable tail, we must free our mind from the sacrilege of worship offered to this unholy power, this evil dragon which can never be the presiding deity of the civilization of man.

I am sure you know that this soulless progeny of greed has already opened its elastic jaws wide over the fair limbs of your country, wider perhaps than in any other part of the world. I earnestly hope that you will develop some means to rescue her from her destination towards the hollow of its interior.

But the danger is not so much from the enemy who attacks, but from the defender who may betray. It fills my heart with a great feeling of dismay when, among your present generation of young men, I see signs of their uccumbing to the depravity of fascination for an evil power which allures with its enormity. They go about seeking for civilization amongst the wilderness of skyscrapers, in the shrieking headlines of news journals, and the shouting vociferation of demagogues. They leave their own great prophets who had afar-seeking vision of truth, and roam in the dusk begging for the loan of light from some glow-worm which can only hold its niggardly lantern for the purpose of crawling towards its nearest dust.

They will learn the meaning of the word *civilization*, when they come back home and truly understand what their great master, Lao-tze, wanted to teach when he said: 'Those who have virtue attend to their obligations; those who have no virtue attend to their claims.' In this saying he has expressed in a few words what I have tried to explain in this paper. Progress which is not related to an inner ideal, but to an attraction which is external, seeks to satisfy our endless claims. But civilization, which is an ideal, gives us power and joy to fulfil our obligations.

About the stiffening of life and hardening of heart caused by the organization of power and hardening of heart caused by the organization of power and production, he says with profound truth: The grass as well as the trees, while they live, are tender and supple; when they die they are rigid and dry. Thus the hard and the strong are the companions of death. The tender and the delicate are the companions of life. Therefore he who in arms is strong will not conquer. The strong and the great stay below. The tender and the delicate stay above.

Our sage in India says, as I have quoted before: 'By the help of anti-dharma men prosper, they find what they desire, they conquer enemies, but they perish at the root.' The wealth which is not welfare grows with a rapid vigour, but it carries within itself the seed of death. This wealth has been nourished in the West by the blood of men and the harvest is ripening. The same warning was also given centuries ago by your sage when he said: 'Things thrive and then grow old. This is called Un-Reason. Un-Reason soon ceases.'

Your teacher has said: *To increase life is called a blessing.* For, the increase of life, unlike the increase of things, never transcends the limits of life's unity. The mountain pine grows tall and great, its every inch maintains the rhythm of an inner balance, and therefore even in its seeming extravagance it has the reticent grace of self-control. The tree and its productions belong to the same vital system of cadence; the timber, leaves, flowers and fruits are one with the tree; their exuberance is not a malady of exaggeration, but a blessing. But systems which mainly are for making profits and not for supplying life's needs, encourage an obesity of ugliness in our society obliterating the fine modulations of personality from its features. Not being one with our life, they do not conform to its rhythm.

Our living society, which should have danced in its steps, music in its voice, beauty in its limbs, which should have its metaphor in stars and flowers, maintaining its harmony with God's creation, becomes, under the tyranny of a prolific greed, like an over-laden market-cart jolting and creaking on the road that leads from things to the Nothing, tearing ugly ruts across the green life till it breaks down under the burden of its vulgarity on the wayside reaching nowhere. For, this is called 'Un-Reason', as your teacher has said, and Un-Reason soon ceases.

（一位中国作家写道："在中国，局势的可怕的悲剧性方面就在于，当中华民族被号召摒弃它自己的文明而采用现代欧洲的文明时，在整个帝国却没有一个有学识之士能够给予一个最清晰的概念，来说明这个现代欧洲文明究竟是什么。"

我在别处读到一篇由一本杂志所转引、由一位法国人所写的评论。他在其中写道，中国不是一个国家，而是一种文明。由于未读到全部的论述，我无法确定他指的是什么。但是在我看来，根据作者所写，他似乎是想说明中国体现了一种理想，而不是某些物品的生产和集合，亦不是有关事物性质中的某一特性的信息；这就是说，它代表的不仅仅是财富、知识与力量的发展，而且是生命的哲学和生活的艺术。

"文明"一词是个欧洲词语，我们几乎尚未来得及费心去弄清它的真实含义。一个多世纪以来，我们接受了它，仿佛是接受了一匹别人赠送的马，由于对它完全信赖，因此从未想到要去数一数它的牙齿。只是在最近，我们才开始怀疑，我们是否真的认识到，当西方人提到"文明"一词时他们指的究竟是什么。我们问自己："它的含义与我们自己语言中用以表示人类至善至美概念一词的含义是相同的吗？"

文明不可能仅仅是偶然采取某一特定形态的、不断增加各种事件的总和，也不可能仅仅是我们认为极好的一种倾向。它应当是我们在我们的社会中为了达到至善至美的目标而逐渐形成的、对于某种指导性的道德力量的一种表现。当"至善至美"一词用于某一无生命的事物时，甚至用于其生命主要是生物学意义上的某种生物时，它具有其单一的确切的含义。但是，由于人类是复杂的，并且总是不断行进在超越自身的道路上，因此，当"至善至美"一词运用在他们身上时，其含义就不可能囿于一成不变的概念之中。这就使得不同的民族对于这一术语可能会有形形色色不同的定义。

我认为，我们自己语言中的梵语词"达摩"（dharma）与"文明"一词的词义最为近似。事实上，大概除了那些既无生命力又缺少氛围的新造词汇，我们也无其他词可用。"达摩"的特定含义指的是那种使我们精诚团结，引导我们获得最大幸福的原则。这个词的一般含义是指某一事物的本质。

对于人类来说，"达摩"是他对处于真理中的最佳表达方式。假如从外在的物质的观点出发，他可以拒绝"达摩"，可以选择动物或机器，由此可以使他不受损害，甚至还可以获得力量和财富。然而，对于作为一个人的他来说，与其如此，还不如死去。我们的圣典中说道："通过非达摩（否定达摩），人们事业发达，诸事遂愿，战无不胜，但在本质上却早已灭亡。"

如果一个人仅仅是一台相当不错的赚钱机器，在他身上是不会体现出人的各种完美品格的。他不啻是金玉其外，败絮其中。他在自己的生活中为裂开大口的、"否定达摩"那又聋又瞎的偶像建立起一座富丽堂皇的圣坛；而所有源源不断敬奉给它的昂贵的祭品都被倾入那犹如无底深渊般的永远也填不满的大口之中。按照我们的圣典所说，即使他趾高气扬，大喊大叫，猛力地做着手势，他也已经灭亡。

同样的思想也由伟大的中国先哲老子以不同的方式表达出来。他说："死而不亡者寿。"①在此他也表明了类似的理论：当一个人体现出他的真理时，他就活着，而那真理本身便是"达摩"。按照这种理想，"文明"就应该是用以对人类在共同生活中的"达摩"的表达方式。

一个多世纪以来，我们一直被繁荣的西方拖在它的战车后面，被它的烟尘窒息，被它的噪音震聋，因我们自己的孤弱无助而地位卑微，又被它的速度所压倒。我们承认，驾驭这一战车就是进步，而这种进步就是文明。假若我们胆敢问一声："进步是为了什么，进步不是为谁？"人们就会认为，对于进步的绝对性竟然会存有这种怀疑，这真是典型而又可笑的东方人所独有的想法。近来，更有一个声音传来，吩咐我们不仅要重视这辆战车上的科学的完美，而且还要重视横在其路途中的沟渠的深度。

不久前，我读了美国的《民族》周刊上的一篇短评。在论述一些英国航空兵对阿富汗的马赫苏德村庄进行轰炸时，在对待事实的真相方面，这篇短评与其说是审慎，倒不如说是率直。被这家周刊所评论的事件发生在当"一架轰炸机迫降在马赫苏德的一个村庄"，以及当"没有负伤的飞行员们从飞机的残骸中出来时。当时他们所面对的只不过是五六个老年妇女，她们正巧在躲避炸弹的袭击，正挥舞着令人胆寒的刀子。"评论撰写人援引了伦敦《泰晤士报》的如下报道：一位可爱的姑娘保护了这些飞行员，将他们带到附近的一个山洞。一位族长正把守在洞口，大声喊叫着，挥舞着刀子，不让聚在周围的大约四十个人靠近洞口。炸弹仍从空中接二连

---

① 此处及以下老子著《道德经》的汉译部分全部引自沙少海、徐子宏译注的《老子全译》（贵州人民出版社1989年版）中的《道德经》中的原文。

三地落下，因此那群人由于眼红山洞的安全，便拼命往洞里拥。飞行员们不顾人们敌意地表示，挤过了人群。……人们向他们提供饮食，附近的族长们还来拜访他们，显得十分友好。一位祭司也来探望他们，他同样也很和蔼可亲。妇女们照管安排他们的饮食。生活用品从拉扎与拉兹马克安全运来。……在24日晚上他们被送往拉扎，并于翌日黎明时分到达。护送者们将他们的俘虏装扮成马赫苏德人，以此防备有人袭击他们。……意味深长的是，飞行员们的保护人首先是在男女青年一代中出现的。

在上述报道中，可以发现这样一个强有力的事实，即西方已经取得了惊人的进步。他已打开了穿越地球上那一神秘莫测的地区的通道。炸弹的爆炸威力所产生的大规模杀伤的机械力量达到这样一种程度，在昔日只有众多人的勇猛所产生的力量才能与之相比。然而，这种巨大的进步却使人类变得渺小。西方得意洋洋地想象，当他展现出他所产生的成就以及他手中所持有的力量时，他也就表现出自己的创造力了。巨大的成果以及机械上的无可挑剔的装备向他隐瞒了这样一个事实——他身上的人性被扼杀了。

在孩提时代，我自由不羁地把一些小物件当作玩具，依靠我的想象创造出我自己的游戏，与我一起做游戏的小伙伴们充分地分享着我的快乐。实际上，我做游戏的全部乐趣都依赖于他们的参与。一天，在我们童年的这片乐土中，闯入了来自成年人世界的一个诱惑物。

一个从英国商店买来的玩具送给了我们的一个同伴，它完美无瑕，体积很大，逼真得令人惊奇。我的这个伙伴开始以这个玩具为荣，对我们的游戏也不那么上心了。他小心翼翼地不让我们接近那个价格昂贵的东西，因自己独占它而扬扬自得，感到自己比只拥有廉价玩具的伙伴们优越。我相信，倘若他能够运用历史上的时髦字眼儿的话，他肯定会说，他比我们文明，因为他已经达到了拥有那个完美得可笑的玩具的程度。

在他的兴奋中，有一点他没有能够认识到，一个当时在他看来是无关紧要的事实，即这一诱惑遮住了某种远比他的玩具完美得多的东西，遮住了完美儿童所应展现的东西。那个玩具只不过表现了他的财富，却没有表现出儿童的创造精神，没有表现出儿童在他的游戏中，在他的游戏世界里对所有小伙伴的敞开心扉邀请时所应有的那种慷慨大方的童趣。那些前去轰炸马赫苏德诸村庄的人，是以作为他们最新发明的科学玩具的那些器具的完美功效去衡量他们的文明的。他们如此强烈地认识到这些东西的价值，以至于他们不惜让本国人民以及那些偶尔有可能亲身尝到这些机器的致命的完美滋味的其他国家的人民，都去承受其忍耐力的极限。这种承受不仅存在于金钱中，而且也存在于人性中。这些人用人类的死亡率换取了玩具的出生率，而他们似乎还很高兴。他们的科学使他们如此轻而易举地获得了物质方面的巨大成就，因此他们不愿再去计算他们的精神所需要付出的代价。另一方面，那些保护了前来大批屠杀他们，屠杀男人、妇女和儿童的飞行员的马赫苏德人，在拥有这种致命的玩具方面却是原始的、未开化的。然而，他们却淋漓尽致地证实了人性的纯真，通过这种纯真他们能够表现出他们的人格。而若从所谓北欧日耳曼民族的观点，从那些自封为人类统治者的人的观点出发，那就是愚蠢。对于一个马赫苏德人来说，好客是被称作一个人所必须具有的品德，因此他不能错过他所遇到的机会。即使在对待某个一贯进行无情的敌对活动的人时也是如此。从实利的观点出发，马赫苏德人为此付出了十分昂贵的代价，如同我们对于我们最珍视的东西所必须付出的代价那样。文明的使命即是要为我们树立正确的价值观标准。马赫苏德人也许会有许多错误，并对此他们应负有责任。然而，在他们身上所体现的更有价值的东西是好客，而不是复仇，这一点不会被称作进步的，却一定是文明的"冷酷",在危急时刻不屑于顾忌太多,而坚决根除制造麻烦的原因。它运用其不分青红皂白的武器,无情对待罪犯与无辜者、战斗人员与平民,在这些方面它确乎是有效用的。通过这种彻头彻尾的冷酷无情的方法,人们事业发达,他们事事遂心如意,他们战胜敌人,然而,他们却停在了那里,是不完全的人。

我们不妨设想一下,下述造物过程中的某一糟糕的实验:它始于尾端,当造完胃时便骤然停止了。这种创造物的消化能力是完美无瑕的,所以它不断地长胖长壮,然而,其结果并不美妙。上次大战之初,当这一类怪物以各种各样千奇百怪的形状出现时,西方人一见,曾一度畏缩不前。但是现在似乎已对它们心生喜爱了,因为它们同其他各种丑类的孵化物一起被慈爱地置于她的育儿室中。由这种缺头少肢的畸形怪物所制造的种种骇人听闻的活动,也许会为那些想要成为人类主宰的人拓宽那条被称作进步的道路,然而它们肯定不属于文明。

有一次,我因事要从100英里以外的一个地方乘汽车去加尔各答。由于汽车的机械故障,迫使我们几乎每隔半个小时就必须给汽车加一次水。在我们被迫停驶的第一个村庄中,我们请求一个人帮助我们找水。这对他颇有些勉为其难,但是当我们付给他酬金时,尽管他很穷,他却拒绝接受。在沿途其他的15个村庄中都发生了同样的事情。在一个炎热的国度中,旅行者们时时都需要水,而在夏季又往往变得供水不足,但是村民们却把为需要水的人提供水视为己任。如若遵循那不可抗拒的供求规律,他们本可以轻易地以此做一笔交易的。然而,他们将其视作他们的"达摩"的那种理想已与他们的生命融为一体。要求他们出卖它,不啻要求他们出卖他们的生命。他们不会因为拥有它而要求承认任何个人的功德。

老子在论及那确实优秀的人物时说道:"圣人……生而不有,为而不恃,功成而弗居。夫唯弗居,是以不去。"我们的身外之物我们可以出售，但是与我们的生命融为一体之物我们却不能出售。这种对于真理的完全的吸收是属于完美无瑕的天国，它远在自我意识的炼狱之外。要想达到它，需要一个亲证文明的漫长过程。

能够不辞千辛万苦去为过往的陌生人送水，却又从不要求什么功德或报酬，这与每分钟都生产出令人咋舌的大批物品的能力相比，似乎简单得荒谬可笑，而又微不足道。一个在食品市场囤积居奇，不惜将整个世界推到濒临饿死的边缘，从而以此大发横财的百万富翁旅游者，在以每小时六十英里的速度驱车从我们的村庄中疾驶而过时，肯定是倨傲得对这种区区小事都不屑一顾。因为它既不像那以其奇长的指状物而引人注目的电线杆那样扎眼，又不似他自己的汽车发动机所发出的无礼地划破寂静的长空的噪音那般刺耳。

这种小事是简单，但是这种简单是数世纪的文化的产物，这种简单是难于模仿的。不出几年的时间我就可能学会如何转动一下机轮，瞬间就在成千上万根针上打出孔来。但是要求一个人对待敌人或者陌生人般勤好客，其中的那种绝对的简单却需要经过几代人的培养。这种简单不会将自己待价而沽，不会要求金钱报酬，因此那些醉心于力量的人是不会认识到这一点的，即"精神表达中的简单正是文明的最高产物"。

分裂瓦解的过程能够扼杀这种更高生活所产生的稀有的果实，犹如拥有某种罕见的美丽的鸟类，会被拥有着文明的武器的贪婪这种卑下的力量所彻底灭绝一般。事实已清楚地向我证明了这一点，这是当我发现了那唯一因向我们供水而收取费用的地方时所认识到的。那个地方是我们所途经的加尔各答的一个郊区，在那里生活要比别处富裕，供水也更容易变得充裕，那里的"进步"已在四面八方各个系统中涌现。我们应当逐步了解这种分裂瓦解的力量，了解它是如何起作用的。

创造是通过律动形式对真理的揭示，它的两重性是由表达与物质两方面构成的。在二者中物质必须绝对忠诚地献身于表达。它必须懂得它自身是不会有止境的，因此，它不应通过其自身的巨大压力而使人们背离他们的创造性活动。

　　在印度，我们有这样一种类型的梵文诗歌，内中专门阐明所有复杂的梵文语法规则。这种诗歌在我们某些读者的心中激发出延绵不绝的勃勃兴致，使他们即便在一件艺术作品当中，也要找出对力量的某种确切的证明，对其表现形式的要求也是近乎确实具体的。这表明，经过专门的培养，便可造成一种仅仅能以展示力量为乐的心理，这种心理乐于操纵各种物质，却忘记了这些物质本身并无价值可言。在现代的西方世界，我们目睹了同样的情况。在那里，进步是以物质增长的速度来衡量的。用马力衡量是一种方法，在它面前，精神力量已变得地位卑微。马力疾驰，精神力量护持。疾驰者被称作进步的原则，护持者被我们称作"达摩"；而"达摩"这个字眼儿，我认为应被译作"文明"。

　　科学家告诉我们，原子的构成方式，是由一个原子核以一种舞动的节律将其同伴吸引在周围，并从而形成一个完美的统一体。只要在一种文明的核心中包含着某种按照相互关系的节律将其成员结合在一起的创造性理想，这种文明就会永葆健康、强壮。这种相互之间的关系是美好的，而不是纯粹功利主义的。当这种身为"达摩"的创造性力量让位于某一压倒一切的情感时，这一文明就会突如其来地燃烧，酿成一场大火灾，犹如一颗点燃了自身的火葬柴堆的一颗火星。这一文明从柔和而适中的光芒中一下子迸发出最耀眼的强光，仅仅因其灼人的火光，就足以使其自身遭受剧烈的灭顶之灾。

　　西方社会在很长一段时间曾经有过一种伟大的精神理想，而不是仅仅把进步的动力作为其主要的动力的。它曾有着积极致力于为发生冲突的社会力量进行调解，使之重归于好的宗教信仰。它所最珍视的是人类关系的完美,这种完美是由克制人类自私的本能,使人类懂得其根本统一的哲学而达到的。然而,在过去的二百年中,西方发现了进入大自然的力量之宝库的通路,自此,它的全部注意力便不可抗拒地被吸引到那个方向。它的内在的文明的理想就这样被对力量的爱恋推到一边。

人类的理想就其活动的领域来说,从上到下都充满着十足的人性。这一理想之光是柔和的,因为它漫射四方;它的生命是温和的,因为它包容一切;它是宁静的,因为它伟大;它是适中的,因为它全面。然而,我们的感情却是狭隘的,它那有限的领域使它具有强烈的冲动性。这种肆无忌惮的贪婪的力量近来已经占据了西方的心灵。这种情况不过是在很短的时期内发生的,却顷刻之间就使物品泛滥成灾,淹没了地球上的一切时间和空间。昔日的一切具有人性的事物都正在被打碎。

为了在这种混乱的分裂状态中保持某种貌似统一的东西,各种组织机构建立起来了,以大批量地制造和平或者虔诚或者社会福利。但是这种组织机构决然不会具有那种完美统一体的性质。毋庸置疑,它们是必需的,正如我们需要我们的水杯一样。然而我们之所以需要水杯是因为我们需要水,而不是水杯本身。这些组织机构原本不过是它们自身制造出来的负担。倘若我们乐于将其数目无限制地增多,其结果也可能是惊人的卓有成效,然而对于生活来说,却是毁灭性的,致命的。

我曾经在某个地方读过柏拉图的一段话,他说:"只有当一个明智的、社会化的团体保持为一个统一体,它才能继续发展。若非如此,发展必会停止,或者团体就会分裂瓦解,不再是一个有机体。"只有当这种统一体的精神的核心是某种具有达摩性质的充满生气的思想感情,并将人们导向合作与对生活的馈赠的共同分享,那统一体的精神才会被保持下去。

老子曾经说过："不知常，妄作凶；……"舒适方便被追求着，物品成倍地增长着，永恒却黯然失色，感情被激起，邪恶乘胜前进，从一个大陆走向另一个大陆。它残害着人们，将生命之花——这一寓居于人性的圣殿之中的母亲之心的产物无情地践踏、碾碎。而我们却还被要求建立起一座座迎接这一死亡进军的凯旋门。让我们至少拒绝承认它的胜利吧，即使我们不能阻止它的前进。让我们去死，一如你们的老子所说的那样，却依然不朽。

我们的圣典说："罪寓于贪，死寓于罪。"你们的哲人也说过："祸莫大于不知足。"这些格言警句中包含着人们长期积累的智慧。当贪婪成为一个民族的主要特征时，也就预示着这个民族的灭亡。仅仅依靠诸如国际联盟这样的组织是绝对挽救不了它的。听任发自那个民族内心的追求私利的洪水自由泛滥，与此同时又企图筑起一座外部堤坝拦住这股洪水的去路，这种方法决不会成功。由于阻塞，这股洪水将会以更大的力量爆发。老子说："以其不自生，故能长生。"生命的法则即存在于此。因此，在一个社会中，一切有助于生活的培养、教导，无非是指那些能帮助我们克制利己的贪欲的事物。

在昔日文明活跃的时期，亦即当它的大部分活动都与一种内在的理想而不是与一种外在的强制相联系时，金钱尚未具有现在所具有的价值。你们难道没有认识到这个事实在我们的生活中造成多么巨大的差异？它又是多么野蛮地贬低了我们遗产中的那些无价之宝吗？我们已经对这种灾难性的变化变得如此习以为常，使我们已经不能充分认识到它强加在我们身上的那种对尊严的损害。

我请你们想象一下，有一天——假设这一天会到来的话——在一次聚会中，当一个人进来时，其他的人全都敬畏地起身离开座位，只因为来人所佩戴的项圈上的人头骨的数目要比他的同伴的多。今天，我们会毫不迟疑地承认，这是纯粹的野蛮风尚。难道就没有象征着人类同样堕落的其他标志吗？难道除了那些野蛮人如此自豪地佩戴的人头骨，就没有其他形式取代人头骨吗？

  昔时，人们从不把仅仅聚敛起无数的钱财看作是富有，除非他拥有某个可用以表明其理想之伟大的荣誉花冠，才可称作富有。无论是在东方还是在西方，人们为了保持其与生俱来的尊严，绝对蔑视那仅仅代表占有的权利却不代表道德的职责的金钱。赚钱作为一种职业无处不受人轻蔑，而那些以获取巨额利润为生活的唯一目标的人，皆为人们所不齿。曾经有一个时期，在印度，我们的婆罗门受人尊敬。这不仅因为他们的学问和纯洁的生活，还因为他们对于物质财富完全漠视的态度。这仅仅表明，当时，我们的社会充分意识到，它的生活是要依赖于它的理想的，而这些理想决不应被任何属于那种追求私利的感情所损害。然而，今天，由于进步被视作文明的代表，又由于这一进步无休止地聚集、增加物质财富，金钱已在全世界建立起统治权。因为，在这个物欲横流的世界上，金钱不啻一座向四面八方输送动力的中央电站。在以往的时代里，君王并不耻于谦恭地向有才智的人或者向有精神才能或创造天赋的人致敬。因为高级生活所具有的特性即是这些时代文明的动力。然而，在今天，人们不论其身份如何，从来不认为对那些腰缠万贯的人表示敬意是什么丢脸的事情。他们这样做，倒不都是因为企望以此得到什么好处，而是因为对方拥有万贯家财这样一个赤裸裸的事实。这意味着完善的人已被物质的人所击败。这一巨大的倒退，犹如一只又黏又滑的爬虫，缠绕着整个人类世界的躯体。在我们能够将人类从它那无尽头的长尾巴的束缚中拯救出来之前，我们必须首先使我们的心灵摆脱对于这一邪恶力量的崇拜，摆脱对于这条决不能成为主宰人类文明之神的恶龙的那种亵渎神圣的崇拜。我相信，你们一定知道，这一没有灵魂的、贪婪的滋生物，已经对你们国家那秀美的肢体张开了它那翕张自如的大口，其贪婪的程度也许甚于对世界上任何其他的地区。我真诚地希望你们能够采取一些措施,以使她得以摆脱被它那血盆大口吞噬的命运。然而,来自进攻的敌方的威胁并不是那么大,倒是来自可能背叛的防御一方的危险要大得多。当我在你们现在年轻一代的身上,看到他们自甘堕落,被一种具有巨大诱惑力的邪恶力量迷惑得神魂颠倒这种迹象时,我感到极为震惊。他们在大片的摩天大楼中,在新闻杂志耸人听闻的大标题中,在政客大叫大嚷、蛊惑人心的煽动中四处寻求着文明。他们将自己的那些对于真理具有远见卓识的伟大的先知抛诸脑后,却在黑暗中徘徊着,乞求某种萤火虫出借它那微乎其微的光亮。而那只萤火虫只能提着它那光线微弱的灯笼,以便使自己能够缓缓地落到最近的尘埃中去。当他们返回家中,真正理解了他们的大师老子在进行教诲时所说的"有德司契,无德司彻"这句话时,他们就会明白"文明"一词的含义了。在这句格言中,他仅用几个词就表达了我试图在这篇文章中所要说明的意思。这并非与一种内在的理想相关,而是与一种外在的诱惑相联系的进步,追求的是满足我们无止境的要求。而那身为一种理想的文明,却给予我们履行我们职责的力量和欢乐。由于权力的组织和生产的组织而使生活变得呆板、心肠变得冷酷。对于这一点,他道出了深刻的真理:草木之生也柔脆,其死也枯槁。故坚强者死之徒,柔弱者生之徒。是以兵强则灭,木强则折。故坚强处下,柔弱处上。 如上所引,我们印度的圣贤说过:"有非达摩相助,人们事业发达,诸事遂愿,战无不胜,然而,他们本质上早已灭亡。"那本身并非为幸福的财富正迅速茁壮地成长着,然而它自身中却已孕育着死亡的种子。这种财富在西方得到了人血的滋养,其果实正在成熟。许多世纪之前,你们的圣贤也已发出同样的告诫,他说:"物壮则老,谓之不道,不道早已。"你们的导师说过:"益生曰祥。"因为"益生"不像物品的增长,决不会超出生活的统一这个界限。高山上的松树长得高大伟岸，它从上到下，每一微小的部分都保持着一种内在平衡的节律。因此，它在外表上虽然极为高大，却别有一种体现出自制力的恰到好处的韵致。那棵松树及其产物属于相同的有节奏的生命体系，其树干、枝叶、花朵和果实都与这棵树浑然一体，它们的丰盛繁茂并不是一种病态的过分，而是一种福祉。但是，那些主要是为了获取利润而不是为了满足生活的需要的体系，却促使我们这种扼杀人性健康发展的社会之中的丑恶现象极度膨胀。由于它们并未与我们的生活融为一体，因而也不符合它的节律。我们现在的生活，本应步如曼舞、声如妙乐、体态优美，本应用群星和花簇来比喻之。因为它应该与天神的创造保持和谐一致。然而，在四处蔓延、不断滋生的贪婪这一暴政的统治下，它变得如同一辆不堪重负的集市上的马车，颠簸着，摇晃着，吱吱嘎嘎地行进在那条从物品通向一无所有的道路上。沿途轧过绿色的生命，留下丑陋的车辙，直到终因其粗野行为的重荷而抛锚在路旁，从而到达不了任何地方。因为，这就叫作"不道"，而正如你们的导师所说的"不道早已"。）

诗人泰戈尔在这篇长文中深刻地揭示了来自欧洲的词语"文明"和梵语词"达摩"的关系，并且表达了自己对欧洲文明的观点。他认为中国古代圣贤老子的观点与"达摩"几乎表达了同样好的意义。诗人对中国青年们说，在印度，他们的婆罗门受人尊敬。这不仅因为他们的学问和纯洁的生活，还因为他们对于物质财富完全漠视的态度。今天，由于进步被视作文明的代表，又由于这一进步无休止地聚集、增加物质财富，金钱已在全世界建立起统治地位。因为，在这个物欲横流的世界上，金钱不啻一座向四面八方输送动力的中央电站。在以往的时代里，君王并不耻于谦恭地向有才智的人或者向有精神才能或创造天赋的人致敬。因为高级生活所具有的特性即是这些时代文明的动力。然而，在今天，人们不论其身份如何，从来不认为对那些腰缠万贯的人表示敬意是什么丢脸的事情。这意味着完善的人已被物质的人所击败。这一巨大的倒退，犹如一只又黏又滑的爬虫，缠绕着整个人类世界的躯体。

　　诗人在这篇文章中表示，他相信，中国青年一定知道，这一没有灵魂的、贪婪的滋生物，已经对中国那秀美的肢体张开了它那翕张自如的大口，其贪婪的程度也许甚于对世界上任何其他的地区。诗人泰戈尔真诚地希望中国青年能够采取一些措施，以便摆脱被那种血盆大口吞噬的命运。印度这位诗人说，来自进攻的敌方的威胁并不是那么强大，倒是来自可能背叛的防御一方的危险要大得多。

　　认真地品味诗人这一段语重心长的讲话，再观察当今一些社会现实，任何一位善良正直的人就不能不生发出很多的感慨，不能不感受到诗人泰戈尔思想的深邃、人格的伟大。

出席清华大学欢迎会并与大家交谈

泰戈尔第一次访华纪实

加尔各答〇--仰光〇--马来亚〇--新加坡〇--香港〇--上海〇--杭卅〇--南京〇--济南〇--北京〇--太原〇--武汉〇--上海〇

5月2日（拜沙克月十九日）星期五，诗人泰戈尔还住在清华大学的时候，一群男女学生又聚集到诗人的身边，向他提出了如下的几个问题：

1. How will love and beauty of the world be kept everlasting?

2.What is the significance of our life?

3. What should be our attitude toward life during the present stage of great transition?

4.1s it a privilege for a person to live? If it is, then how can we avoid sorrow and gain happiness?

5.In the near future, can the materialism conquer the spiritualism in the far East?

（1. 世界上的爱和美如何保持永恒？

2. 我们生命的意义是什么？

3. 在这个大转型的阶段，我们的生活态度应该是什么？

4. 一个人活着是一种荣幸吗？如果是，那么我们如何避免悲伤而获得快乐呢？

5. 在不久的将来，远东的唯物主义能否战胜唯心主义？）

诗人泰戈尔又推心置腹地与大学生们进行了交谈，并且一一回答了他们的问题。

5月3日（拜沙克月二十日）星期六，这一天，清华大学学生会举行晚会，欢迎诗人泰戈尔。他们发给诗人泰戈尔这样的邀请函：

The students of Tsing Hua College have the greatest pleasure and honor to invite the venerable presence of Mr. Tagore to a social to be given on the college lawn in front of the Auditorium, at eight o'clock in the afternoon, on Saturday, May the third.

（清华大学的学生们十分高兴和荣幸地邀请泰戈尔先生出席定于五月三日（星期六）下午八时在大礼堂前的学院草坪上举行的联谊活动。）

晚会的节目单：

STUDENTS SOCIAL & RECEPTION IN HONOR OF RABINDRANATH TAGORE/

May 3rd 1924/ PROGRAMME

Part I/ Students Mass Dinner Time 6:30 p.m. Dining Hall, H.S.

Part II/ Social/ Time 7:45 p.m. Place: Auditorium

1.Opening Remarks: Wang Tsao Shih//2.College Song in Chinese 3.Welcome Address in Honor of Tagore : Chi Chao Ting//4.Music//5.Play etc.

4 May Hsiang Yu Lee：...I dare not trouble you any more, for you are very old and we, innocent boys, have troubled you enough already. My question is "What trainings are necessary for a young man who is sentimental in nature and poetical in thinking in order to expect him become

a poet?"

学生会为欢迎泰戈尔而举行的晚会（1924年5月3日）节目单：

第一部分：学生聚餐时间下午六点半，餐厅；

第二部分：晚会开始时间晚上7:45，地点：礼堂；

1. 开幕致辞：王曹石（Wang Tsao Shih的音译）；2. 唱大学校歌（中文）；3. 迟朝亭（Chi Chao Ting的音译）致词，欢迎纪念泰戈尔；4. 音乐；5. 演出节目等。

5月4日 向玉莉（Hsiang yu Lee的音译）给诗人写了一封信，信中提出了一个问题："…I dare not trouble you any more, for you are very old and we, innocent boys, have troubled you enough already. My question is what trainnings are necessary for a young man who is sentimental in nature and poetic in thinking in order to expect him become a poet?"

（我不敢再麻烦您了，因为您已经年迈了，而我们这些无辜的孩子已经麻烦您够多了。我的问题是："对于一个天性多愁善感、思想富有诗意的年轻人，要想成为诗人，需要接受什么样的训练？"）

1924年4月30日至5月5日，印度大诗人泰戈尔访问清华并做讲演，在"水木清华"留影。后排右为校长曹云祥，中排左起辜鸿铭、泰戈尔，前排左起王文显、张歆海、徐志摩、张彭春。

5月5日晚上,清华一群学生陪同诗人泰戈尔围坐在荷花畔旁边的工字厅外。署名"德"的记者在《清华周刊》1924年第214期上报道了这次聚会:

5月5日,傍晚五时许,夕阳反照着环拥荷花池畔的苍茵,山堤树影横斜。而池面之微波亦因之成明阴错综、金光浮荡的美趣。时则印度诗人泰戈尔,因他的从客士女数人,正围坐后工字厅槛外,临风茶叙。我跟本校同学数十余,亦照预定时间,到荷花池旁边伫候。过了几分钟,泰氏乃拥客离席,同学们亦跟着上前。于是泰氏入后工字厅当中,背着槛外的石山坐下,诸同学多环坐席上。先由同学高君起问,被西洋文明迫成之饥窘问题,应当何样解决?泰氏用流利之英文,滔滔叙说印度这个问题的始末,极感兴趣。现在我冒昧译述如下:"我(泰氏自称)对这个问题,因为不十分明了中国的经济情况,所以只能根据印度的经过情形来讲。印度的情形,与中国亦有许多相同的地方。当我年少的时候,印度人大都住在乡村,而当时的村庄生活虽然朴实,而确是很快乐的!那个时候,凡与我们家庭稍有一点亲戚关系的人,都可以到我们家里吃住,所以我们往往有极大的家庭。因为那时风俗,各庄家都愿意尽他们的力量所及,供给来客饭食。那时候印度人耕种所收获的粮食既然丰裕,而且全储存印度境内,为本地人消用。所以各农家见有行旅过客,没有不乐意招待、厚款饭菜的。再讲村居的生活状况,各农家除田事以外,亦还有社交同娱乐的时间。其中最重要的就是戏剧的艺术。多数农民虽没有享过学校的教育,但是他们因为受戏剧的陶冶感移,亦很能发展赏美乐善的心情。可见这种戏剧,实在是很富于教育上、艺术上的价值了。

一般有名学者,都是住在自己的村居,要从他的学生,就到他那里住,同他领教。这些学生,不特不预交纳修金,而且连伙食、住宿都是由师长供给的。当时的社会,因为明白了培养起一个学者,是要替社会造幸福的缘故,都以支持青年求学为社会的责任。民间既然是衣食丰饶，风气亦称醇厚，凡庆祝良辰喜事，或因别的缘故请客的时候，无论什么人，都可以到这一家吃酒看戏、享受娱乐。固然食品只是当时的简单果肉，然而供食百千的宾客请帖真算公开的呢。

富豪人家，当喜事宴请的时候，习例都要先请远近有名的学者到会，不特以厚礼宴请，而且亦在此时送给学问家酬谢的金钱。这些学者之间，此时亦常发生辩论，往往让各处来之学生辩驳，而先生们只在旁边观察之。但辩论之胜负，于各先生之名誉亦稍有关系的。凡此都是印度没有同西方接触时候的景象。

后来印度受西方人工商业的侵入，到了近几年来，印度人几乎都被时势逼着去做苦工，以保持他的生活。印度受西方物质文明的压制，使少数人发财、据有资本，而普通人民，都要做苦工制造许多不在本国消耗的物品输运出口。一方面风气亦渐尚浮华，生活程度日高。同时与西方通商后，几个大城都发展得非常兴旺，而旧日乡村之半乐生活，即随之一落千丈。原来有大城市的国家，往往把全国的精华皆萃集在一块地面。结果，城市一部分的居民单独兴盛，而郊野中大多数的人口都处在零落苦役的地位。印度从城市发展以来，以前守着家园的学者、医生，亦都被牵诱到城市里去做事。而乡村的生活亦就日行干枯憔悴了。刚才所举的这几种恶趋势，所由生产，全是因为他们发展失去了均衡的准则。因此，劳动者与农主之阶级悬殊，城市之过分发展，都是亏失均衡之道。"

尚君起问泰氏，他所信仰的上帝究竟是否与耶稣教的上帝有分别？

泰氏答曰：他所信的上帝，与耶稣教旧约圣经中所讲的偏狭的上帝不同，但他与新约中耶稣所信奉之上帝大略相似。

尚郡复问："则何以证明上帝之存在？"

泰氏侃侃解说，听者莫不觉得他讲时神趣之锐敏。他先说明物质部分的人身与体外之物质世界的关系作为引证，大意说：人们的生理上的有机体之外,就有万有物体之大世界去供给他生活的需要,和满足他的官觉。凡人体所有的十几种物质,都是这大物体世界里边所包括而有的同一物质。譬如人身上血液里的水,在大物体世界里,则为奔腾河海及空中之雨水。而且我们的身体总永远在感觉那体外之较大的实在体——物体的世界。假如人世间没有物体的世界的存在,我们这有机物质的身体便要完全失去它的存在意义了。人们身体上的灵动官能,全在继续着要求和自体之外质物接触。例如人们的眼睛必定是时常喜欢能看见外界的东西,耳朵则要求时常能够听见外界的声音。况且眼睛所以能看见东西,全靠自然界的物质世界中有光之存在。若是宇宙间没有光,则眼睛天然就丧失它的官能了。由此我们可以明白人体有机物质的身体,这个小实体(smaller reality)是永远在感觉、需要和寻求着自体之外的那个大实体(greater reality)——大物体世界。我们都知道人类的存在,绝不是单来满足身体上、生理上的作用就算完事的,我们生活的大部分,是为我们的精神和心性所支配的。这一部分就叫作人们的人格或灵性(personality or soul)。我们已经明白人身上生理的肉体,不能离开它的较大的实在体——大物体的世界。同一道理,我们就可见我们的人格或灵性,亦不能够没有它的大实在来做我们这个小实在存在的根据。这就是伟大无量的人格或上帝(Infinite Personality of God)……同他人们可以借爱做不断的交通、结极雄固的友谊。

这时候。钟先生问泰氏对人猿同祖说的真假有何见解。

泰氏答曰:他认此问题殆专为生物学家所急欲解决的,不过无论人类曾与猿猴同祖或否,皆非他所特别关心的。因为他认为,不管人类先前经过了多少蛟龙或狲猴的时期,我们现在总明白,我们已经到了这个人类的世界,我们就应该自己想求领导我们真美的生活就是了。

复次马君问他对于基督教中所谓罪恶(sin)有何主义?

泰氏答曰：基督教所讲的罪恶，他不认为十分紧要。他对罪恶的观念，似乎很近佛家那平等看待众生、虽蚊蚁都禁杀害的慈悲，但他实在却认凡是能得爱的障魔，就算罪恶。除杀了这个罪恶，依旧是合于仁爱的举动，所以杀了一个猛虎不算有罪恶，因为猛虎是吃杀动物和人的野兽，是爱的大蟊贼，今除杀戕贼"爱"的怪物，当然不谓之罪恶。

"人们的生存在世，是不是特幸？"这个问题为王君提起后，全座都带上笑脸，双目都疾守着泰氏的仪容，急要一下子把答案看出。泰氏微笑着稍停歇一下，乃以恺悌清爽的音调，畅谈人生之真美的享乐。意谓："他自己承认的确人生是一个大特幸。凡宇宙色相，万千奇幻，天然的美丽，都是供人赏尚，无代价的享乐。可惜人们常忘弃这许天然界的灿烂，而不见觉其宝贵。假使一旦太阳失落了，人们必定愿意出极重价去买回来它。你若说：'我的事情太忙，我要预备考几何、英文，没有工夫去享受。'那就似乎有点儿可怜。"

高君问泰氏对"自由"与"爱"之确凿的界说及其相互的关系，答复大意说：绝对的自由与绝对的爱，都是人们灵性对自己以外的实在而言，实际上爱是终极，而自由只是如方针一般，能够使爱的旅程平安达到宇宙美满的境遇罢了。

泰氏谈到这儿已经6点30分了，同学恐他老人家太辛苦，大家就向他道谢并告别。

泰戈尔第一次访华纪实

在燕京女师大的谈话

加尔各答○----○仰光○----○马来亚○----○新加坡○----○香港○----○上海○----○杭州○----○南京○----○济南○----○北京○ 太原○ 武汉○ 上海○

5月6日上午，胡适来会见诗人泰戈尔。这一天中午，华北英语教师在燕京女子师范大学设午宴招待诗人泰戈尔。午餐后，诗人泰戈尔会见了燕京女师大同学和教师，并且发表了讲话，他的讲话全文如下：

When I am invited to speak at any meeting, I always try to avoid it. You will sympathize with me when you know the reason. The language in which I have to speak is not my own.Yet, by some chance, I achieved a reputation which I have to live up to, and I am always afraid of being found out. But when I heard that this was to be an opportunity of meeting the girl students here, I cheerfully took a chance, and risked the possibility of making a fool of myself.

I do not know what you expect from me this afternoon. I have been told that you would like to hear of the educational mission I have taken up, but it will be difficult for me to give you a distinct idea of my institution which has grown gradually during the last twenty-four years. With it my own mind has sympathize with me when you know the reason. The language in which I have to speak is not my own. Yet, by some chance, I achieved a reputation which I have to live up to, and I am always afraid of being found out. But when I heard that this was to be an opportunity of meeting the girl students here, I cheerfully took a chance, and risked the possibility of making a fool of myself. I do not know what you expect from me this afternoon. I have been told that you would like to hear of the educational mission I have taken up, but it will be difficult for me to give you a distinct idea of my institution which has grown gradually during the last twenty-four years. With it my own mind has grown and my own ideal of education has come to its fullness, so slowly, and so naturally, that I find it difficult now to analyse and put it before you.

The first question you may all ask is: what urged me to take up education. I had spent most of my time in literary pursuits till I was forty or more. I had never any desire to take my part in practical work, because I had a rooted conviction in my mind that I had not the gift. Perhaps you know the facts, or how I make a confession? When I was thirteen I finished going to school. I do not want to boast about it, I merely give it you as a historical fact.

So long as I was forced to do so, I felt the torture of going to school insupportable. I often used to count the years that must pass before I should find my freedom. My elder brothers had passed through their academic career and were engaged in life, each in his own way. How I used to envy them when, after a hurried meal in the morning, I found the inevitable carriage, that took us to school, ready at the gate. How I wished that, by some magic spell, I could cross the intervening fifteen or twenty years and suddenly become a grown-up man. I afterwards realized that what then weighed on my mind was the unnatural pressure of the system of education, which, prevailed everywhere.

Children's minds are sensitive to the influences of the great world to which they have been born. Their subconscious. Mind is active, always imbibing some lesson, and with it realizing the joy of knowing. This sensitive receptivity of their passive mind helps them, without their feeling any strain, to master language, that most complex and difficult instrument of expression, full of ideas that are undefinable and symbols that deal with abstractions. And through their natural gift of guessing they learn the meaning of words which we cannot explain. It may be easy for a child to know what the word *water* means, but how difficult it must be for it to know what idea is associated with the simple word *yesterday*. Yet how easily do they overcome innumerable such difficulties owing to the extraordinary sensitiveness of their subconscious mind. Their introduction to this great world of reality has been easy and joyful because of this.

But it is just at this critical period that the child's life is brought into the education factory, lifeless, colourless, dissociated from the context of universe, within bare white walls staring like eyeballs of the dead. We had that God-given gift of taking delight in the world, but such delightful activity was fettered and imprisoned, stilled by a force called discipline which kills the sensitivity of the child mind, the mind which is always on the alert, restless and eager to receive first-hand knowledge from mother Nature. We had to sit inert, like dead specimens of some museum, whilst lessons were pelted at us from on high, like hailstones on flowers.

I rebelled, young though I was. Of course this was an awful thing for a child to do—the child of a respectable family! My elders did not know how to deal with this phenomenon. They tried all kinds of persuasion, vigorous and gentle, until at last I was despaired of and set free. Through the joy of my freedom I felt a real urging to teach myself. I undertook the task of playing schoolmaster to myself, and found it to be a delightful game. I pored over books that came my way—not school-selected textbooks, most often books that I did not understand, and I filled up the gaps of understanding out of my own imagination. The result may have been quite different from the author's meaning, but the activity itself had its own special value.

At the age of twelve I was first coerced into learning English. Most of you here are perhaps blissfully unconscious of the difficulties of your own language. You will admit, however, that neither its spelling, nor its syntax, is perfectly rational. The penalty for this I had to pay, without having done anything to deserve it, with the exception of being born ignorant.

When in the evening time my English teacher used to come, with what trepidation I waited! I would be yearning to go to my mother and ask her to tell me a fairy story but instead I had to go and get my text book, with its unprepossessing black binding, and chapters of lessons, followed by rows of separated syllables with accent marks like soldiers' bayonets. As for that teacher, I can never forgive him. He was so inordinately conscientious! He insisted on coming every single evening—there never seemed to be either illness or death in his family. He was so preposterously punctual too. I remember how the fascination for the frightful attracted me every evening to the terrace facing the road; and, just at the right moment, his umbrella, for bad weather never prevented him coming—would appear at the bend of our lane.

One day I discovered, in a library belonging to one of my brothers, a copy of *Dickens Old Curiosity Shop*. I persisted in reading it and, with the help of the illustrations supplemented by contributions made by my own imagination, I made out some kind of story. In this manner, with no help from my teacher, but just as a child learns by sheer guessing, I went on reading and reading and a twilight atmosphere of colourful vision was produced in my mind.

This was the experience of my own young days and I believe that a large part of such success or reputations as I may have acquired, I owe to that early freedom, won with wilfulness. Thus you can see that I had little or no experience of school-teachers and therefore I should have been the last person to take upon myself this task of conducting a school.

I chose a delightful spot and used to hold my classes under some big shady tree. I taught them all I could. I played with them. In the evening I recited our ancient epics and sang my own songs. I trusted to the presence of the spirit of freedom in the atmosphere. I had to fight the teachers who assisted me, who had been brought up in a different environment to that of mine, who had no faith in freedom, who believed that it was impertinence for the boys to be boys.

Then I tried to create an atmosphere of culture. I invited renowned artists from the city to live at the school, leaving them free to produce their own work, which I allowed the boys and girls to watch if they so felt inclined. It the same with my own work. All the time I was composing songs and poems, and would often invite the teachers round, to sing or read with them. Our boys would also come, and peep in since they were not invited, and listen to the poems and songs fresh from the heart of their composer. This helped to create an atmosphere from which they could imbibe something impalpable, but life-giving.

We have there the open beauty of the sky, and the different seasons revolve before our eyes in all the magnificence of their colour. Through this perfect touch with nature we took the opportunity of instituting festivals of the seasons. When nature herself sends her message we ought to acknowledge its compelling force. When the kiss of rain thrilled the heart of the surrounding trees, if we had still behaved with undue propriety and paid all our attention to mathematics, it would have been positively wrong, impious.

The season of the rains often brought us unexpected release from duty some voice suddenly would proclaim from the sky: 'Today is your holiday!' We submitted gladly and would run wildly away. Such sympathy is so easily crushed by routine which takes no count of nature's claims, and does not keep open the path for this great world to find its place in the soul of man. I do not believe in such barbarity.

I have spoken enough on this most important aspect, but there is one more idea I have not yet mentioned—the ideal of the age—which must find in its place in the centre of education.

When races come together, as they have done in the present age, it should not be merely the gathering of a crowd. There must be some bond of relation, otherwise they will knock against one another. They will be an ill-formed and unfinished body whose limbs are league of peoples engaged in robbing the world for their own aggrandize-internal friction. We are now waiting for a peace from within, and not for a ill-formed and unfinished body whose limbs are disjointed, causing constant internal friction. WE are now waiting for a peace from within. And not for a league of people engaged in robbing the world for their own aggrandizement .

Our education must enable every child to grasp and to fulfil this purpose of the age, not to defeat it by acquiring the habit of the age, not to defeat it by acquiring the habit of creating divisions, and of cherishing national prejudices. There are of course natural differences in human races which should be preserved and respected and the mission of our education should be to realize our unity in spite of them, to discover truth through the wilderness of their contradictions.

This we have tried to do in Visva-Bharati. Our endeavor has been to include this ideal of unity in all the activities in our institution, some educational, some that comprise different kinds of artistic expression, some in the shape of service to our neighbours by way of helping the reconstruction of village life. As I wanted this institution to be interracial, I invited there great minds from the West. They cordially responded, and some have some permanently to join hands with us and build a place where men of all nations and countries may find their true home, without molestation from the prosperous who are always afraid of idealism, or from the politically powerful who are always suspicious of men who have the freedom of spirit.

（当我被邀请在任何会议上发言时，我总是尽量逃避。你们知道原因后也会同情我的。我讲话所要使用的语言不是我自己的母语。然而，机缘巧合下，我获得了声誉，我必须对得起这份声誉。我总是害怕被发现我是由于这个原因才不想发言的。不过，当我听说这是一个与这里的大学生们见面的机会时，我欣然接受了，并且冒着可能出丑的风险。

我不知道你们今天下午想从我这里得到什么。有人告诉我，你们想听听我所承担的教育使命，但我很难向你们清楚地介绍我的学校，因为它在过去24年里逐渐发展起来。随着它的发展，我自己的思想也得到了成长，我自己的教育理想也丰满起来，这个过程是如此地缓慢、如此地自然，以至于我在你们面前现在很难对其做出清晰的分析和阐述。

你们可能会问的第一个问题就是：什么原因促使我从事教育？直到我40多岁，我的大部分时间都是在文学的追求方面度过的。我从来不曾想参加实际工作,因为我心里根深蒂固地认为,我没有这方面的天赋。也许,你们都知道这些事实,或者我可以坦诚地向你们告白?当我十三岁时我就不去上学了。我并不想炫耀这一点,我只是想把它作为一个历史事实告诉你们。我只是被迫去上学,我感到这种折磨无法忍受。我常常计算着:还得挨过多少年华我才能得到自由。我的哥哥们都已完成学业,正以各自的方式谋生。每当我匆匆忙忙吃完早餐,发现那辆送我们去上学的、躲也躲不开的马车已停在大门口时,我是多么妒忌它啊!我多么希望能有一个魔咒,能使我一下子跨越这中间的15或20年而变成一个大人。后来我才认识到,当时压在我心头的重负正是那种违反自然的教育制度。而这一制度却到处都在盛行。儿童的心灵易于感受到他们所降生的这个伟大世界的影响。他们潜意识里的心理活动是积极主动的,总是在汲取着什么知识,并以此认识到吸收知识的欢乐。他们那被动的头脑所具有的这种敏感的、善于接受的天性,帮助他们不用费什么力气就能掌握语言——这种充满着许多不可定义的概念以及用以应付各种抽象概念的、最复杂最困难的表达工具。通过孩子们与生俱来的想象力,他们认识到许多我们无法解释的词语含义。对于一个儿童来说,要懂得单词"水"是什么意思,可能很容易。但是要理解什么概念与一个简单的词"昨天"相联系,该会是多么困难啊!然而,由于他们那潜意识心理所具有的非凡的敏感,他们又是多么轻而易举地克服了无数诸如此类的困难啊!正因为如此,他们就轻松愉快地被引进了这个现实的伟大世界。然而,正是在这个关键时期,孩子们的生活却被带入一种教育的工厂——单调沉闷、索然无味,与天地万物的各种联系被割裂开来,被禁闭在仿佛是死人的眼珠所凝视的光秃秃的四面白墙之内。我们生来就被天神赋予在人世间求得欢乐的能力。但是,这种令人欢快的活动却被束缚,被禁锢,被一种扼杀儿童敏感头脑的被称作纪律的力量所禁止。而儿童的头脑原本总是很机灵、很活跃,渴望着从大自然那里获得第一手的

在燕京女师大的谈话　　239

知识。我们毫无生气地坐着,犹如某个博物馆中的无生命的标本,而功课则铺天盖地而来,倾泻在我们身上,犹如冰雹砸落在花朵上。在孩提时代,我们借助于全部身心吸取知识,全部感官都被充分调动起来,积极而又热切。当我们被送往学校时,自然的知识信息之门便向我们关闭了。我们的眼睛见到的是字母,我们的耳朵听到的是抽象的课程,然而我们的头脑却错过了从自然的本质中流淌出来的永恒的思想之泉流。因为,教师们从他们的智慧出发,认为这些只会使人分心,认为其背后并无远大的目标。当我们接受了任何一条为我们制定的纪律时,我们都试图回避接受任何事物,除非它对实现我们的目标必不可少。而正是出于这种属于成人心理的目的性,我们才强迫孩子们去上学。我们说:"千万不要让你的头脑太活跃了,只须注意摆在你面前的是什么,你得到的是什么。"这对孩子来说不啻成为一种折磨,因为它违反大自然的规律。而大自然,这位一切教师中最伟大的教师,其每行一步都会受到只相信刻板的课程而不相信生活的课程的人类教师的阻挠,从而使得儿童心灵的整个成长过程不仅受到损害,而且还被人为地强行搞糟了。我认为围绕在孩子身边的应该是有其自身教育价值的自然界的事物。应允许他们的头脑对今天的生活中发生的每一件事表示困惑或惊奇。新的明天将会促使他们去关注生活中的新的事实。这对儿童来说是最好的学习方法。然而,在学校中发生的情况却是,每天在同样的时刻拿来同样的书,并将书本知识一股脑儿灌输给他们。他们从来未有机会去注意大自然中那些令人惊奇的事物。我们成年人的头脑中总是装满了我们必须安排与之应付的事情。因此,我们周围发生的事物——由音乐与鲜花预示的清晨的来临,丝毫不会引起我们的注意。我们不允许它们进入我们的头脑,因为我们的头脑已经被塞得满满的了。从大自然的本质中不断流淌出的课程之泉流不会打动我们,我们只挑选那些有用的事物,而将余下的作为不合需要者剔除,因为我们需要获得成功的最近的捷径。儿童不会这样心神烦乱，他们敞开心扉，迎接每一个新事实或事件的到来，富有极大的接受能力。通过这种丰富多彩、不偏不倚的接受，他们在很短的时间内就认识了无数的事实，与我们自己的慢慢吞吞相比，他们的速度简直令人咋舌。这些是生活中至为重要的课程，它们就是这样被学会的。而更为令人称奇的是，其中的大部分还是抽象的真理。儿童之所以学得如此轻松，是因为他们具有天生的才能。而成年人，由于他们是暴君，就无视这种天生的才能，说什么孩子们必须经历与他们相同的过程才能学到知识。我们坚持填鸭式的智力教育，使得我们的课程变成了一种折磨人的形式。这是人类一个最残忍、最易造成浪费的错误。由于我小的时候经历了这一过程，对它所造成的痛苦铭心刻骨，因此我力图建立一所这样的学校——它虽然是学校，却会使孩子们感到无拘无束。由于了解大自然本身为她所创造的一切生物而提供的自然学校的一些情况，我将我的学校建立在一处风景优美的地方。它远离城镇，在那里孩子们享有最大限度的自由。而首要的是，在这里我不去强迫孩子们学习不适合于他们心理的课程。我并不想夸大事实，我必须承认，我没有能够在每一方面都按照我的计划行事。由于我们不得不生活在一个本身就很专制的社会里，而这一事实往往是无可置疑的，我不得不常常被迫对我所不相信的，而我周围的人又坚持要做的事情做出让步。但是我无时不在想着要营造一种氛围，我觉得这比课堂教学更为重要。氛围一直就在那儿，我怎么能营造它呢？鸟儿欢唱着唤醒晨光，在夜色中星星带来安宁，而夜晚又带来自身的静谧。在那里我们有寥廓明丽的天空，不同季节的景色在你眼前转换，那种各具特色的瑰丽色彩令人叹为观止。通过与大自然的这种完美的接触，我们不失时机地设立了与季节有关的几个节日。我谱写歌曲庆祝春天和历时数月的漫长的旱季之后那奇妙的雨季的到来。随着季节的变换，我们进行各种不同的化装戏剧表演。我邀请城里著名的画家来到学校居住，让他们自由自在地创作他们的作品。如果男孩子女孩子们也有此种爱好的话，我就允许他们前去观摩。对于我自己的作品我也采取了相同的做法。所有的时间我都用于创作歌曲和诗歌，并经常邀请周围的教师来吟唱朗诵一番。这有助于营造一种氛围，使他们可以从中吸收一些虽然不可捉摸，却可使万物苏醒的东西。对于这个最重要的方面，我已经讲得够多的了。不过，还有一种思想，我尚未提及，即时代的理想，它应该被摆在一切教育的中心地位。当各民族走到一起来之时，正如他们在当今时代已经做到的那样，应该不只是一群人的汇集，而必须有一个相互关系的某种契约，否则他们彼此之间将会发生冲突。我们的教育应当使每一个儿童领会并实现这一时代的目标，而不是要学那些制造分裂、怀有民族偏见的习性，从而破坏这一目标的实施。不言而喻，人类各民族之间存在着不少天然的差别，它们应当被保持，被尊重。而我们教育的使命就是，尽管有这些差别，我们还是应当实现我们的统一，应当通过他们之间的大量矛盾去发现真理。这一点我们在国际大学中已经努力实施了。我们一直力图将这统一的理想贯穿到我们学校的一切活动中去。这些活动有些是教育方面的，有些包括了各种艺术表现形式，有些则采取了帮助我们的邻居重建乡村生活，并以此为服务于他们的方式。孩子们已开始能为我们的邻居帮忙了。他们开始用各种方式帮助邻居，并不断接触到周围的生活。他们有了自己成长的自由，这是我们对儿童生活所能给予的最伟大的礼物。此外，我们的目的还旨在另一种形式的自由，即与全人类保持和谐一致的自由，去除一切种族与民族的偏见的自由。儿童的头脑通常都被囚禁在牢房中，致使他们变得不能理解具有不同语言与风俗的其他民族的人民。其结果，就导致了当我们成长中的心灵有需要时，我们就在黑暗中相互搜索，在愚昧中相互伤害，遭受这个时代中最坏形式的盲目所造成的痛苦。传教士本身就已经将自己出卖给邪恶。他们打着兄弟关系的旗号，在一派盛气凌人的教派优越感之中，制造着误解。他们还将这些做法写入他们的教科书，来毒害儿童的心灵。当儿童失去他们心灵的自由之时，也就是套上了最为有害的枷锁之日。我努力从这种离间儿童的思想感情的邪恶方法中，从通过书本，通过历史、地理和充满民族偏见的课程而养成的其他偏见中将孩子们拯救出来。在东方，人们往往对其他种族积怨甚深。在我国，人们常常是在敌意的情绪中长大的。我力图在来自西方的朋友们的帮助下，使孩子们摆脱这种情绪。而由于那些西方朋友善解人意，富有人类的同情心与爱心，从而使我们得到了极大的帮助。我们正在一切民族的精神统一这一理想的基础之上，逐步完善我们的学校。我想要在所有其他民族的帮助之下建设它。当我在欧洲大陆时，我曾求助于西方的伟大学者，我十分幸运地获得了他们的帮助。他们离开了自己从事学术活动的地方，来到这所物质条件很差的大学，帮助我们将它逐步建立起来。我所建立的不仅仅是一所大学——这不过是我们国际大学的一个方面——而且还是为来自一切国家的人们欢聚一堂所提供的聚会场所。

我们的努力是将这种团结的理想纳入我们教育机构的所有活动，有些是教育活动，有些是包括不同形式的艺术表现，有些是通过帮助重建乡村生活来服务我们的邻居。因为我希望这个机构是跨种族的，所以我邀请了来自西方的伟大思想家。他们真诚地回应了，有些人永久地与我们携手，建立一个地方，让所有民族和国家的人都能找到真正的家园，不受那些总是害怕理想主义的富人骚扰，也不受那些总是怀疑拥有精神自由的人的政治权势骚扰。在这里，相信我们所倡导的精神统一的人们可以来与他们的邻人和睦友好地相处。确实存在着这种理想主义者。当我在西方旅行时，即使在不少边远的地方，也有许多没有显赫名声的默默无闻的人士想要参加这项工作。当人类各民族彼此更为接近时，当通过他们的相会而展现出新的真理，摆脱我们内心卑劣情感的刺激时，我们就会有一个伟大的前程。真理的朝阳将会再度升起，而爱也将会通过那种地位卑微的小人物展现出来。这些小人物为了人类而殉难,一如那位伟大的人物,他只在渔人中有为数很少的门徒。在他一生结束之时,展现出一幅彻底失败的悲惨图景。其时,正当罗马帝国处于全盛时期的巅峰。他被那些有权势的人辱骂,被大众忽视,他的死亡充满了耻辱。然而,正是这种彻底的失败才象征着他的永生。今天的殉道者是这种人:他们被投入监狱,遭受迫害,他们不是有权有势的人,然而他们却属于不朽的未来。)

诗人泰戈尔在5月6日午餐之后会见了燕京女师大同学和英语教师,并且发表了这篇即兴讲话。他在这篇讲话中回顾了自己童年上学时所感受的痛苦经历,并且因此于13岁逃离了当时自己就读的学校。他在40岁时开始创办自己的学校。他系统地简述了自己为什么要创办自己的学校以及自己的办学理想。

诗人泰戈尔认为,他童年时代的学校就是"一种教育的工厂——单调沉闷、索然无味,与天地万物的各种联系被割裂开来",孩子们"被禁闭在仿佛是死人的眼珠所凝视的光秃秃的四面白墙之内",因此他才逃学,他实在无法忍受那种痛苦。他还对当时在印度盛行的西方传教士的宣传教育进行了抨击,他指出:"传教士本身就已经将自己出卖给邪恶。他们打着兄弟关系的旗号,在一派盛气凌人的教派优越感之中,制造误解。他们还将这些做法永久写入他们的教科书,来毒害儿童的心灵。当儿童失去他们心灵的自由之时,也就是套上了最为有害的枷锁之日。"于是他在40岁时创办了自己学校,他要让孩子们在与大自然接触过程中自由地学习,他要"努力从这种离间儿童的思想感情的邪恶方法中,从通过书本,通过历史、地理和充满民族偏见的课程而养成的其他偏见中将孩子们拯救出来"。

后来他的这所学校发展成为著名的国际大学。他指出:"我所建立的不仅仅是一所大学,……而且还是为来自一切国家的人们欢聚一堂所提供的聚会场所。"诗人泰戈尔的理想就是把国际大学变成一所交流和传播世界文化的平台,促进世界各民族和平相处的一个教育机构。

泰戈尔第一次访华纪实

庆祝泰戈尔的生日

加尔各答　仰光　马来亚　新加坡　香港　上海　杭州　南京　济南　北京　太原　武汉　上海

1924年5月8日是孟加拉历的拜沙克月二十五日，这一天是诗人泰戈尔的生日。这一天，诗人泰戈尔从郊区返回了北京城里。上午诗人的随行者们以家庭的方式为他庆祝了生日。依德拉尔将自己画的一幅画作为生日礼物赠送给诗人，迦利达斯·纳格朗诵他自己创作的一首诗《赞美诗人》（কবিপ্রশস্তি），基迪莫洪朗读了他创作的梵语颂词。

　　当天晚上，为庆祝诗人泰戈尔64岁生日，在北京师范大学礼堂——位于北京东单三条的协和礼堂举行一场晚会，有四百多位著名的客人出席。诗人泰戈尔身穿深蓝色丝质长袍，头戴绛红色印度罩帽，美须皓然，慈祥地坐在第三排中间，著名京剧大师梅兰芳先生陪坐在他的身边。

　　晚会由胡适博士主持，梁启超致祝词，他说："……泰翁要我替他起一个中国名字。从前印度人称中国为震旦，原不过是支那的译音，但选用这两个字却有很深的象征意味。从音喑氛害的状态中霁然一震,万象昭苏,刚从扶桑浴过的丽日,从地坪下面上涌现出来(旦字末笔代表地平线),这是何等境界。泰戈尔原文(名字)整合这两种意义,把他意译称'震旦'两个字,再好没有了。又从前自汉至晋的,西来古德(古德就是有道德的高僧)都有中国名,大率以所来之国为姓,如安世高来自安息便姓安,支娄迦谶从月支来便姓支,康僧会从康居来便姓康,而从天竺——印度来的都姓竺,如竺法兰、竺佛念、竺法护都是历史上有功于文化的人。今天我们所敬爱的天竺诗圣,在他所爱的震旦地方过他六十四岁生日,我用极诚恳极喜悦的情绪,将两个国名联起来,赠给他一个新名曰'竺震旦'。(全场鼓掌)我希望我们对他的热爱,跟着这名字,永远嵌在他的心灵上,我希望印度人和中国人的旧爱,借竺震旦这个人复活起来。"[①]随后诗人致答词。梁启超送给诗人泰戈尔两枚贵重石料印章,上面刻有"竺震旦"三个中文字。梁启超解释这三个中文字的含义时说,"竺"是中国古代人称呼印度为"天竺"一个字,"旦"字的词义是朝阳升起,同诗人孟加拉语名字中的"罗比"(太阳)词义相同,"震"的词义是"雷声",与诗人孟加拉语名字中"因陀罗"即"雷神"也有联系,因此"竺震旦"这名字的含义与诗人孟加拉语名字"罗宾德罗"(রবীন্দ্র=রবি+ইন্দ্র)有相同的含义,其另一个含义就是"云雾雷鸣唤醒的晨曦"。

梵语学家基迪莫洪·森教授朗诵了两首梵语赞美诗;迦利达斯·纳格教授朗诵诗人泰戈尔《鸿雁集》原文第5首诗《旧岁憔悴疲惫之夜》,其译文如下:

旧岁的憔悴疲惫之夜
已经过去,哦,旅游之人,
照耀在你旅途上的骄阳带来
召唤,也带来湿婆的歌音。

---

① 梅兰芳:《忆泰戈尔》,《人民文学》1961年5月号。

从远处到更远处的旅途中
回荡着低沉激越的悠长幽韵,
 仿佛是一位无欲的迷路歌者
在弹奏着独弦琴。
 哦,旅游之人,
路上那灰蒙蒙的尘土
就是你的慈母娘亲,
就让她用旋风撩起的衣襟
把你抱入她的怀里贴心。
在地平线之上明月高悬,
那不是给你的贝壳手镯
象征着家庭幸福的美满好和,
不是爱妻含泪的眼神秋波,
也不是黑夜灯火的闪烁。
一路上期待着拜沙克月的祝福,
期待着斯拉万月黑夜雷鸣之歌。
一路上遇有带刺的欢迎,
一路上有藏匿着的毒蛇。
谴责是赐给你的胜利号音,
那是湿婆馈赠与你的礼盒。

每一步挫折都带来无价无形的礼赞。
人民不朽的权利曾经是你的期盼,
可那不是平和,哦,也不是快乐
不是安宁,也不是慰藉。

死亡将会对你进行袭击。

在家家户户的门前你会

得知对你的新年祝福，

那就是湿婆赠给你的礼物。

旅游之人，不必害怕，不必惊恐，

离家迷路的厄运就是天神对你的祝福。

旧岁的憔悴疲惫之夜

已经过去，哦，旅游之人。

残酷已经降临，

就让大门早早关闭吧，

还要将酒杯打碎。

对他不理解，不了解，不认识，

你要抓住他的手臂。

让他那闪光谏言在心动时发声吧。

哦，旅游之人，旧岁之夜正在消逝，

那就让它消逝吧。①

依德拉尔·巴苏赠送给诗人一幅他创作的画作。中国画界尊爱泰戈尔的一些朋友赠送给诗人泰戈尔十五六幅精美的绘画、一套画有各种鲜花的瓷器茶具和其他物品。

在晚会的最后演出了诗人泰戈尔的剧作《齐德拉》。诗人泰戈尔对中国朋友们为他举办生日庆祝晚会表示感谢，他说今天的活动是令人难忘的，朋友赐给他的中文名字具有历史意义，将在中印关系史上留下浓墨重彩的一笔。随后他对《齐德拉》这部作品做了介绍，并且讲述这部剧作的意义。

《齐德拉》剧本的故事取材于印度大史诗《摩诃婆罗多》，大史诗中的情节很简单：曼尼普尔国王没有儿子，只有一个美丽的女儿齐

---

① 译自বিশ্বভারতীপত্রিকা (গুপুরবংখ্যা), ৬শ৩, ১৯৬-১৯৭;．《泰戈尔作品全集》原文普及版，第6卷，第196—197页。

德拉，国王将女儿许配给流放中的般度族五兄弟中的老三阿周那，三年后阿周那离开曼尼普尔王国。后来齐德拉和她生育的儿子先后继承曼尼普尔国的王位。

诗人泰戈尔借用大史诗《摩诃婆罗多》中这个故事框架，以自己的想象，创造一部情节曲折、动人的戏剧性很强的一部十一场的诗剧《齐德拉》，其主要情节是：国王没有儿子，只有一个女儿齐德拉。国王把她当儿子一样抚养，让她穿上男人的服装，学习骑马射箭，因此齐德拉练就了一副硬朗的身躯，成为武艺高强的巾帼英雄。有一次她在森林中遇到阿周那，为阿周那的英雄气概所倾倒，内心萌发了爱慕之情。她换上女装，向阿周那示爱，遭到了阿周那的拒绝。这时她明白了，男人喜欢的是女人的妩媚、温柔，于是她求助于春神的帮助，春神赐给她一年的美丽外貌，随后她赢得了阿周那的爱情。最初她感到很幸福很快乐，可是她逐渐萌生厌倦之情。阿周那听说附近村庄来了强盗，于是前去迎战，强盗们闻讯而逃走。村民们向他讲述了女英雄齐德拉为保护村民们的生命财产安全，同强盗们战斗的故事。阿周那听后十分感动。这时一年期已到，相爱的两人聚在一起，阿周那向自己的爱人讲述他听到的关于齐德拉的英武故事。他的爱人将面纱掀起说，她就是齐德拉，并且向阿周那讲述了一年前春神赐给她美丽相貌之实情。齐德拉对阿周那说："我不是神，也不是普通女人。……如果在危险的道路上你让我留在你身边，如果你让我分担你的忧虑，如果你让我在艰巨的事业中助你一臂之力，不论在顺境还是逆境中你如果让我做你的助手，那么，你就能真正认识我。我腹中已经孕育着你的孩子，如果他是男孩儿，我就会将他培养成人，使他成为阿周那的第二代。"阿周那不但没有嫌弃，而且更加爱恋自己这位英武刚强的妻子。他对自己的爱妻说："亲爱的，今天我成为最幸福的人。"

诗人泰戈尔在这部剧中所要表达的主要思想是：女人的青春魅力

是她的身外之物，是不能持久的，唯有她内心的良好品德和力量，才是两人相爱的支柱，才能相爱到白头。

当时《齐德拉》尚无适合演出的中文好译本，所以刚成立不久的新月社[①]就决定用英语演出《齐德拉》，因为新月社的成员中有十几位通晓英语的俊男靓女。他们商定由青春靓丽的林徽因女士扮演女主角齐德拉，男主角阿周那由青年才俊张歆海扮演，爱神由徐志摩扮演，春神由林徽因的父亲林长民扮演，林徽因的表姐王孟瑜女士、戏剧家丁西林等也参加了演出。依德拉尔·巴苏为中国演员们提供了印度服装并且帮助他们化妆。林徽因、徐志摩、张歆海三位青年人是从海外留学归来的才子，都讲一口流利的英语，所以演出非常成功。

诗人泰戈尔看了演出，赞不绝口，非常高兴。林徽因和林长民父女一起同台演出这部诗人名剧，更是引起京城文化界的轰动，一时传为佳话。

[①] 新月社于1923年成立于北京，活动地点是西单石虎胡同7号院，是五四以来以探索新诗理论与新诗创作为主的文学社团。主要成员有胡适、徐志摩、张歆海、林徽因、王孟瑜、闻一多、梁实秋等。前期把《晨报副刊》作为阵地，后期创办《新月》月刊（1928.03.10）等。

泰戈尔第一次访华纪实

在真光剧场的第一次讲演

加尔各答 ○――― 仰光 ○――― 马来亚 ○――― 新加坡 ○――― 香港 ○――― 上海 ○――― 杭州 ○――― 南京 ○――― 济南 ○――― 北京 ○――― 太原 ○ 武汉 ○ 上海 ○

从5月9日星期五起，应北京讲学社的邀请，诗人在北京真光剧场开始他的系列讲座的第一场。全文如下：

"Lately I read an observation in one of your papers that, being a philosopher, I was half an hour late in attending a particular meeting. I could satisfactorily explain my conduct if the complaint were restricted to this one casual event, but I believe the writer took it to be a symbol of some truth bout me which was not accidental. I suppose that what gave him more serious concern was that according to him I was altogether out of date in this modern age, that I ought to have born 2000 years ago when poets dreamed over their brimming wine cups in the moonlight, and philosophers ignored everything immediate, time and space.

This has caused me some surprise, which I am sure will grow into amusement when I have more leisure than I have now. Almost from my boyhood I have been accustomed to hear from my own countrymen angry remonstrances that I was too crassly modern, that I had missed all the great lessons from the past, and with it my right of entry into a venerable civilization like that of India. For your people I am obsolete, and therefore useless, and for mine, newfangled and therefore obnoxious. I do not know which is true.

Dr. Hu Shih, yesterday, in the capacity of astrologer, calculated from the sun and stars some augury on my visit to this country. I suppose he will be able to tell from the antics of the stars, under what auspices, and what contradictory influences I was born. He will let me know why this unfortunate being has been so continually suspected to be contraband—smuggled on to the wrong shore of time, not only by his own countrymen to whom he is too familiar, but by others to whom he could hardly have yet given any occasion for grave anxiety. Because of this misunderstanding, I have been asked by my friends to introduce myself to you with some biographical details so that my ideas may not appear to you too visionary, and frighten you as does an apparition that has lost its context of life.

I was born in 1861, that is not an important fact of history, but it was a great period in our history in Bengal. You do not know perhaps that we have our places of pilgrimage in those spots where the rivers meet in confluence, the rivers which to us are the symbols of the spirit of life in nature, and which in their meeting present emblems of the meeting of spirits, the meeting of ideals. Just about that time the currents of three movements had met in the life of our country.

One of these movements was religious, introduced by a very greathearted man of gigantic intelligence, Raja Rammohan Ray. It was revolutionary, for he tried to re-open the channel of spiritual life which had been obstructed for many years by the sands and debris of creeds that were formal and often materialistic, fixed in external practices lacking spiritual significance.

There was a great fight between him and the orthodox who suspected every living idea that was dynamic. It has its analogy in the modern West where the prosperous are afraid of idealism because they believe in certain things they call wealth, things that can be hoarded in iron safes, secured in banks and watched over by armed guards. Ideas cause movement and all movements forward they consider to be a menace against their warehouse security.

People who cling to an ancient past also have their pride in the antiquity of their accumulations, in the sublimity of time-honoured walls around them. They grow nervous and angry when some great spirit, some lover of truth, breaks open their enclosure and floods it with the sunshine of thought and the breath of life.

This was happening about the time I was born. I am proud to say that my father was one of the great leaders of that movement, a movement for whose sake he suffered ostracism and braved social indignities. I was born in this atmosphere of the advent of new ideals, which at the same time were old, older than all the things of which that age was proud.

There was a second movement equally important. A certain great man Bankim Chandra Chatterjee who, though much older than myself, was my contemporary and lived long enough for me to see him, was the first pioneer in the literary revolution which happened in Bengal about that time.

Our self-expression must find its freedom not only in spiritual ideas but in literary manifestation. But our literature had allowed its creative life to vanish. It lacked movement and was fettered by a rhetoric rigid as death.

This man was brave enough to go against the orthodoxy which believed in the security of tombstones and in that perfection which can only belong to the lifeless. He lifted the dead weight of ponderous forms from our language and with a touch of his magic wand aroused our literature from her age-long sleep. What a vision of beauty she revealed to us when she awoke in the fullness of her strength and grace.

There was yet another movement started about this time in my country which was called "National". It was not fully political, but it began to give voice to the mind of our people trying to assert their own personality. It was a voice of indignation at the humiliation constantly heaped upon us by people who were not oriental, and who had, especially at that time, the habit of sharply dividing the human world into the good and bad according to what was similar to their life and what was different.

This contemptuous spirit of separateness was perpetually hurting us and causing great damage to our own world of culture. It generated in the young men of our country distrust of all things that had come to them as an inheritance from their past. The old Indian pictures and other works of art were laughed at by our students in imitation of the laughter of their European schoolmasters.

Though latterly our teachers themselves have changed their mind, their disciples have not yet fully regained confidence in the merit of our art tradition even where such merit is permanent. They have had a long period of encouragement in developing an appetite for third-rate copies of French pictures, for gaudy oleographs abjectly cheap, for the pictures that are products of mechanical accuracy of a stereotyped standard, and they still consider it to be a symptom of superior culture to be able disdainfully to refuse oriental works of creation. There has been cultivated the same spirit of rejection, born of utter ignorance, in most other departments of our culture.

You must know, my friends, when you class things as modern or old, that you make a great mistake in following your calendar of dates. Don't you know that the flowers of spring are old, that they represent the first dawn of life on the earth, but are they therefore symbols of the dead and discarded? If you follow your standard of chronology in your craving for the modern, would you rather replace them with artificial flowers made of rags, because they were made 'yesterday'?

But the modern young men of India nodded their heads and said that true originality lay not in the discovery of the rhythm of the essential in the heart of reality but in the full tips, tinted cheeks and bare breasts of imported pictures. It is the result of the hypnotism exercised upon the minds of the younger generation which is ready to sell its soul for the cheap things that are brought to its door by people who are loud of voice and strong of arm. We were cowed down, we accepted their verdict and said yes.

Reaction had just set in when I was born and some people were already trying to stem the tide. This movement had its leaders in my own family, in my brothers and cousins, and they stood up to save the people's mind from being insulted and ignored by the people themselves.

We have to find some basis that is universal, that is eternal, and we have to discover those things which have an everlasting value. The national movement was started to proclaim that we must not be indiscriminate in our rejection of the past. This was not a reactionary movement but a revolutionary one because it set out with a great courage to deny and to oppose all pride in mere borrowings. When we have filled our drawing-rooms with foreign furniture, aren't we proud of inviting guests to contemplate their value, not in terms of spiritual or mental effort, but of some standard of approval belonging to a foreign race, of having been bought from some expensive shop in the Legation Quarter? It needs a spirit of martyrdom to stand up against the pride of the crude who are ready to pelt you with maxims from their modern schoolbooks.

These three movements were on foot and in all three the members of my own family took active part. We were ostracized because of our heterodox opinions about religion and therefore we enjoyed the freedom of the outcaste. We had to build our own world with our own thoughts and energy of mind. We had to build it from the foundation, and therefore had to seek the foundation that was firm.

We can't create foundations, but we can build a superstructure. These two must go together, the giving of expression to new life and the seeking of foundations which must be in the heart of the people themselves. Those who believe that life consists in change because change implies movement, should remember that there must be an underlying thread of unity or the change, being unmeaning, will cause conflict and clash. This thread of unity must not be of the out side, but in our own soul.

As I say, I was born and brought up in an atmosphere of the confluence of three movements, all of which were revolutionary. I was born in a family which had to live its own life, which led me from my young days to seek guidance for my own self-expression in my own inner standard of judgment. The medium of expression doubtless was my mother tongue. But the language which belonged to the people had to be modulated according to the urging which I as an individual had.

No poet should borrow his medium ready-made from some shop of spectability. He should not only have his own seeds but prepare his own soil. Each poet has his own distinct medium of language, not because the whole language is of his own make, but because his individual use of it, having life's magic touch, transforms it into a special vehicle of his own creation.

The races of man have poetry in their heart and it is necessary for them to give, as far as is possible, a perfect expression to their sentiments. For this they must have a medium, moving and pliant, which can freshly become their very own age after age. All great languages have undergone and are still undergoing changes. Those languages which resist the spirit of change are doomed and will never produce great harvests of thought and literature. When forms become fixed, the spirit either weakly accepts its imprisonment within them, or rebels. All revolutions consist of the fight of the within against invasion by the without. The spirit which is the sovereign must have conviction in its own dignity of life, in order to resist the dominance of the external and to find freedom in the world it perpetually creates for itself.

There was a great chapter in the history of life on this earth when some irresistible inner force in man found its way out into the scheme of things, and sent forth its triumphant mutinous voice, with the cry that it was not going to be overwhelmed from outside by a huge brute beast of a body. How helpless it appeared at the moment, but has it not nearly won? In our social life, also, revolution breaks out when some power concentrates itself in outside arrangements and threatens to enslave for its own purpose the power which we have within us.

When an organization which is a machine, becomes a central force, political commercial, educational or religious, it obstructs the free flow of inner life of the people and waylays and exploits it for the augmentation of its own power. Today such concentration of power is fast multiplying on the outside and the cry of the oppressed spirit of man is in the air which struggles to free itself from the grip of screws and bolts, of unmeaning obsessions.

Revolution must come and men must risk revilement and misunderstanding, especially from those who want to be comfortable, who believe that the soul is antiquated, and who put their faith in materialism and convention. These will be taken by surprise, these stunted children who belong truly to the dead past and not to modern times, the past that had its age in distant antiquity when physical flesh and size predominated, and not the mind of man.

Purely physical dominance is mechanical and modern machines are merely exaggerating our bodies, lengthening and multiplying our limbs. The modern child delights in such enormous bodly bulk, representing an inordinate material power, saying: "Let me have the big toy and no sentiment which can disturb it." He does not realise that we are returning to that antediluvian age which revelled in its production of gigantic physical frames, leaving no room for the freedom of the inner spirit.

All great human movements in the world are related to some great ideal. Some of you say that such a doctrine of spirit has been in its death throes for over a century and is now moribund, that we have nothing to rely upon but external forces and material foundations. But I say, on my part, that your doctrine was obsoleted long ago. It was exploded in the springtime of life, when mere size was swept off the face of the world, and was replaced by man, brought naked into the heart of creation, man with his helpless body, but with hisindomitable mind and spirit.

The impertinence of material things is extremely old. The revelation of spirit in man is modern: I am on its side, for I am modern. I have explained how I was born into a family which rebelled, which had faith in its loyalty to an inner ideal. If you want to reject me, you are free to do so. But I have my right as a revolutionary to carry the flag of freedom of spirit into the shrine of your idols—material power and accumulation.[①]

（最近，我在你们报纸上的一篇文章中读到这样一段话：作为一名哲学家，我参加一个特别的会议时迟到了半个小时。如果对我的抱怨仅限于这件偶然的事情，我可以很好地解释我的行为，但我相信写信人把它看作是我的某种真相的象征，而这种真相并非偶然。我想，更让他担心的是，在他看来，我在这个现代时代完全过时了，我应该出生在2000年前，那时诗人在月光下对着斟满酒的杯子做着美梦，哲学家们忽略一切眼前的事物、时间和空间。

这使我有些惊讶，我相信当我拥有比现在更多空闲的时候，那将成为一种乐趣。几乎从孩提时代起，我就经常听到同胞们愤怒的抗议，我太过粗陋，错过了过去的一切伟大教诲，也错过我进入像印度这样一个古老文明的权利。对你们来说，我是过时的，因此是无用的；对我的人来说，我是新潮的，因此是令人讨厌的。我不知道哪种说法是真实的。

胡适博士昨天以占星家的身份，从太阳和星座方面为我这次对这个国家访问做了预测。我想，他可以从星象中看出，我是在什么样的庇护下出生的，以及受到什么样的相互矛盾的影响。他会告诉我，为什么我这个不幸的人会被怀疑是"违禁品"——被走私者劫持到错误时间的彼岸。不仅是他非常熟悉的同胞有这样的怀疑，还有他没有理由感到严重担忧的那些人也有这样的怀疑。因为有这种误解，我的朋友让我给你们讲一讲有关我生活方面的一些细节，以免我的想法对你们来说太虚幻，也不至于像一个失去了生活背景的鬼魂一样，会把你们吓倒。

....
① The English writings of Tagore, 2/, 663-667. 《泰戈尔英文作品集》第2卷，第663—667页。

我出生于1861年，这不是一个重要的历史时期，但这是我们孟加拉历史上的一个伟大时期。你们也许不知道，我们的朝圣地就在河流交汇的地方，这些河流对我们来说是自然界生命精神的象征，它们的交汇象征着精神的交汇，象征着理想的交汇。大约就在那个时候，我国的生活中出现了三股运动的潮流。

这三大运动潮流中有一个运动是宗教性的，是由一个非常善良、有着巨大智慧的拉姆莫汉·拉伊①所倡导的。那是一场革命性的运动，因为那场运动试图重新打开精神生活的通道，这条通道多年来被教条的沙子和碎片所阻碍，那些教条是正统的，往往是物质主义的，是固定在缺乏精神意义的外部实践中的。

他和正统派之间展开一场激烈的斗争，正统派怀疑一切有活力的思想。现代西方也有类似的情况，富裕的人害怕理想主义，因为他们相信他们称之为财富的某些东西可以储存在铁保险柜里，放在银行里，由武装警卫看守。思想会引发行动，而一切向前发展的行动，他们都认为是对他们仓库安全的威胁。

那些沉湎于古老过去的人，也会为他们积累的古老东西而自豪，为他们周围历史悠久的城墙的崇高而自豪。当某个伟大的灵魂，某个热爱真理的人打破他们的藩篱，让思想的阳光和生命的气息洒满周围世界的时候，他们就会变得紧张而愤怒。

这种情况就发生在我出生的时候。我可以自豪地说，我的父亲是这场运动的伟大领袖之一，为了这场运动，他遭受过排斥，但是他勇敢地面对社会的侮辱。我是在新理想出现的气氛中出生的，那些新理想同时也是古老的，比那个时代引以为傲的一切事物都要古老。

还有第二个同样重要的运动。一个伟大的人——般吉姆琼德

---

① 拉姆莫汉·拉伊（1774—1833），印度孟加拉人，宗教改革家，梵社的创始人，反对偶像崇拜，主张废除寡妇殉葬，发展教育等。

罗·丘多巴泰[①]，虽然比我大很多，但他和我是同时代的人，而且他活得足够长久，我同他会过面，他是当时发生在孟加拉的文学革命的第一个先驱。

我们的自我表达不仅要在精神观念中找到自由，而且要在文学表现中找到自由。但是我们的文学却让其创作的生命消逝了。这个人有足够的勇气去反对那种相信墓碑是安全的，相信那种只属于死去之人的完美的正统观念。他把沉重的形式从我们的语言中移开，用魔杖一点，把我们的文学从长久的沉睡中唤醒。当我们的文学带着充沛的力量和优雅醒来的时候，她向我们展示出一幅多么美丽的景象啊！

大约在这个时候，在我的国家又开始了另一场运动，叫作民族主义运动。它不完全是政治性的，但它一开始就让我们的人民表达自己的想法，努力维护自己的个性。这是人们发出的一种义愤填膺的声音，因为那些非东方人，尤其是在那个时候就习惯于按照与自己生活相似和不同，把人类世界泾渭分明地划分为好的与坏的两种。

这种轻蔑的划分思想不断地伤害着我们，对我们自己的文化世界造成了巨大的破坏。它使我们国家的年轻人对他们从过去继承下来的一切都产生了怀疑。我们的学生模仿他们的欧洲老师的笑声，嘲笑古老的印度绘画和其他艺术作品。

近年来虽然我们的老师们自己已经改变了看法，但他们的弟子们还没有完全恢复对我们艺术传统优点的信心，即使这种优点是永恒的。长期以来，他们一直受到鼓励，对三流的法国画儿产生了兴趣，对可怜的平版印刷出来的庸俗的、廉价的东西，对千篇一律的精度机械产品，产生了兴趣，而且他们仍然认为，能够轻蔑地拒绝东方的创

[①] 般吉姆琼德罗·丘多巴泰（1838—1894），印度孟加拉语著名小说家，印度独立前国歌《向母亲致敬》（*Bande Mataram*）的创作者。

作作品是优越文化的表现。在我们文化的大多数其他部门中，也培养出了同样的拒绝精神，这种精神源于完全的无知。

印度的现代青年却点点头说，真正的独创性不在于发现现实生活核心中的本质节奏，而在于舶来品中的丰唇、红颊、裸乳。这是对年轻一代的思想施加催眠的结果，他们准备出卖自己的灵魂，以换取那些声音响亮、臂力强大的人带到他们家门口的廉价商品。我们被吓倒了，我们接受了他们对审美的判断。

在我出生的时候，对这场运动的反应刚刚开始，一些人已经在试图阻止这股潮流。这场运动的领导者在我自己的家里，在我的兄弟和堂兄弟中间，他们挺身而出，拯救人民的思想，使其免受人民自己的侮辱和忽视。

我们必须找到一些普遍的、永恒的基础，我们必须发现那些具有永恒价值的东西。民族运动的开始是为了宣告我们不能不分青红皂白地拒绝过去。那不是一场具有反动性的运动，而是一场革命运动，因为它以巨大的勇气否认和反对一切以单纯借用舶来品为骄傲的行为。当我们的客厅里摆满了外国家具时我们难道能自豪地邀请客人来品评它们的价值吗？不是从精神上或努力从精神方面去观看，而是从属于外国种族的某种认可标准去观看，难道那不是从公使馆区某个昂贵的商店买回来东西吗？我们需要一种殉难的精神来对抗那些准备用现代教科书上的格言来攻击你们是野蛮人的傲慢。

这三个运动当时都是同步进行的，我的家人都积极参与其中。由于我们对宗教持有非正统观点，所以我们被排斥在外，因此我们享受着种姓外的自由。我们必须用我们自己的思想和精神力量来建立我们自己的世界。我们必须从基础开始建造它，因此必须寻找坚固的基础。

我们不能创造基础，但我们可以建造一个上层建筑。赋予新生命以表现，并在人民心中寻找基础——这两者必须并行不悖。那些认为生活就是变化、变化意味着运动的人应该记住，必须有一个潜在的统一线索，否则变化是毫无意义的，而且会导致对抗和冲突。这条统一之线不应该来自外部，而应该来自我们自己的灵魂。

正如我所说的，我是在上述三种运动汇合的气氛中出生和长大的，这三种运动都是革命性的。我出生在一个独立过自己生活的家庭，这让我从小就在自己的内心判断标准中寻求自我表达的方式。自我表达的媒介无疑是我的母语。但是，使用属于人民的语言必须根据我个人的愿望加以调整。

任何诗人都不应该从一些体面的铺子里借用现成的媒介。他不仅要有自己的种子，而且要准备自己的土壤。每个诗人都有自己独特的语言媒介，不是整个语言都是他自己创造的，而是因为他个人使用语言要具有生活的魅力，把它变成他自己创造的特殊工具。

人类各种族的心中都存在诗意，他们需要尽可能完美地表达自己的情感。为此，他们必须有一个既能变通又具有适应性的媒介，这种媒介应该是新颖的，同他们自己的年龄一样。所有伟大的语言都是一代又一代经历过发展变化的，并且仍然继续经历着发展变化。那些抗拒变革精神的语言是注定僵化的，永远不会产生伟大思想和获得文学丰收。当形式变得固定时，精神要么软弱地接受它的禁锢，要么进行反抗。一切革命都是内部反对外部入侵的斗争。作为主权者的精神必须坚信自己的生命尊严，以便抵抗外部的统治，并在不断为自己创造的世界中找到自由。

在这个地球上的生命史中曾经有过这样一个伟大的篇章：人的某种不可抗拒的内在力量，在事物的发展中找到了自己的道路，发出了反叛的胜利声音，大声疾呼，敢于说自己不会被一个巨大的野兽般的躯体从外面压倒。那时它显得多么孤立无助啊，可是它不是差一点儿就要赢得胜利了吗？在我们的社会生活中，当某种权力集中在外部并威胁要为自己的目的而奴役我们内在的力量的时候，革命就会爆发。

当一个像机器一样的组织成为政治、商业、教育或宗教的中心力量时，它就会阻碍人们内心生活的自由流动，并阻碍和利用这种流动来扩大自己的权力。今天，这种权力集中在外部并迅速扩大，空气中回荡着人类被压迫精神的呼号，人们挣扎着要摆脱螺丝钉和螺栓似的束缚，摆脱毫无意义的强迫。

革命必然会到来，人们必须冒着遭受辱骂和误解的风险，尤其要冒着那些想要舒适的人、相信灵魂已经过时的人、相信物质主义和习俗之人的辱骂和误解。一些发育不良的孩子们将会感到惊讶，他们真正属于死去的过去，而不是现代，在过去遥远的古代是属于他们的时代，那时候肉体和体型占据主导地位，而不是人的思想。

纯粹的身体优势是机械性的，现代机器只是扩大了我们身体的机能，延长和增加了我们的四肢。现代的孩子喜欢这种巨大的身躯，它代表着一种超乎寻常的物质力量，他们说："让我拥有这个大玩具吧，任何情感都无法妨碍它。"他们没有意识到，我们正在回到那个沉迷于生产巨大的物质的旧时代，没有给内在精神的自由留下空间。

世界上一切伟大的人类运动都与某种伟大的理想相联系。你们有些人说，这种精神方面的学说已经在垂死挣扎一个多世纪了，现在已经奄奄一息，我们没有任何别的依靠，只有外部力量和物质基础。但我要说，就我而言，你们的学说早就过时了。它是在生命的春天爆发的，那时单纯的庞然大物从世界的表面上消失了，取而代之的是人，是赤裸裸地进入创造的中心的人，尽管人的身体是孤立无助的，但是人的思想和精神却是不屈不挠的。

不合时宜地坚持物质性是极其陈腐的，展现人的精神才是真正现代的。我站在它这一边，因为我是现代的。我已经解释过我是如何出生在一个叛逆的家庭，这个家庭对自己内心的理想提供了忠诚的信念。如果你们想拒绝我，你们可以这么做。但作为一名革命者，我有权利将精神自由的旗帜高举到你们偶像的殿堂——物质权力和财富积累的神龛中。)

5月10日星期六的《远东时代》（*Far Eastern Times*）刊物写道："The pit of the Chen Kwang Theatre and a couple of score of seats in the gallery were filled with the audience that attended the first of Rabindranath Tagore's public lectures yesterday morning. It was a pity that the gathering was not much larger, for the utterance was a remarkably fine one, delivered with a rhetorical perfection that enhanced its acceptability, and made arresting by its quiet and indirect but eviscerating criticism of the accepted standards."

［昨天上午，泰戈尔（Rabindranath Tagore）首次公开演讲，听众坐满了真光剧场（Chen Kwang Theatre）的大厅和旁听众席上的几十个座位。遗憾的是，聚集的人还不是特别多，他的演讲非常精彩，言辞完美，使人更容易接受，他对公认的现代性标准进行了平静、间接而又尖锐的批评，因而引起了人们的注意。］

泰戈尔第一次访华纪实

有人散发反对泰戈尔的传单

加尔各答 ○――○ 仰光 ○――○ 马来亚 ○――○ 新加坡 ○――○ 香港 ○――○ 上海 ○――○ 杭州 ○――○ 南京 ○――○ 济南 ○――○ 北京 ○ 太原 ○ 武汉 ○ 上海 ○

很可惜，当时中国社会中的一些人士，硬是把诗人泰戈尔的访华政治化，他们硬说北京讲学社邀请诗人泰戈尔来华访问是为他们的守旧的玄学势力助威彰目。简直是毫无道理的无稽之谈。他们鼓动和指使一小部分青年学生散发反对诗人泰戈尔的传单。

在5月9日星期五的讲演现场也有人散发传单，这种行为引起在场的广大听众的不满，因此引起讲演会场的骚乱。诗人泰戈尔当场问徐志摩怎么回事。徐志摩只好如实相告。诗人泰戈尔听了笑着说，好啊，有人反对我，说明他们重视我。后来一位印度朋友得到了传单，并且将其翻译成英文，诗人泰戈尔看了之后很是吃惊。这封传单的内容后来在加尔各答出版的《孟加拉人》杂志上刊出了，内容共有5点：

1. 我们在古老的东方文明下受尽了苦，包括男尊女卑、崇拜皇帝、压迫百姓、封建制度、等级制度及盲从礼教。泰戈尔博士企图维护我们文明的这些腐朽无用的方面，我们只好反对他。

2. 我们接触到现代文明后感受到很大羞辱。我们必须改进：人力耕种、手工业制造、舟楫慢行、印刷落后、道路崎岖、卫生差劲。我们是为了现代文明进步而反对泰戈尔博士。

3. 所谓的东方精神文明只不过是内战、自私的割据、伪善、欺骗、掠夺、罪恶的孝道以及鄙视女性的裹足。我们怎么能不反对这些害人事情呢？

4. 中国人对列强的侵略与国内军阀的压迫麻木不仁，他们的生命与安全濒临危险。泰戈尔博士要废除民族与政治，用灵魂的安慰来取代。这是逃避现实，是懒汉聊以自慰之道，不适合我们。泰戈尔博士用这些来使我们民族短命，我们非反对他不可。

5. 泰戈尔博士和同善会亲善，这是一个中国道教、佛教联合的卑鄙邪恶组织。泰戈尔口口声声'天国''上帝''灵魂'。如果靠这些可以使我们不受苦，那人类就不必致力于改造世界了？我们反对阻碍受压迫阶级与民族的自觉与斗争的泰戈尔博士。

这份传单最后写道："Therefore we protest, in the name of all the oppressed peoples, in the name of all the persecuted classes, against Mr. Tagore, who works to enslave them still more by preaching to them patience and apathy. We also protest against the semi-offcial literati who have invited Mr. Tagore to come to hypnotize and drug out Chinese youth in this way, these literati who use his talent to instill in Young China their conservative reactionary tendencies."[1]

（因此，我们以所有被压迫人民的名义，以所有受迫害阶级的名义，向泰戈尔先生提出抗议，他通过向他们鼓吹耐心和冷漠来进一步奴役他们。我们也抗议那些半官方的文人，他们邀请泰戈尔先生来用这种方式催眠和麻醉中国青年，这些文人利用泰戈尔的才能在青年中

---

[1] Krishna Dutta & Andrew Robinson, *Rabindranath Tagore: The Myriad-minded Man*, 2009,New York:Tauris Parke Paperback, pp.251-2. 克里什那·杜多和安德鲁·罗宾逊著《罗宾德罗纳特·泰戈尔——有丰富思想的人》。

国灌输保守反动的倾向。）

　　这份反对泰戈尔的传单中所列出的五点理由，都是强加在诗人泰戈尔身上的不实之词，没有一条能站得住脚。传单的作者把一些封建社会恶俗陋习都贴上了"东方精神文明"的标签。难道"东方精神文明"就是"内战、自私的割据、伪善、欺骗、掠夺、鄙视女性的裹足"吗？难道真正属于中华文明的"孝道"也是罪恶吗？诗人泰戈尔何时阻碍过"受压迫阶级与民族的自觉"和正义斗争？简直是一派胡言乱语！

　　诗人泰戈尔已经知道在前几次讲演的时候，有人散发传单反对他，他就晓得现在中国也有人不理解他，所以他这一次讲演中重点讲述了他自己的经历：他出生的时候正值印度处在一个激荡的时代，国内先后爆发了三次大规模的革命性运动：宗教改革运动、文艺改革复兴运动和民族主义运动。他的家庭成员，他的父亲和他的兄长以及堂兄们都积极投身于上述运动之中。他自己深受这种革命家庭的熏陶，成为推动上述三大运动的推手。因此遭到印度社会守旧人士的反对，所以诗人认为自己就是革命者。诗人泰戈尔指出："我是在上述三种运动汇合的气氛中出生和长大的，这三种运动都是革命性的。我出生在一个独立过自己生活的家庭，这让我从小就在自己的内心判断标准中寻求自我表达的方式。自我表达的媒介无疑是我的母语。但是，使用属于人民的语言必须根据我个人的愿望加以调整。"也正因为这样，他才能创造出新颖的反映现实生活的文学作品，其中包括诗歌。诗人坚信，革命必然会到来，"人们必须冒着遭受辱骂和误解的风险，尤其要冒着那些想要舒适的人、相信灵魂已经过时的人、相信物质主义和习俗的人的辱骂和误解"。诗人通过自己的经历，用事实来说明，自己不是顽固不化的守旧分子，而是一个勇于创新的革命者。

泰戈尔第一次访华纪实

徐志摩的讲话

加尔各答○──仰光○──马来亚○──新加坡○──香港○──上海○──杭州○──南京○──济南○──北京○──太原○──武汉○──上海○

讲学社与诗人泰戈尔本来决定：上周五（5月9日）讲座之后，再讲演四场：从5月12日星期一到星期四每天上午讲一场。可是上周五讲座时发生散发反对他的传单事件之后，诗人泰戈尔宣布，取消剩下的四场讲座。

得知这一消息后，北京各大学的男女学生2000多人于次日来到真光剧场。徐志摩和胡适会见了大学生。徐志摩首先支持诗人泰戈尔的决定；胡适要求同学们应该给予客人应有的尊重。徐志摩发表长篇讲话，他对同学们说：

我有几句话想趁这个机会对诸君讲，不知道你们有没有耐心听。泰戈尔先生快走了，在几天内他就离别北京，在一两个星期内他就告辞中国。他这一去大约是不会再来的了。也许，他永远不能再到中国来了。

他是六七十岁的老人，他非但身体不强健，他并且是有病的。所以他要到中国来，不但他的家属，他的亲戚朋友，他的医生，都不愿意他冒险，就是他欧洲的朋友，比如法国的罗曼罗兰，也都有信去劝阻他。

他自己也曾经踌躇了好久,他心里常常盘算他如其到中国来,他究竟能不能够给我们好处,他想中国人自有他们的诗人、思想家、教育家,他们有他们的智慧、天才、心智的财富与营养,他们更用不着外来的补助与戟刺。他说:"我只是一个诗人,我没有宗教家的福音,没有哲学家的理论,更没有科学家实利的效用,或是工程师建设的才能,他们要我去做什么,我自己又为什么要去,我有什么礼物带去满足他们的盼望。"他真的很觉得迟疑,所以他延迟了他的行期。但是他也对我们说道,冬天完了春风吹动的时候(印度的春风比我们的吹得早),他不由地感觉到一种内迫的冲动,他面对着逐渐滋长的青草与鲜花,不由的抛弃了、忘却了他应尽的职务,不由的解放了他歌唱的本能,和着新来的鸣雀,在柔软的南风中开怀的讴吟。同时他收到我们催请的信,我们青年盼望他的诚意与热心,唤起了老人的勇气。他立即定夺了他东来的决心。他说:"趁我暮年的肢体不曾僵透,趁我衰老的心灵还能感受,决不可错过这最后唯一的机会。这博大、从容、礼让的民族,我幼年时便发心朝拜,与其将来在黄昏寂静的境界中萎衰的惆怅,毋宁利用这夕阳未暝的光芒,了却我晋香人的心愿?"

他所以决意东来,他不顾亲友的劝阻,医生的警告,不顾自身的高年与病体,他也撇开了在本国一切的任务,跋涉了万里的海程,他来到了中国。

自从4月12日在上海登岸以来,可怜老人不曾有过一半天完整的休息,旅行的劳顿不必说,单就公开的演讲以及较小集会时的谈话,至少也有了三四十次!他的讲话,我们知道,不是教授们的讲义,不是教士们的讲道,他的心府不是堆积货品的栈房,他的辞令不是教科书的喇叭。他是灵活的泉水,一颗颗颤动的圆珠从他心里兢兢地泛登水面,都是生命的精液;那是瀑布的吼声,在白云间,青林中,石罅里,不住地欢响;那是百灵的歌声,他的欢欣、愤慨、响亮的谐音,弥漫在无际的晴空。但是他是疲倦了。终夜的狂歌已经耗尽了子规的精力，东方的曙色亦照出他点点心血染红了蔷薇枝上的白露。

老人是疲乏了。这几天他睡眠也不得安宁，他已经透支了他有限的精力。他差不多是靠散拿吐瑾过日的。他不由得不感觉风尘的厌倦，他时常想念他少年时在恒河边沿拍浮的清福，他想望椰树的清荫与芒果的甜瓢。

但他还不仅是身体的愈劳，他也感觉心境的不舒畅。这是很不幸的。我们做主人的只是深深的负歉。他这次来华，不为游历，不为政治，更不为私人的利益，他熬着高年，冒着病体，抛弃自身的事业，备尝行旅的辛苦，他究竟为的是什么？他为的只是一点看不见的情感，说远一点，他的使命是在修补中国与印度两民族间中断千余年的桥梁。说近一点，他只想感召我们青年真挚的同情。因为他是信仰生命的，他是尊崇青年的，他是歌颂青春与清晨的，他永远指点着前途的光明。悲悯是当初释迦牟尼证果的动机，悲悯也是泰戈尔先生不辞艰苦的动机。现代的文明只是骇人的浪费，贪淫与残暴，自私与自大，相猜与相忌，飓风似的倾覆了人道的平衡，产生了巨大的毁灭。芜秽的心田里只是误解的蔓草；毒害同情的种子，更没有收成的希冀。在这个荒惨的境地里，难得有少数的丈夫，不怕阻难，不自馁怯，肩上抗着铲除误解的大锄，口袋里满装着新鲜人道的种子，不问天时是阴是雨是晴，不问是早晨是黄昏是黑夜，他只是努力地工作，清理一方泥土，施殖一方生命，同时口唱着嘹亮的新歌，鼓舞在黑暗中将渐次透露的萌芽。泰戈尔先生就是这少数中的一个。他是来广布同情的，他是来消除成见的。我们亲眼见过他慈祥的阳春似的表情，亲耳听过他从心灵底里迸裂出的大声，我想只要我们的良心不曾受恶毒的烟煤熏黑，或是被恶浊的偏见污抹，谁不曾感觉他至诚的力量，魔术似的，为我们生命的前途开辟了一个神奇的境界，点燃了理想的光明？所以我们也懂得他深刻的懊怅与失望，如其他知道部分的青年不但不能容纳他的灵感，并且存心诬毁他的热忱。我们固然奖励思想的独立，但我们决不敢附和误解的自由。他生平最满意的成绩就在他永远能得到青年的同情,不论在德国,在丹麦,在美国,在日本,青年永远是他最忠心的朋友。他也曾经遭受种种的误解与攻击,政府的猜疑与报纸的诬捏与守旧派的讥评,不论如何的谬妄与剧烈,从不曾扰动他优容的大量;他的希望,他的信仰,他的爱心,他的至诚,完全地托付青年。"我的须,我的发是白的,但我的心却永远是青的。"他常常对我们说,"只要青年是我的知己,我理想的将来就有着落,我乐观的明灯永远不致黯淡"。他不能相信纯洁的青年也会坠落在怀疑、猜忌、卑琐的泥涸,他更不能相信中国的青年也会沾染不幸的污点。他真不预备在中国遭受意外的待遇。他很不自在,他很感觉异样的怆心。

因此,精神的懊丧更加重他躯体的倦劳。他差不多是病了。我们当然很焦急地期望他的健康,但他再没有心境继续他的讲演。我们恐怕今天就是他在北京公开讲演最后的一个机会。他有休养的必要。我们也决不忍再使他耗费有限的精力。他不久又要长途跋涉,他不能不有三四天完全的养息。所以从今天起,所有已经约定的集会,公开与私人的,一概撤销,他今天就出城去静养。

我们关切他的,一定可以原谅,就是一小部分不愿意他来作客的诸君也可以自喜战略的成功。他是病了,他在北京不再开口了,他快走了,他从此不再来了。但是同学们,我们也得平心地想想,老人到底有什么罪,他有什么负心,他有什么不可容赦的犯案?公道是死了吗?为什么听不见你的声音?

他们说他是守旧,说他是顽固。我们能相信吗?他们说他是"太迟",说他是"不合时宜",我们能相信吗?他自己是不信的,真的不能信。他说这一定是滑稽家的反调。他一生所遭逢的批评只是太新,太早,太激进,太激烈,太革命的,太理想的,他六十年的生涯只是不断地奋斗与冲锋,他现在还只是冲锋与奋斗。但是他们说他是守旧,太迟,太老。他顽固奋斗的对象只是暴烈主义、资本主义、帝国主义、武力主义、杀灭性灵的物质主义;他主张的只是创造的生活,心灵的自由,国际的和平,教育的改造,普爱的实现。但他们说他是帝国政策的间谍,资本主义的助力,亡国奴族的流民,提倡裹脚的狂人!肮脏是在我们的政客与暴徒的心里,与我们的诗人又有什么关系?昏乱是在我们冒名的学者与文人的脑里,与我们的诗人又有什么亲属?我们何妨说太阳是黑的,我们何妨说苍蝇是真理?同学们,听信我的话,像他的这样伟大的声音,我们也许一辈子再不会听着的了。留神目前的机会,预防将来的惆怅!他的人格我们只能到历史上去搜寻比拟。他的博大的温柔的灵魂,我敢说永远是人类记忆里的一次灵绩。他的无边的想象是辽阔的同情,使我们想起惠德曼;他的博爱的福音与宣传的热心,使我们记起托尔斯泰;他的坚韧的意志与艺术的天才,使我们想起造摩西像的密仡郎其罗;他的诙谐与智慧使我们想象当年的苏格拉底与老聃!他的人格的和谐与优美使我们想念暮年的歌德;他的慈祥的纯爱的抚摩,他的为人道不厌的努力,他的磅礴的大声,有时竟使我们唤起救主的心像,他的光彩,他的音乐,他的雄伟,使我们想念奥林必克山顶的大神。他是不可侵凌的,不可逾越的,他是自然界的一个神秘的现象。他是三春和暖的南风,惊醒树枝上的新芽,增添处女颊上的红晕。他是普照的阳光。他是一派浩瀚的大水,从来不可追寻的渊源,在大地的怀抱中终古地流着,不息地流着,我们只是两岸的居民,凭借这慈恩的天赋,灌溉我们的田稻,苏解我们的干渴,洗净我们的污垢。他是喜马拉雅积雪的山峰,一般的崇高,一般的纯洁,一般的壮丽,一般的高傲,只有无限的青天枕藉他银白的头颅。

　　人格是一个不可错误的实在,荒歉是一件大事,但我们是饿惯了的,只认鸠形与鹄面是人生本来的面目,永远忘却了真健康的颜色与彩泽。标准的降低是一种可耻的堕落:我们只是蹲坐在井底的青蛙,但我们更没有怀疑的余地。我们也许端详东方的初白,却不能非议中天的太阳。我们也许见惯了阴霾的天时,不耐这热烈的光焰,消散天空的云雾，暴露地面的荒芜，但同时在我们心灵的深处，我们岂不也感觉一个新鲜的影响，催促我们生命的跳动，唤醒潜在的想望，仿佛是武士望见了前峰烽烟的信号，更不踌躇地奋勇向前？只有接近了这样超轶的纯粹的丈夫，这样不可错误的实在，我们方始相形自愧我们的口不够阔大，我们的嗓音不够响亮，我们的呼吸不够深长，我们的信仰不够坚定，我们的理想不够莹澈，我们的自由不够磅礴，我们的语言不够明白，我们的情感不够热烈，我们的努力不够勇猛，我们的资本不够充实……

我自信我不是恣滥不切事理的崇拜，我如其曾经应用浓烈的文字，这是因为我不能自制我浓烈的感想。但是我最急切要声明的是，我们的诗人，虽则常常招受神秘的徽号，在事实上却是最清明，最有趣，最诙谐，最不神秘的生灵。他是最通达人情，最近人情的。我盼望有机会追写他日常的生活与谈话。如其我是犯嫌疑的，如其我也是性近神秘的（有好多朋友这么说），你们还有适之先生的见证，他也说他是最可爱最可亲的个人：我们可以相信适之先生绝对没有"性近神秘"的嫌疑！所以无论他怎样的伟大与深厚，我们的诗人还只是有骨有血的人，不是野人，也不是天神。唯其是人，尤其是最富情感的人，所以他到处要求人道的温暖与安慰，他尤其要我们中国青年的同情与情爱。他已经为我们尽了责任，我们不应，更不忍辜负他的期望。同学们！爱你的爱，崇拜你的崇拜，是人情不是罪孽，是勇敢不是懦怯！

徐志摩这篇满怀深情的讲话，表达了当时中国知识界广大青年对诗人泰戈尔的真爱之情，赞美了诗人泰戈尔的伟大人格，也从侧面回击了所谓邀请诗人泰戈尔来华是为中国保守势力助威的杂音说。北京讲学社之所以要邀请泰戈尔前来访华，是想以此来表达对这位东方第一位荣获诺贝尔文学奖的伟大诗人泰戈尔的尊敬和厚爱，也想借鉴他作为伟大诗人成功的经验，促进我们中国文学事业的发展和繁荣。最后他对同学们说，诗人泰戈尔无论"怎样的伟大与深厚，我们的诗人还只是有骨有血的人，不是野人，也不是天神。唯其是人，尤其是最富情感的人，所以他到处要求人道的温暖与安慰,他尤其需要我们中国青年的同情与情爱。他已经为我们尽了责任,我们不应,更不忍辜负他的期望。同学们!爱你的爱,崇拜你的崇拜,是人情不是罪孽,是勇敢不是懦怯!"

徐志摩讲完,诗人泰戈尔发表了以 Judgement(意见)为题的即兴讲话。后来将其修改为 The Challenge of Judgment(意见的挑战),打印出来后,作者又进行了修改和压缩,形成打印的讲话稿。

诗人泰戈尔以快乐的姿态开始讲道:"The young generation of men in the East are everywhere attracted by what they imagine is modern. And they have convinced themselves that Western life modern. They are seeking from its manners and mentality the magic formula of how to grow modern. They believe that what is called modern represents the principle of indefinite growth and freedom—it is youth, it is life."

(东方的年轻一代到处都被他们想象中的现代所吸引。他们确信西方的生活是现代的。他们正在从年轻人的举止和心态中寻找如何实现现代性的神奇配方。他们相信所谓的现代性代表着无限成长和自由的原则——这就是青春,这就是生命。)

可是,如果是这样的话,那么,他们就应该明白,现代性绝不会局限在某个特定的时期,现代性存在于一个特殊的现实之中——由于缺少这种现实,尽管存在最现代的设计和华彩,实际上它也会面临着过时和毁灭。

诗人泰戈尔反问道:"Are we sure that the same thing has not happened to the West, and that the atmosphere of turmoil which we find there is not due to the conflict between, their present history, which is no longer modern, and the messenger of the future, which was come with its sovereign claim?"

〔我们能肯定同样的事情没有在西方发生吗?我们在那里发现的动荡气氛难道不是由于他们现在的历史(不再是现代的)和未来的使

者（伴随着其主权要求而来）之间的冲突吗？］

诗人泰戈尔在这里再次抨击了西方所谓的现代性所追求的是自私自利的机械化。他说："All that is deeply human is never old. It has the perpetual freshness of imperishable life."

（所有人性深处的东西永远不会衰老。它具有生命永恒的不朽的新鲜感。）

过去一百年来，西方那些贪婪的民族掠夺了东半球国家的财富并且侮辱了东方人，我们又怎么能相信，他们是在寻找生活的无限情趣呢？他们来到外国住下来，并且继续住在别的国家赖着不走。"The West has come to us like an engineer…with the primary object of making easy his work of exploitation…The West, in its relationship with non-western peoples, has for its constant meditation-text: They are radically and eternally different from ourselves."

（西方像一个工程师一样来到我们这里，主要目的是使他们的剥削工作变得容易，西方在与非西方民族的关系中，有一个不断沉思的文本：他们与我们根本不同，永远不同。）

欧洲有一些有思想的人士也在思考这类问题，诗人泰戈尔作为例子提到了其中一位作者所写的文章Christian Missions（基督教的使命），并且从该文引用了很长的一段话。

不过，可能是因为想到甘地先生及其追随者，所以他就在文章的最后提醒大家注意不要盲目地反对西方："But we must guard against antipathy that produces blindness. We must not disable ourselves from receiving truth. For the West has appeared before the present-day world not only with her dynamite of passion and cargo of things but with her gift of truth. Until we fully accept it in a right spirit we shall never even discover what is true in our own civilization and make it generously fruitful by offering it to the world. The culture, the humanity of the West do not belong to the Nation but to the People."

（但我们必须防止产生盲目的反感。我们不能使自己丧失接受真理的能力。因为西方出现在当今的世界面前，不仅带着激情的炸药和物欲之货，而且带有真理的天赋。除非我们以正确的精神完全接受它，否则，我们甚至永远不会发现我们自己的文明中什么是真实的，并通过将其慷慨地奉献给世界而使其富有成果。西方的文化和人性不属于国家，而属于人民。）

诗人泰戈尔认为，当一些西方列强为了扩展自己的权利在争斗的时候，人民群众渴望交流自己的真理财富。而西方所有这些人民内心中的真诚友爱和活跃的人类之爱等等最美好的品德，我们都应该努力地去继承，因为最终我们就能将这种富有前途和理想的生命力带入我们的生活之中。

诗人泰戈尔在北京与朋友们的合影：左起恩厚之、胡适、泰戈尔、钢和泰（Baron Alexander Wihelm Von Stael Holstein）等。

会见俄国代表加拉罕

泰戈尔第一次访华纪实

加尔各答○──仰光○──马来亚○──新加坡○──香港○──上海○──杭州○──南京○──济南○──北京○──太原○──武汉○──上海○

恩厚之先生的计划是从日本乘轮船和火车去俄罗斯。俄罗斯当局会派官员来接师尊泰戈尔。泰戈尔告诉他自己会提前做好准备，师尊泰戈尔准备明年前往俄国。恩厚之先生作为国际大学的代表将会再次前往中国，商谈进行长期乡村重建工作——情况就这样。恩厚之在寄给朋友的一封信中写道："……师尊他很好。报纸上突然发布消息：他已停止讲演，因为生病了。对此你不必担心，师尊他很好。"恩厚之叫国内的人不必为他的健康担心，他并没有生病，只是报纸报道说他生病了。

对于恩厚之的这封信中提到的"俄罗斯当局会派官员来接师尊"这句话需要做些解释。一位名叫廖尼德·加拉罕的苏维埃俄国政府的代表当时正在北京，他与中国一些怀有现代思想的青年人联系相当密切。5月11日，诗人泰戈尔在离开北京前会见了加拉罕。*Japan Chronicle*（《日本纪实报》）5月12日发布了一则信息："Mr. Rabindranath Tagore paid a visit to Mr. Karakhan yesterday and, it is understood, expressed a wish to visit Russia in order to study the conditions there and to furture among the Russian people the study of the civilization of India and the East. The Russian representative is reported to have expressed himself in favour of the India poet's idea, and to have promised to convey Tagore's wish to his government in Moscow…During the conversation Mr.Karakhan, it is stated, urged the establishment of closer relation between Russia and India."

（罗宾德罗纳特·泰戈尔先生昨天访问了加拉罕先生，据了解，为了研究俄国的情况，他表达了想访问俄罗斯的愿望，并为将来俄罗斯人对印度和东方文明的研究做些准备。据报道，俄罗斯代表表示赞成这位印度诗人的想法，并承诺将泰戈尔的愿望转达给莫斯科的俄罗斯政府。据说，加拉罕先生在谈话中希望俄罗斯和印度建立更密切的关系。）

诗人泰戈尔对加拉罕说："Russia's territory is mostly in the East, her traditional civilization is quite close to Eastern civilization, and Russia is completely different from the countries of Western Europe, who insistently advocate materialistic civilization. Therefore, I very much wish to visit Soviet Russia, both for sightseeing and to plant there the spirit of Eastern civilization."

（俄罗斯的领土大部分在东方，她的传统文明与东方文明相当接近，俄罗斯与西欧国家完全不同，西欧国家坚持崇尚物质文明。因此，我非常希望访问苏维埃俄国，我既可以观光，也可以在那里种下东方文明精神的种子。）

加拉罕向诗人泰戈尔许诺，他会向自己的政府转达诗人泰戈尔的愿望。他说，由于政治方面的原因，他的国家渴望全世界所有被压迫国家的帮助，因为最近几年来在西方物质主义文明的操控下俄罗斯遭受到相当大的损失。在19世纪，托尔斯泰曾经想放弃物质文明，然而他希望诗人泰戈尔将来在俄罗斯的讲话也会涉及这个方面。诗人泰戈尔的办学主张也得到了加拉罕的赞赏,可是诗人泰戈尔并不喜欢这样的主张:把俄罗斯所有农村都效仿莫斯科的样子进行建设。

为了前往俄罗斯访问,这次与加拉罕的会见,是诗人泰戈尔自己主动提出的,其原因之一,可能是他想去俄罗斯亲眼看一看,弄清楚苏维埃俄国究竟有什么特别的地方,居然能够如此地吸引中国青年学生们,让他们迷恋。加拉罕许诺,他要设法让诗人泰戈尔于明年访问俄罗斯。可是,诗人泰戈尔并未能在1925年实现访问苏维埃俄国的愿望,而在过了6年之后,即在1930年9月才实现这一愿望。

5月12日诗人泰戈尔宣布自己要休息之后,就前往北京西郊的西山了。报纸上刊登这样一则声明:"On the advice of his physician, Dr. Rabindranath Tagore has cancelled all his public and private engagements and after his last lecture at the Chen kuang Theatre this morning, he left for the Western Hill. Because of his physical and mental fatigue, DR. Tagore will remain in the hills until next Sunday when he will return to Peking and next morning."[1]

(在医生的建议下,泰戈尔博士取消了所有公共和私人活动,今天上午在真光剧场做完最后一场演讲后,他动身前往西山。泰戈尔先生因身心疲惫,将在山上留宿到下星期天,然后于次日上午返回北京。)

不过,身心疲惫的说法纯属借口,这一点从5月13日基迪莫洪写给诗人之子罗廷德罗纳特的信里就可以得知:"……我们来到中国青年们中间,他们都更迷恋地陶醉于机械之中。机械就是他们的一切,那就是他们崇拜的对象,而且他们并没有从政治的漩涡中摆脱出来,进入更高的境界。……师尊做过2—3次讲演之后今天就前往西

---

[1] 参见: Stephen N. Hay: Asian Ideal of East and West:Tagore and his critics in japan, China and India /73-74. 东方和西方的亚洲思想: 泰戈尔及其在日本、中国和印度遭遇的批评, 第73—74页。

山——前往距离这里20英里的一个宁静的地方。5月18日他将回到这里。然后于5月20日经过汉口，走长江水路去上海。途中将会见吴佩孚将军。……"

5月13日，诗人泰戈尔离开北京城里的喧嚣环境，住进了北京西山清澈的泉水旁边一栋新建的别墅里，在这里休息几天有助于消除诗人泰戈尔的疲劳。但是林长民和北京讲学社的其他成员十分关心诗人泰戈尔的身心健康，所以常常去西山看望诗人。在宾馆里他们一起共进午餐，诗人泰戈尔谈到印度和中国农村的问题，诗人讲述了自己振兴农村的理想。

5月16日，北京佛教讲习会的几位会员前往西山诗人的住处拜访诗人泰戈尔，当时有议员黄攻素、陈铭鉴、张树丹等人在场。来者向诗人泰戈尔提出一些问题，诗人一一作答，徐志摩和邓高镜二人为其翻译。

林长民（1876—1925）

何雯：印度最近佛教及婆罗门教之状况如何？

泰戈尔：印人崇拜佛教，故近今婆罗门教所有之仪式，多已归纳于佛教之中。

何雯：印度九十六种道外，现尚存在否？

泰戈尔：派别甚多，不胜列举，然多皈依佛法也。

何雯：世界哲学，莫高博于佛理，中印两国人士，欲发扬东方文化，宜宣传佛教，为世界消除劫难，此意当否？

泰戈尔：此意极是，余深望世人倾向为善，互相亲爱，尊重道德和平，俾不致魔鬼以物质的实利主义，破坏我精神上之文明。且魔鬼之所为，实地狱之种子也。

黄攻素：素食究于吾人有益否？

泰戈尔：余在本土，曾素食25年，极能保养健康。后游美国，因种种不便，遂不恪守严格之素食。其实肉食极不洁净，每为败德致病之源，故素食实最所主张也。

沈钧儒：此次来游北京之感想如何？

泰戈尔：前观纽约、伦敦、巴黎、加尔各答、上海等大都会，见皆提倡恶浊知识，人人以牟利为能事，建筑设备，尽物质上之工巧。殊不若北京之自然开化，花草树木，有天然之美观，余极表好感。盖予深望世人返璞归真，生活上力求节俭，重农作而不重工巧，应不为讲物质实利者所支配也。

张相文：我欲发展佛教，使向西方传布，益令东方文明真有价值，于意云何？

泰戈尔：予信真理为一，本无东方、西方之分，故尝劝印度佛教徒及学者努力向西方宣传教化。予所办之学院，容纳十数国之士子，即灌输善的知识，倡导和平。中印均为世界文明古国，颇望设法结合，一以谋精神教育之发展，一以谋农业生活之安全。有某君素研究农业，将来可请其来华，同时望中国学者，亦多往印度为幸。

何雯：一切科学，出于哲学。哲学固最精于印度之释迦牟尼，彼能解决宇宙中现在未来，又能救拔世人，使了生脱死。现在世界，魔鬼之力正盛，吾人应负救世之责，从事于感化与宣传，将来可组织一中印学会，互通声气，请问此法善否？

泰戈尔：予此次来华，本有斯意。希望中印两国人士为精神之结合，共谋发扬东方文化，实最心祷。

恩厚之于5月17日写给拉奴·奥提加里的信中透露出以下一些信息：

...Gurudev is better now than I have ever known him before. He has delievered over twenty speeches and addresse and given countless interviews and at the moment when he seemed to be getting tired, we persuaded him to cut all the engagements, as he did that day at Benares, you remember & boit for this little hotel in the country with its hot sulphur spring. They have done him a world of good and he no longer talks of leaving this existence at an early date, but of going to Italy and Russia and heaven knows where. Most of his speeches I have taken down word by word and am slowly transcribing them. He quickly revises them and is thereby adding volumes to the comparatively small stock of authentic English works hitherto published. Mere translation always ruins them.

（师尊现在比我认识他的任何时候都要好。他已经发表了20多次演讲和谈话，接受了无数次采访。在他似乎感到疲倦的那一刻，我们说服他取消所有会面，就像他在贝拿勒斯那天所做的那样，你还记得吧，他住进了那个有硫磺温泉的乡村小旅馆。这让他好了起来，他不再说要早日离开这个世界，而是要去意大利、俄罗斯还有其他我不知道的地方。他的大部分演讲我都逐字逐句地记下来，慢慢地抄写过。他很快对其做了修改，从而为迄今为止已出版的相对较少的正宗英语作品增加数量。只是翻译总会有损原文。）

前面提到，诗人泰戈尔准备5月18日回到北京城里。早在这之前的5月14日宗教联合会会长Gilert Reid就给他发出了邀请函。他在邀请函中写道："Here with the formal invitation which I mentioned to you early after your arrival...We desire a message from you that will help on the moral and spiritual regeneration of China. From your wide experience you will be able to emphasize those great principles that belong to the whole human race. Then as your farewell message, you are free to point out what China needs along these religious lines...It is your presence that we all wish...Our Committee will be ready to welcome you at any time before half past three in the room adjoining the theatre. Over 900 tickets have been applied for and distributed among these various organizations. I am sure you will have one of the most sympathetic and appreciative audiences you have ever had."①

（随函附上在您抵达后早些时候我就提到的要发给您的正式邀请函……我们希望从您那里得到有助于中国道德和精神复兴的信息。从您丰富的经验中您将能够强调指出那些属于全人类的伟大原则。然后作为您的告别信，您可以自由地指出中国在这些宗教方面需要做些什么……我们希望您能出席……我们联合会随时准备在三点半以前在剧院旁边的房间欢迎您。超过900张门票已分发给申请者和一些不同的组织。我敢肯定，您会遇到一群不曾见过的富有同情心和感激之情的观众。）

---

① 见：রবীন্দ্রভবনে রক্ষিত মূল পত্র বা উপকরণ. 泰戈尔纪念馆保存的主要信件和物品。

泰戈尔第一次访华纪实

意外遇到北京大学的学生们

加尔各答 ○－－仰光 ○－－马来亚 ○－－新加坡 ○－－香港 ○－－上海 ○－－杭州 ○－－南京 ○－－济南 ○－－北京 ○－－太原 ○ 武汉 ○ 上海 ○

正如所计划的那样,5月18日上午诗人泰戈尔回到了北京城里。北京大学的一群男女学生突然来到他的身边,请求诗人泰戈尔再讲点儿什么。诗人泰戈尔对于一些没有礼貌的青年是很反感的,因此他就取消三次讲演,而离开了北京城,去西山休息了。因此他向来拜访他的青年人问道:"你们想从我这里得到什么?为什么你们还要请我讲话?"

　　诗人泰戈尔一生的经历都可以证明,他不是演说家。他平生的很多时间都是在寂静的大自然怀抱中和独自思考中度过的。这一次他对这次意外遇到的北京大学同学们发表了即兴讲话,全文如下:

　　"What do you want from me? Why do you ask me to give you a speech? I am honest when I say that I am not a speaker. My conduct contradicts the very idea. Most of my life I have spent in giving expression to thoughts born of solitude and communion with nature. When I was young as you I was a recluse, living alone in a houseboat on a river, like your Yang Tse. I had developed the habit of thinking in the heart of solitude. I was shy of crowds, and whenever I was asked to speak it made me feel miserable. I had not the gift and yet it became my fate to talk.

I wish I could have come to you today in my true capacity as a poet, you would not then have asked me for a speech, but for something better, a poem. I don't know your language, or I would have tried it with poet or I would have tried it with poetry. But it is too late for me to learn, and anyhow I never learnt anything. Whatever you do, don't follow my example. When I was young I gave up learning, and ran away from my lessons. I was only thirteen then.

That saved me, and I owe all that I possess today to that courageous step taken when I was young. I fled the classes which gave me instruction, but which did not inspire. As for information, you know your mathematics, your logic and your philosophy, while I know nothing, and would fail miserably before your examiners. But one thing I have gained, a sensitivity of mind which has never been impaired, the touch of life and of nature, who speak to me.

Wise people put their thoughts in books and I acknowledge their superiority; but sensitiveness of mind is a precious gift. It is a great world to which we have been born, and if I had cultivated a callousness of mind, if I had smothered this sense of touch under a pile upon pile of books, I should have lost the whole world. We can ignore what is scattered in the blue of the sky, in the basket of flowers from the seasons, in the delicate relationships of love, of sympathy and of mutual friendship, only if we have killed and smothered the sensitiveness that thrills us when we come into touch with reality, the reality which is everywhere in this great world, in man, in nature, in everything. This sensitiveness I have kept.

If mother Nature could do it, she would crown me, she would bless me, she would kiss me. She would say, "You have loved me." I have lived in this great world not as member of society or of a group, but as a scamp, as a vagabond, and yet free in the heart of the world, which I have seen face to face. I have lived into the mystery of its being, of its heart and soul. You may call me uneducated, uncultured, just a silly poet; you may grow great as scholars and philosophers; and yet I think I would have the right to laugh at your pedant scholarship.

How at the age of thirteen, could I have been blessed with the wisdom to realize the value of sensitiveness? I was not fully conscious, at the moment, of the way to go about it, nor did I know that I would have to give up erything else to earn my freedom to live in the heart of things. It only came through intensity of feeling itself direct, not from books or teachers.

I know, really, that you do not despise me, because I know less of mathematics than you; for you believe that I have come to the secret of existence in some other way, not through analysis, but as the mother's chamber can be approached by a child, rather than by even the honoured guest. I had kept the spirit of the child fresh within me; because of this I have found entry to my mother's chamber wherein a light burns in the dark, where some symphony of awakening light sang to me from the distant horizon, in response to which I also sing."

（你们想从我这里得到什么？为什么你们还要请我讲话？我说我不是一个演说家，我说这话是很诚实的。我的行为与我的这种想法是相矛盾的。我一生的大部分时间都花在表达那些产生于孤独和与大自然交融的思想上。当我像你们一样年轻的时候，我是一个隐士，独自住在一条河上的一艘船屋里，那条大河就如同你们的扬子江一样。我已经养成了在孤独中进行思考的习惯。我对人群很害羞，每当我被要求发言的时候，我都感到很痛苦。我没有这种天赋，但是我命中注定是要发表讲话的。

我希望，我今天能以诗人的真正身份来见你们，那样你们就不会要求我发表演讲,而是要求我写一首诗。我不懂你们的语言,否则我会尝试以诗人身份或者用诗歌来表达我的思想。可是现在学习太晚了,而且我什么也没学到。无论你们做什么,都不要学我。当我年轻的时候放弃了学习,逃离了我的学校大门。那时我只有13岁。

这倒是救了我,我今天所拥有的一切都归功于我年轻时迈出那勇敢的一步。我逃离了那些给予我指导、却不能激励我的课堂。至于知识,你们懂得数学、逻辑学和哲学,而我这些都不懂,在你们这些考官面前我会惨败的。但有一种东西我却得到了,那是一种从未受到伤害的心灵之敏感,这种心灵的敏感对我来说就是接触生活和大自然。

学者们把他们的思想写在书里,我承认他们的思想是有价值的;但心灵的敏感是一种珍贵的天赋。我们出生在一个伟大的世界里,如果我培养了一颗麻木不仁的心,如果我把这种触觉压在一堆又一堆的书里,那么,我就会失去整个世界。当我们接触现实生活时,我们的敏感会使我们兴奋不已,而且现实在这个伟大的世界、在人们的身上、在自然界、在一切事物中是无处不在的,只有当我们扼杀和窒息这种敏感时,我们才会忽略那种散落在蔚蓝天空、散落在四季的花篮、散落在爱恋同情和相互友爱的微妙关系中的东西。我一直保持着这种敏感性。

如果大自然母亲能做到这一点,她会给我戴上王冠,她会祝福我,她会亲吻我的。她会说:"你爱过我。"我生活在这个伟大的世界上,不是作为某一个社会组织或一个群体的成员,而是作为一个周游世界者而生活,然而我在世界的心中是自由的,这是我亲身经历过的。我生活在现实世界中,生活在它的心灵和灵魂的神秘之中。你们可以说,我没有受过教育,没有文化,只是一个愚蠢的诗人;你们可以成为伟大的学者和哲学家,但是我认为我有权利嘲笑你们那种的学究式的学问。

在13岁的小小年纪,我怎么会有智慧认识到敏感的价值呢?当时我还没有完全意识到应该怎么做，也不知道，我必须放弃其他一切，才能获得在事物中心生活的自由。这种自由只是来自于强烈的感觉本身——来自于直接的感触，而不是来自于书本或老师。

我知道，真的，你们看不起我，不是因为我的数学知识比你们少，而是因为你们相信，我不是通过精神分析，而是通过别的途径了解存在的秘密。我心里一直保持着儿童心理，因此我找到了通往母亲房间的入口，那里有一盏灯在黑暗中燃烧着，在那里，从遥远的地平线上传来了某种唤醒我的光明交响乐曲，作为对其的回应。）

诗人泰戈尔对同学们说，他希望今天能以诗人的真正身份来见他们，那样同学们就不会要求他发表演讲了，而是要求他奉献更好的东西——诗歌。如果能够懂得同学们的语言，并且用这种语言写诗，那么，他就能容易表达自己的情感。可是他没有时间学习这种语言，实际上他一生都没有按照传统的方法进行学习，他13岁时就逃离了学校大门。他不懂数学、逻辑学和哲学，但是他说，有一件事他得到了，一种从未受到损伤的心灵之敏感，一种对生活和大自然的触摸，这种触摸是在与他谈话。学者们将他们自己的思想都写在书本里，他们思想的价值是无限的，但是喜欢对自然的这种感觉也是巨大的收获；他们出生在一个宏大的世界，若不接受这种感觉，总是被压在外部的一堆物质下面，就会丧失感知这个世界的一切。在这个世界上，他——诗人泰戈尔不是任何社团组织的成员，他是一个周游世界者，但是他感悟到世界存在的乐趣，感悟到她的心灵、她的精神。诗人泰戈尔对大家说，他们可以说他没受过教育，没有文化，只是一个愚蠢的诗人，但是诗人觉得他有权利嘲笑他们那种的学究式的学问。

诗人泰戈尔在这次讲话中对于中国青年们所崇尚的物质主义表达了自己犀利的嘲讽，讲述了自己生活的深刻的真实感受，并以此结束了这次讲话。

泰戈尔第一次访华纪实

出席北京大学的送别茶话会

加尔各答〇—仰光〇—马来亚〇—新加坡〇—香港〇—上海〇—杭州〇—南京〇—济南〇—北京〇—太原〇—武汉〇—上海〇

5月18日下午，北京大学的校长蒋梦麟[①]和教师们举行茶话会，为诗人泰戈尔送行。诗人泰戈尔在这次茶话会上发表了讲话，全文如下：

"The time for taking leave has come, leave from friends with whom I have lived and at whose hands I have received much kindness. I cannot tell you how much I have felt at home with those who have taken the trouble to introduce me to this great land and its people. Yet I feel today a discontent, as of something not accomplished, as of my mission not completed. But it is not I who am to blame. The present age is the great obstacle.

I may tell you now that when my people heard I had received an invitation from China, there was great rejoicing and excitement amongst them. Most of you are aware that I have had, before this, other invitations

---

[①] 蒋梦麟（1886—1964），原名梦熊，字兆贤，号孟邻，浙江余姚人。美国哥伦比亚大学教育学博士，曾任国民政府第一任教育部部长、行政院秘书长，长期担任北京大学校长。

from countries in the West, but this time the feeling of rejoicing was not restricted to that small circle which knows England, it came from those who had no knowledge of England at all, and yet who England at all, and yet who were full of admiration at your generosity in inviting a man from the East, at a time when most people are infatuated with Western culture. They felt that this was a great opportunity for us to reopen the ancient channel of spiritual communication once again.

Our simple-minded people are not sophisticated. They know nothing of world affairs, they think it quite a simple matter for nations to come together, and rather feel that it is the building up of hostile relationships which requires the greatest amount of energy. Some will smile at such credulity of theirs.

"Sir, do speak to the people of China, for we can never forget the relationship which was established in those distant ages·"—that was their charge to me. It is a great fact that they should feel thus. They thought it absolutely easy for me to let you, through the length and breadth of China, now how we in India have a love for you, and how we long to be the recipients of our love. They did not know that times were hard, and that there might be insurmountable difficulties. In the simplicity of their hearts they thought it possible for me, one individual, to bind together the hearts of both countries.

It has become so easy for us to approach each other. We have come to you in only a few days time. But this very ease of communication takes away from our minds the realization of the fact. Our visit becomes a picnic. We attend parties, amuse one another, hold teas, lectures, and keep engagements. Then we go back. It is all too easy.

But things that are valuable you have to pay for. Our ancestors had a great ideal of the spiritual relationship between peoples, but there were no end of difficulties in their way; they could not carry their message in a comfortable manner. Nevertheless, a thousand years ago, they could speak in your language. Why? Because they realized the importance of the work in hand—how invaluable was this bond of unity between nations, which could surmount the difference of languages. It is the one bond that can save humanity from the utter destruction with which it is threatened today, through the selfishness which is torturing mankind and causing misery in the world.

Is it not marvellous how these men at all arrived, and having come, translated their metaphysical ideas into Chinese, a language so utterly different from Sanskrit that the difficulties thereby encountered were far more insurmountable than the mountains they climbed, the deserts they traversed, the seas they navigated?

Our ancestors, thus, had to pay for the truth they served. I never had to pay—everything is made so easy and comfortable for me. I have spoken to you, I have read a few lectures, I have enjoyed travelling in your railway carriages which have hurried me to my destination. And yet I say this is not natural. I have had no opportunity to know my fellow passengers, who, in the days of caravans, would have been real to me. As for my audience—are not they mere shadows? Do I ever know them, or they me? Every man has his own language—do they, can they understand mine? For three quarters of an hour I pour down a torrent of words upon their hapless heads. It is this that civilization has made so easy.

But ideas, to be fruitful, must have the collaboration of hearer and speaker. All real union consists of a binding of two hearts. If I could live among you, I could speak to you and you to me, and our thoughts would live through our close contact. They would bear fruit, not immediately, but in the process of time. Obstacles would vanish, misunderstanding would not be possible. Our relation would no longer be one-sided. We would work and produce together from the mutual contact of our hearts and minds. But our professors and schoolmasters demand lectures, from which no deep impression remains but only some faint outlines upon the memory merely events, which find their paragraphs in the newspapers, but do not leave their mark on the hearts of men.

The truths that we received when your pilgrims came to us in India, and ours to you—that is not lost even now. We may feel that those ideas have to be adapted to the present changed conditions, and we cannot accept in their totality the thoughts and teachings of thousands of years ago. We may even grow angry over them, considering them mischievous, but we can never forget them completely because they were mutually assimilated to our lives. They are there for good or for evil, the result of a real meeting for which our ancestors paid.

What a great pilgrimage was that! What a great time in history! Those wonderful heroes, for the sake of their faith, risked life and accepted banishment from home for long, long years. Many perished and left no trace behind them. A few were spared to tell us their story, but most had no opportunity to leave a record behind. For such relics of theirs as have been spared to us, we should be thankful, as well as for something in them which we may call primitive because their primitive condition of life had one great advantage—the coverings were less.

Modern civilization, like a tailoring department has produced all kinds of covering—veils of prejudice which make it very difficult for us to come into touch with those outside, and which cause us even to misunderstand our own countrymen. When life was simple, when people were hospitable and not suspicious, they could share their wealth and happiness, and their lives were welded in a mutual destiny. This was so easy then. Now it is so difficult and therefore we, who still believe in idealism, feel it so keenly.

The bringing of the different human races close together in bonds of love and cooperation, we all believe in; and yet it is difficult because life has become so conventional. You have not the leisure to listen. Even if one of those great teachers, one of those same old monks had come, you would not have had the opportunity, nor perhaps even the curiosity to listen to them. Your days would have been occupied with all kinds of engagements, which are not essential to the true life, a part of which merely goes to fill up so many gaps, like the sawdust that fills the inside of a doll.

Can you even imagine a great messenger today coming and settling down at the foot of your western hills, on the bank of the lake? You would say he was an eccentric man; you would send the police to take him in charge and your foreign embassies would deport him, or put him in safe custody. Would you come close to him? No. Your attitude of mind is completely changed.

Let me confess this fact, that I have my faith in higher ideals. I believe that through them we can best serve the higher purpose of life. At the same time, I have a great feeling of delicacy in giving utterance to them, because of certain modern obstacles which make it almost a disreputable thing to be frank and free in the expression of ideas. We have nowadays to be merely commonplace and superficial. We have to wait on the reports in the newspapers; so representative of the whole machinery which has been growing up all over the world for the creation of misunderstanding, and for the making of life superficial. It is difficult to fight through such obstructions and to come to the centre of humanity.

This is a gathering of intimate friends. Never think that this is a complaint at not finding a place in your hearts. I have never been so happy nor so loosely in touch with any other people, as I have with you. Some I feel as though I had known all my life. My stay here has been made pleasant, beautiful, and I am happy. But in the depth of my heart there is pain, I have not been serious enough. I have had no opportunity to be intensely, desperately serious about your most serious problem. I have been pleasant, nice, superficial. I have followed the spirit of the time which is also easy and superficial, when I ought to have come as one making penance, to take up the heart of life, to prove that I was sincere, not merely literary and poetical.

But it is true I have not had that opportunity; I have missed it. At the same time I hope that something has been done, that some path has been opened up which others may follow, and along this path I also hope that some of you will find your way to India.

I have this one satisfaction that I am at least able to put before you the mission to which these last years of my life have been devoted. As a servant of the great cause I must be frank and strong in urging upon you this mission. I represent in my institution an ideal of brotherhood, where men of different countries and different languages can come together, I believe in the spiritual unity of man and therefore I ask you to accept this task from me. Unless you come and say, "We also recognize this ideal", I shall know that this mission has failed. Do not merely discuss me as a guest, but as one who has come to ask your love, your sympathy and your faith in the following of a great cause, If I find even one among you who accepts it, I shall be happy.

（告别的时候到来了，我要告别那些和我生活在一起的朋友们，我从他们的手中得到了很多的恩惠。对于那些不厌其烦地把我介绍给这片伟大的土地及其人民的人士们,我无法告诉你们,我感到多么像在家里一样的自由自在。然而,今天我感到一种不满足,好像有些事情我还没有做完,好像我的使命也没有完成。但这不是我的过错,这是当前时代制造的最大障碍。

我现在可以告诉你们,当我国人民听说我收到了来自中国的邀请时,他们非常高兴和兴奋。你们大多数人都知道,在此之前,我收到过西方其他国家的邀请,但这一次的欢欣感觉并不局限于了解英国小圈子里的人,而是来自那些根本不了解英国的那些人,他们对此充满了钦佩,因为你们在大多数人迷恋西方文化的时候,你们慷慨地邀请了一位来自东方的人。他们觉得,这对我们重新打开精神沟通的古老渠道是个很好的机会。

我们中那些头脑简单的淳朴人并不会老于世故。他们对世界事务一无所知,他们认为各国走到一起是一件很简单的事情,相反,他们认为建立敌对关系倒需要花费最大的精力。有些人会对他们的这种轻信回报以嘲笑。

"先生,请告诉中国人民,我们永远不会忘记在那些遥远时代建立起来的关系。"这是他们对我的嘱托。他们理所当然地会这样想,因为这是千真万确的事实。他们认为,我通过走遍中国,使你们知道我们印度人是多么爱你们,我们是多么渴望得到你们的友爱。这对我来说是不容易做到的。他们不知道时局艰难,也不知道可能会出现无法克服的困难。他们认为,我这个人有可能把印中两国人民的心凝聚在一起。

我们是那么容易地彼此接近起来。我们到你们这里来,才不过几天的时间。可是正是这种交流的便利让我们忘记了这样一个事实:我们的访问变成了轻松愉快的乐事。我们参加聚会,互相逗乐,饮茶,演讲,赴约会。然后我们返回。这一切都太轻松了。

可是,但凡有价值的东西,你必须得花钱购买。我们祖先对民族间的精神方面的关系曾经怀有伟大的理想,可是在他们的道路上却存在着无穷无尽的困难;他们不能以舒适的方式传递信息。然而,1000年前,他们就会说你们的语言。为什么?因为他们意识到正在进行的工作的重要性,这种超越语言差异的民族间团结的纽带是多么宝贵啊!这是唯一的纽带,正是这种纽带,才能将人类从今天濒临彻底毁灭的绝境中拯救出来。这种出于自私目的的毁灭的威胁正在折磨人类,并在世界上制造痛苦。

这些人是如何到达这里的?又是如何将他们的玄学思想翻译成中文的?这简直是不可思议的。你们的这种语言与梵语完全不同,因此他们遇到的困难远比他们爬过的高山、走过的沙漠、航行过的海洋要多得多。

因此,我们的祖先必须为他们所献身的真理付出代价。而我却从来不用付出代价,一切都为我安排得那么轻松舒适。我曾经对你们说过,我宣读过几篇演讲稿,我享受过乘坐你们的火车去旅行的快乐,火车把我迅速送到目的地。不过,我要说,这是不合情理的。我没有机会去认识我的旅伴们,他们在乘车旅行的日子里本应同我真诚相见。至于说到我的听众,难道他们不纯粹是些影子吗?我真认识他们吗?或者,他们认识我吗?每个人都有自己的语言,他们能听懂我讲的话吗?整整45分钟,我滔滔不绝地将我的话语之雨倾泻在他们倒霉的头上。就这样,文明使这一切都变得如此地容易了。

但是,要想使思想结出丰硕的果实,就必须有听者和讲者双方的合作。所有真正的结合都是两颗心的融合。如果我能生活在你们中间,我就能和你们对话,你们也能和我对话,我们的思想就会通过我们的密切接触而彼此了解。我们的思想就会结出果实,但不是立刻,而是在时间流逝的过程中逐渐结出果实。障碍将会消失,误解将不复存在。我们的关系将不再是单方面的。我们将通过心灵和思想的相互交流共同工作和生产。可是,我们的教授和校长却要求讲演,这些讲演不会留下深刻的印象,只能在记忆中留下一些模糊的轮廓——仅仅是一些事件而已,可以在报纸上找到记载它们的段落,但不会在人们的心中留下深刻的印记。

当你们的朝圣者来到我们印度的时候,我们得到了真理,我们对你们的友爱,即使到现在也没有丢失。可能,我们会觉得,这些思想观念必须适应今天变化了的条件,我们不能全盘接受几千年前的思想和学说。我们甚至会对其生气,认为他们搞的是恶作剧,但我们永远不会完全忘记他们,因为他们已经深深地融入我们双方的生活之中。在那些思想中有好的有坏的,但那都是我们的祖先为之付出辛劳的真实聚会的结果。

那是多么伟大的朝圣壮举啊!那是历史上多么伟大的时代啊!那些了不起的英雄们,为了他们的信仰,冒着生命危险,接受了长期的跋涉、长期的流放。许多人死亡了,没有留下任何痕迹。少数人幸免于难地向我们讲述了他们的故事,但大多数人都没有机会留下记录。对于他们留给我们的这些遗物遗迹,我们应该感激,同时也应该感谢他们身上的那种我们可以称之为原始的东西,因为他们原始的生活条件有一个很大的优势,那就是他们身上的覆盖物比较少。

现代文明就像服装生产车间一样,制造着各种各样的身体覆盖物——这种掩饰偏见的覆盖物,使我们很难与外界接触,甚至使我们对自己的同胞产生误解。当生活简单的时候,当人们热情好客、不存在多疑的时候,他们可以分享财富和幸福,他们的生活被一种共同的命运联结在一起。这在当时是很容易做到的。现在却是如此地困难,所以我们这些仍然相信理想主义的人,对此就会感受如此强烈。

我们都相信,通过友爱与合作,不同的人类种族可以走得更近一些,然而,做起来是困难的,因为生活已经变得如此地循规蹈矩。你们没有闲工夫聆听对方发言。即使那些伟大的导师,那些高僧大德来了,你们也不会有机会,甚至也不会有好奇心去听他们的讲演。你们的时日会被各种各样的事情所占据，而那些事情对真正的生活来说并不重要，其中的一部分只是用来填补许多空白，就像是填充玩偶里边的锯末一样。

今天有一个大信使来到你们西山的脚下，并在湖岸上安顿了下来，你们能想象到吗？你们会说他是个古怪的人，你们会把他送交警察，你们的外交部门会把他驱逐出境，或者把他拘禁在一个保险的地方。你们还愿意接近他吗？不会的。你们的思想态度完全改变了。

让我承认这个事实，我信仰更高的理想。我相信，怀有这种理想，我们就可以最好地为更高的人生目标服务。同时，我也有一种非常微妙的感觉来对其进行表达，因为某些现代障碍使得坦率和自由地表达思想几乎成为一件不光彩的事情。我们现在都显得平庸而浅薄。我们必须等待报纸的报道，那是整个政治机器的代表，整个政治机器在世界各地不断发展，制造误解，使生活变得浅薄。要想克服这些障碍，走进人类的中心是很困难的。

这是一次亲密朋友的聚会。永远不要认为这是我在抱怨我在你们心里找不到位置。我从来没有感到过同你们在一起时如此快乐过，也没有像同你们在一起时这样轻松过。有些事情，我觉得好像一辈子都会记得的。我在这里过得很愉快、很美好，我很开心。但是在我内心深处也有痛苦，我还不够认真严肃。我还没有机会对你们最严重的问题进行严肃的、十分认真的对待。我一直感到很愉悦、很好，但是我也很浅薄。我追随的是时代的精神，这种精神既容易理解又肤浅，而我本应该像一个苦行者那样来到这里，应该是以生活，而不仅仅是以文学和诗歌来证明，我是真诚的。

但是我确实没有这样的机会了，我错过了这样的机会。与此同时，我已经做了一些事情，开辟了一条道路，其他人可以遵循，我也希望你们中的一些人能够沿着这条道路找到前往印度之路。

我感到满意的是，我至少能够把我生命中最后几年为之献身的使命摆在你们面前。作为伟大事业的仆人,我必须坦率而有力地敦促你们完成这一使命。在我的教育机构里,我代表着一种兄弟般情谊的理想,在这里,来自不同国家、说不同语言的人可以走到一起。我相信人类的精神团结,因此我请求你们接受我的这项任务。如果你们不来,只是说,"我们也赞同这个理想",那我就知道,我这个使命失败了。不要把我当作客人,而要把我当作一个来请求你们的友爱、同情和深信一项伟大事业的人。如果我在你们中间发现哪怕只有一个人接受它,我也会感到很欣慰的。)

接着胡适博士致答词。

他说:"我相信,我们大家都被这位客人的演讲深深打动了。我也相信,我能代表所有在场的人说,我们大家都真诚地希望泰戈尔博士和他的朋友们回来时,如此同情地、如此深情地感到,他们今天摆在我们面前的伟大任务没有失败。相反,我希望他们回国时能确信,他们已经高尚而令人钦佩地完成了自己的任务。

确实存在着误解,甚至是愚蠢的反对,但这些事情是不可避免的。甚至对我们自己来说,让别人理解我们也常常是困难的,而我们试图向自己的人民传递信息,也常常经历被误解的考验。

如果允许我做个人参考性的讲话,我想补充一点,就我自己而言,我自己已经被我们的客人们完全解除了武装,从一个相当冷漠和愿意站在远处的人,变成了一个通过个人接触而成为诗人和他的朋友们的热情崇拜者。我从诗人本人的个性中得到了他的温暖。所以,我可以用我自己的例子来证明,我们的客人的访问确实是成功的。你在我们中间找到了一个,如果有一个,我相信你已经使更多的人皈依了。

这是一项艰巨的任务,宣讲真理,巩固两国关系已经中断10个世纪的伟大民族相互同情和理解的纽带。我想指出诗人是多么正确,他说,这必须通过语言的相互学习来完成。因为相互理解不可能在短时间内完成。他已经开创了一个美丽而成功的开端,这个开端将不断发展,并显示出远远超出今天在座的所有人期望的结果,包括诗人本人。

我们知道,伟大的革命都是由一两个伟大的大师发起的,少数人的工作产生了具有世界意义的成果。通过我们的朋友,我们与印度的关系得到了极大的恢复。他们就是派给我们的最伟大的代表,难道不是比任何民族派给任何国家的代表都要伟大吗?我们欢迎他们,不是因为他们拥有完全的真理,而是因为他们是人民、教授、学生和人类交流中的一系列最优秀代表的先驱。从一开始,就已经在我们心中播下的友谊种子永远不会丢失,它被播撒在肥沃的土壤里,在未来的岁月中,它将结出硕果。我真诚地希望,泰戈尔博士和他的朋友们回到印度时会坚信他们已经高尚地完成了自己的使命。"

(**Reply from Dr. Hu Shih**

I am sure we are all deeply touched by the speech of our guest, and I am sure I speak for all present when I say that all of us sincerely hope Dr. Tagore and his friends will return feeling that they have not failed in the great task they have put before us today, so sympathetically and so feelingly. Rather I would ask them to return with the assurance that they have succeeded nobly and admirably in their task.

It is true that there has been misunderstanding, even foolish opposition; but these things are unavoidable. It is often difficult even for us ourselves to make ourselves understood, and we who try to impart messages to our own people, have often undergone the trial of being misunderstood.

If a personal reference is allowed, I may add that I myself, for one, have been completely disarmed by the presence of our guests and converted from one who was rather unsympathetic and who was willing to stand aloof, to one who from personal contact has become a warm admirer of the poet and his friends. his warmth I have received from the personality of the poet himself. So I may, use my own case as an example with which to prove that the visit of our guests has really been a success. You have then found one among us, and if one, I am sure you have converted many more.

The task is a tremendous one, this task of preaching truth, in cementing two great peoples, whose relationship has been interrupted for ten centuries, in bonds of mutual sympathy and understanding. I wish to point out how right the poet is when he says that this must be accomplished through the mutual study of language. For mutual understanding cannot be accomplished in a short period of time. He has made a beautiful and a successful beginning, one that will grow and show results far beyond the expectation of all those present here today, not excepting the poet.

We know that the great revolutions are made by one or two great masters; that the work by a few produces results of worldwide importance. A renewal of our relationship with India, has through our friends been made with great grandeur. Have they not sent to us the greatest representative that any people ever sent to any nation? We welcome their embassy, not as the possessors of complete truth, but as the forerunners of a long series of the best representatives of the people, of an interchange of professors, of students, of men. A beginning has been made and the seed that has been sown in our hearts will never be lost. It has been placed in fertile soil and it will bear fruit n the ages to come. I sincerely hope that Dr. Tagore and his friends will return to India with the conviction that they have succeeded nobly in the mission they set out to accomplish.)

泰戈尔第一次访华纪实

参加宗教界人士的欢送会

加尔各答〇──仰光〇──马来亚〇──新加坡〇──香港〇──上海〇──杭州〇──南京〇──济南〇──北京〇──太原〇──武汉〇──上海〇

诗人泰戈尔一行要离开北京了。5月19日星期一（孟加拉历杰斯塔月初五），这一天北京大乘佛教的一群僧人会见了诗人泰戈尔，他们带来印度教和佛教的一些画像，并且对诗人泰戈尔说，通过心灵沟通和简朴生活方式的遵循，人们是可以在发展中国和印度文明方面一起做一些工作。

当天下午3点在真光剧场为诗人一行举行送别会。《北京日报》在报道中写道："The meeting lasted from three o'clock to six…after the address of Dr. Tagore, listened to by over thousand attentive listeners, there was intermission of ten minutes, during which, as for half an hour before the meeting, music was rendered by a Chinese band of thirty persons rendering Western music. Then the address was able translated by Mr. C. S. Chang of the Chinese Y. M. C. A., after which Prof. Sen spoke briefly on 'Human Brotherhood' translated by Dr. George Wilder, and Prof. Nagspoke on 'Religious Reformers of India', translated by Dr. Reid."会议从下午3点一直持续到6点……然后是泰戈尔博士的演

讲，听众超过了1000多人，诗人讲演结束后，有10分钟的中场休息，在此期间，一个由30人组成的中国乐队演奏西方音乐，就像会议前半小时一样，由中华基督教青年会的张C.S.担任翻译。随后，基迪莫洪·森教授做了简短的发言，由乔治·怀尔德博士担任翻译，题目是《人类的兄弟情谊》，迦利达斯·纳格教授讲了《印度的宗教改革家》，由雷德博士翻译。印度教、拜火教、儒教、道教、大乘佛教、佛教、基督教、东正教、伊斯兰教等九大宗教的代表都穿着自己的宗教服装坐在剧场的舞台上。雷德博士在介绍诗人泰戈尔时称谓诗人泰戈尔是当代最杰出的宗教导师。诗人泰戈尔在这次会上谈到了自己对宗教的体验（*Religious Experience*）。全文如下：

"I am glad that when I am about to take my farewell from China, Dr. Reid has given me this opportunity to speak to you about something which lies deep in my heart, something to which I have not yet been able to give expression in China.

I have been given to understand that China never felt the need of religion. This I find hard to believe. People very often judge their neighbour's religion from their own narrow sectarian definition. I am sure that if it had been my good fortune to stay longer I should have been able to realize those deeper chords in the heart of China, whence the music of the spirit comes. But my visit has been short and unfortunately interrupted with engagements that have prevented me from coming into a close personal touch with the people who in the simplicity of their mind keep alive their country's tradition.

I have been asked to let you know something about my own view of religion. One of the reasons why I always feel reluctant to speak about this is, because I have not come to my own religion through the portals of passive acceptance of a particular creed owing to some accident of birth. I was born to a family who were pioneers in the revival in our country of a great religion, based upon the utterances of India sages in the *Upanishads*. But, it was through my idiosyncrasy of temperament that I refused to accept any religious teaching, simply because people in my surroundings believed it to be true. I could not persuade myself to imagine that I had a religion because everybody whom I might trust believed in its value.

Thus my mind was brought up in an atmosphere of freedom, freedom from the dominance of any creed that had its sanction in the definite authority of some scripture, or in the teaching of some organized body of worshippers. And therefore, when I am questioned about religion, I have no prepared ground on which to take my stand, no training in a systematic approach to the subject.

Since my arrival in China, only once have I been asked to give justification for my religious faith. Some university student wanted from me the arguments upon which I based my belief in God. I did try to give him my arguments, but I must confess that arguments are wholly different from realization, as is the the perception of light from the theory of light. If my arguments go wrong that does not nullify the truth of my spiritual faith, for the evidence of its reality is in vision and not in logic. And therefore the man who questions me has every right to distrust my vision and reject my testimony. In such case, the authority of some particular book venerated by a large number of men may have greater weight than the assertion of an individual, and therefore I never claim any right to preach, and never consider myself a preceptor of men in the path of religion.

My religion essentially is a poet's religion. Its touch comes to me through the same unseen and trackless channel as does the inspiration of my music. My religious life has followed the same mysterious line of growth as has my poetical life. Somehow they are wedded to each other, and though their betrothal had a long period of ceremony, it was kept secret from me. Then suddenly came a day when their union was revealed to me.

At that time I was living in a village. The day came with all its drifting trivialities of the usual commonplace. The ordinary work of my morning had come to its close and before going to take my bath I stood for a moment at my window, overlooking a market place on the bank of a dry river bed. Suddenly, I became conscious of a stirring of soul within me. My world of experience in a moment seemed to become lighted, and facts that were detached and dimmed found a great unity of meaning. The feeling which I had was like what a man, groping through a fog without knowing his destination, might feel when he suddenly discovers that he stands before his own house.

I remember the day in my childhood when, after the painful process of learning my Bengali alphabet, I unexpectedly came to the first simple combination of letters which gave me the words: "It rains, the leaves tremble." I was thrilled with the delight of the picture which these words suggested to me. The unmeaning fragments lost their individual isolation and my mind revelled in the unity of a vision. In a similar manner, on that morning in the village, the facts of my life suddenly appeared to me in a luminous unity of truth. All things that had seemed like vagrant waves were revealed to my mind in relation to a boundless sea. From that time I have been able to maintain the faith that, in all my experience of nature or man, there is the fundamental truth of spiritual reality.

You will understand me if I tell you how unconsciously I had been travelling towards the realization which I stumbled upon that day. I hope you will excuse me and not think that I am boasting when I confess to my gift of poesy, an instrument of expression delicately responsive to the breath that comes from depth of feeling. From my infancy I had the keen sensitiveness which always kept my mind tingling with consciousness of the world around me, natural and human.

We had a small garden attached to our house; it was a fairy land to me, where miracles of beauty were of everyday occurrence. Almost every morning in the early hour of the dusk, I would run out from my bed in a hurry to greet the first pink flush of the dawn through the trembling leaves of the cocoanut trees which stood in a line along the garden boundary, while the grass glistened as the dewdrops caught the first tremor of the morning breeze. The sky seemed to bring to me the call of a personal companionship, and all my heart, my whole body in fact, used to drink in ata draught the overflowing light and peace of those silent hours. I was anxious never to miss a single morning, because each one was precious to me, more precious than gold to the miser.

I had been blessed with that sense of wonder which gives a child his right of entry into the treasure house of mystery which is in the heart of existence. I neglected my studies because they rudely summoned me away from the world around me, my friend and my companion, and when I was thirteen I freed myself from the clutch of an education system that tried to keep me imprisoned within the stone walls of lessons.

This perhaps will explain to you the meaning of my religion. This world was living to me, intimately close to my life. I still remember the shock of repulsion I received when some medical student brought to me a piece of human windpipe and tried to excite my admiration for its structure. He tried to convince me that it was the source of the beautiful human voice and I rejected that information with an intense disgust. I did not want to admire the skill of the workman, but rather to revel in the joy of the artist who concealed the machinery and revealed his creation in its ineffable unity.

God does not care to keep exposed the record of his power written in geological inscriptions, but he is proudly glad of the expression of beauty which He spreads on the green grass, in the flowers, in the play of colours on the clouds, in the murmuring music of running water.

I had a vague notion as to who or what it was that touched my heart's chords, like the infant which does not know its mother's name, or who and what she is. The feeling which I always had was a deep satisfaction of personality that flowed into my nature through living channels of communication from all sides.

It was a great thing for me that my consciousness was never dull about the facts of the surrounding world. That the cloud was the cloud, that a flower was a flower, was enough, because they directly spoke to me, because I could not be indifferent to them. I still remember the very moment, one afternoon, when coming back from school I alighted from the carriage and suddenly saw in the sky, behind the upper terrace of our house, an exuberance of deep dark rain clouds lavishing rich cool shadow on the atmosphere. The marvel of it, the very generosity of its presence, gave me a joy which was freedom, the freedom we feel in the love of our dear friend.

There is an illustration I have made use of in another paper, in whichi suppose that astranger from some otherplanet has paid a visit to our earth and happens to hear the sound of a human voice on the gramophone. All that is obvious to him, and most seemingly active, is the revolving disk; he is unable to discover the personal truth that lies behind, and so might accept the impersonal scientific fact of the disk as final—the fact that could be touched and measured. He would wonder how it could be possible for a machine to speak to the soul. Then, if in pursuing the mystery, he should suddenly come to the heart of the music through a meeting with the composer, he would at once understand the meaning of that music as a personal communication.

That which merely gives us information can be explained in terms of measurement, but that which gives us joy cannot be explained by the facts of a mere grouping of atoms and molecules. Somewhere in the arrangement of this world there seems to be a great concern about giving us delight, which shows that, in the universe, over and above the meaning of matter and force, there is a message conveyed through the magic touch of personality. This touch cannot be analysed, it can only be felt. We cannot prove it any more than the man from the other planet could prove to the satisfaction of his fellows the personality which remained invisible, but which, through the machinery, spoke direct to the heart.

Is it merely because the rose is round and pink that it gives me more satisfaction than the gold which could buy me the necessities of life, or any number of slaves? You may, at the outset, deny the truth that a rose gives more delight than a piece of gold. But you must remember that I am not speaking of artificial values. If we had to cross a desert whose sand was made of gold, then the cruel glitter of these dead particles would become a terrorfor us, and the sight of a rose would bring to us the music of paradise.

The final meaning of the delight which we find in a rose can neyer be in the roundness of its petals, just as the final meaning of the joy of music cannot be in a gramophone disk. Somehow we feel that through a rose the language of love reaches our heart. Do we not carry a rose to our beloved because in it is already embodied a message which unlike our language of words cannot be analyzed? Through this gift of a rose we utilize a universal language of joy for our own purposes of expression.

In India the Vaishnava religion is a religion of symbolism in which the Supreme Lover has his flute which with its different stops gives out the different notes of beauty that are in nature and in man. These notes bring to us our message of invitation. They eternally urge us to come out from the seclusion of our self-centred life into the realm of love and truth. Are we deaf by nature? or is it that we have been deafened by the claims of the world of self-seeking, by the clamorous noise of the market place? We miss the voice of the Lover and we fight, we rob, we exploit the weak, we chuckle at our cleverness when we can appropriate for our use what is due to others, we make our life a desert by turning away from our world that stream of love which pours down from the blue sky and wells up from the bosom of the earth.

In this region of reality, by unlocking the secret doors of the workshop department, you may come to that dark hall where dwells the Mechanic and help yourselves to attain usefulness, but through it you will never attain finality. Here is the storehouse of innumerable facts and however necessary they may be they have not the treasure of fulfilment in them. But the hall of union is there where dwells the Lover in the heart of existence. When you reach it you at once realize that you have come to Truth, to immortality and you are glad with a gladness which is an end, and yet which has no end.

Mere information of facts, mere discovery of power, belongs to the outside and not to the inner soul of things. Gladness is the one criterion of truth and we know when we have touched Truth by the music it gives, by the joy of the greeting it sends forth to the truth in us in dogma. As I have said before it is not as ether. That is the true foundation of all religions. it is not waves that we receive our light: the morning does not wait for some scientist for its introduction to us. In the same way, we touch the infinite reality immediately within us only when we perceive the pure truth of love or goodness, not through the explanation of theologians, not through the crude discussion of ethical doctrines.

I have already confessed to you that my religion is a poet's religion; all that I feel about it, is from vision and not from knowledge. I frankly say that I cannot satisfactorily answer your questions about evil, or about what happens after death. And yet I am sure that there have come moments when my soul has touched the infinite and has become intensely conscious of it through the illumination of joy. It has been said in our *Upanishad* that our mind and our words come away baffled from the supreme Truth, but he who knows That, through the immediate joy of his own soul, is saved from all doubts and fear.

In the night we stumble over things and become acutely conscious of their individual separateness, but the day reveals the great unity which embraces them. And the man, whose inner vision is bathed in an illumination of his consciousness, at once realizes the spiritual unity reigning supreme over all differences of race and his mind no longer awkwardly stumbles over individual facts of separateness in the human world, accepting them as final; he realizes that peace is in the inner harmony which dwells in truth, and not in any outer adjustments; that beauty carries an eternal assurance of our spiritual relationship to reality, which waits for its perfection in the response of our love. [1]"

（我很高兴，在我即将告别中国的时候，雷德博士来了，给了我这个机会，让我跟你们谈谈深藏在我心里的一种我在中国还没能表达的东西。

我听说，中国从来就没感受到宗教的需要，我觉得这一点很难使人相信。人们常常从自己狭隘的宗派定义出发，来判断邻居的宗教信

---

[1] The English writings of Tagore, 2/ 672-677. 《泰戈尔英文作品集》第2卷，第672—677页。

仰。我敢肯定,如果我的运气好,若能在这里待得长久一点,我就能触摸到那些奏出精神乐曲的中国人内心深处的合音之弦。但是,我的访问时间很短,而且不幸的是,常常被一些约会所打断,使我无法与那些头脑朴实、保持着自己国家传统的人们进行密切的个人接触。

你们要求我向你们讲一讲关于我自己的宗教观。我总是不愿意谈论这个问题的原因之一,就是我并没有因为出生在由于意外事件而被动地接受某种特定宗教信仰的家庭,从而形成了自己的宗教观。我出生在这样一个家庭,它是那场旨在复兴我国宗教伟大运动的一个先驱,而那场运动的开展是以《奥义书》中印度圣贤言论为基础的。但是,正是由于我独特的性情,我不可能仅仅因为我周围的人都确实相信那种宗教就接受它。而我无法说服我自己,因为我信任,每个人都有相信宗教的理由就去信仰某种宗教。

因此,我的思想是在一种自由的气氛中形成的,不受任何信条的支配,即便这些信条受到某些经典权威或某些有组织的宗教团体的认可。因此,当有人问起我关于宗教问题的时候,我没有现成的根据来表明我的立场,我也没有受过系统宗教方面的训练。

自从我来到中国,我只有一次被要求为我的宗教信仰提供理由。一些大学生想从我这里得到我信仰上帝的论据。我确实尝试着给他们提供我的理由,但我必须承认,理由与现实是截然不同的,正如对光的感知与光的理论是完全不同的。如果我的理由出错,那也不能否定我的精神信仰的真实性,因为它的真实性的证据是存在于直观中的,而不是存在于逻辑推理之中。所以向我提问题的人有权怀疑我的直观感受,拒绝我的证据。在这种情况下,受到许多人尊敬的某本书的权威可能比个人的主张更有分量,因此我从不认为,我有任何说教的权利,也从不认为,自己是人们在宗教道路上的导师。

我的宗教本质上是诗人的宗教。对它的触感和我对音乐的灵感一样,是通过一条看不见的、没有轨迹的通道来到我这里的。我的宗教生活和我的诗歌生活一样，遵循着同样神秘的成长轨迹。不知怎么的，他们彼此结为伉俪，虽然他们的订婚仪式进行了很长一段时间，但他们一直瞒着我。突然有一天，我知道了他们的结合。

那时我住在一个村庄。那一日像往常一样，是平淡无奇的一天。早晨处理日常工作，在去洗澡之前，我在窗前伫立片刻，俯瞰着干涸河床岸边的一个市场。突然，我感到自己心灵一阵悸动。刹那间，我的经验世界仿佛变得明亮起来，而那些超然而漫漶的事实也变得模糊了，我找到了真正意义上的伟大统一。我的感觉就像一个人在雾中摸索，不知道目的地在何处，突然发现它就位于自己的房屋之前。

我记得童年的那一天，在痛苦地学习了孟加拉字母之后，我意外地学会了第一个简单的字母组合，它给了我这样的词语："雨在淅沥地下着，树叶在微微颤抖。"这句话给我的印象使我兴奋不已。毫无意义的碎片失去了它们个体的隔离，我的心灵陶醉在一种愿景的统一之中。同样，在村子里的那个早晨，我生活中的现实突然以一种统一的真实面貌出现在我面前。一切曾经仿佛是浪涛似的东西，都映入了我那无边无际的脑海。从那时起，我就能够保持这样的信念：在我对大自然或人类的所有经验中存在着精神世界的基本真实。

如果我告诉你们，我是多么不自觉地朝着我那天偶然发现的东西前进，你们就会理解我了。我希望你们能原谅我，当我承认我具有诗歌天赋时，不要认为我是在自夸，诗歌是一种表达情感的工具，能够微妙地回应来自情感深处的气息。从孩提时代起，我就有一种敏锐的感觉，这种感觉使我的头脑对周围的世界——无论是对自然世界还是对人类世界，都充满了敏感意识。

我们家附近有一个小花园。对我来说，那是一个仙境，在那里每天都有美丽的奇迹发生。几乎在每天早晨，在朦胧的清晨，我都会从床上爬起来，匆匆跑出来，从沿着花园边缘排列的椰子树的颤动的树叶中间迎接黎明的第一缕红色晨曦，而露珠伴随晨风的第一次颤动在草地上闪闪发光。天空仿佛在召唤我独自与之相伴，我的整个心灵，实际上，是我的整个身体，都习惯于一口气喝下那些寂静时刻洋溢着的光明与宁静。我渴望不要错过任何一个早晨，因为，每一个早晨对我来说都是珍贵的，甚至重于守财奴对金子的感情。

我有幸拥有一种奇妙的感觉，这种感觉使一个孩子有权进入存在于心中的神秘宝库。我忽略了学习，因为那种学习粗暴地把我从周围的世界、我的朋友和同伴中隔离开来。我13岁时就摆脱了教育体系的束缚，这种体系试图把我禁锢在课程的石墙里。

这也许可以向你们解释我信仰的含义。这个世界对我来说是活生生的，离我的生活很近。我仍然记得，当一个医科学生给我带来一段人的气管，试图激发我对它的结构的兴趣，当时我萌生了强烈的排斥。他试图说服我，那是人类美妙声音的来源，我以强烈的厌恶拒绝了那个信息。我并不想欣赏工匠的技艺，而是陶醉在艺术家的喜悦中，这种喜悦遮盖了机器，却揭示出其创作就存在于不可言喻的统一性之中。

天神不愿意把他在地质上刻下的铭文所记载的巨大能量暴露在世人面前，但他却为自己能在青草、鲜花、云彩上的色彩变幻和流水的潺潺乐声中所表现的大美而感到骄傲和欣慰。

我不清楚，触动我心弦的是何人，是何物，对此我有一个模糊的概念，就好像婴儿不知道母亲的名字，不知道母亲是谁，长什么一样。我一直有一种感觉，那就是一种对我的个性深感满足，这种满足通过来自各个方面的交流渠道流入我的本性之中。

对我来说，我对周围世界诸事物的感悟意识从不迟钝，这是一个巨大的事实。云就是云，花就是花，这就足够了，因为它们直接对我说话，因为我不能对它们漠不关心。我还记得，有一天下午，放学回家，我下了马车，突然看见在我们家楼上的露台后面的天空中飘浮着一片浓密的乌云，在向空气中投下浓浓的凉爽阴影。它的奇妙，它的慷慨，给了我一种自由的快乐，这种自由的快乐就像我们在钟爱自己亲爱的朋友时所感受到的那种快乐一样。

我在另一篇论文中引用了一个例子，在那个例子中，我假设一个来自其他星球的陌生人访问了我们的地球，碰巧听到留声机上发出的一个人的声音。对他来说，一切显而易见的，似乎最活跃的就是旋转的圆盘；他无法发现隐藏在背后的个人真实，因此可能会接受圆盘这个非个人的科学事实作为最终的真相：一个可以触摸和测量的事实。他想知道，机器怎么可能与灵魂对话。然后，如果他在探索神秘的过程中，通过与作曲家的会面突然达到了音乐的核心，他就会立即理解音乐作为个人交流的意义。

那些仅仅给我们提供信息的东西，是可以用测量来做解释的，但那些给我们带来快乐的东西，却不能仅仅用原子和分子的一组事实来解释。在这个世界的安排中，似乎有一种给予我们快乐的极大关注。这表明，在宇宙中，除了物质和力量的意义之外，还有一种信息是通过人格的魔力来传递的。这种接触不能被分析，只能被感觉到。我们无法证明这一点，就像一个来自另一个星球的人无法向他的同伴证明他的个性是看不见的，但是他可以通过机器直接与心灵对话。

仅仅因为玫瑰花又圆又呈粉红色，难道它给我的那种满足感就超过了我要购买的生活必需品吗？或者超过多少服务人员吗？一开始，你可能会否认这样一个事实：一朵玫瑰花比一块金子更能给人带来快乐。但你必须记住，我说的不是人为的价值。如果我们必须穿越一片沙漠，那里的沙子是金子，那么这些死去的颗粒发出的残酷的光芒就会使我们感到恐怖，而看到的一朵玫瑰花就会给我们带来天堂音乐之感。

在印度，崇信毗湿奴的宗教流派是一种象征主义的宗教，在这个宗教里，至尊爱人有他的笛子，随着不同指法的变换笛子就会发出存在于自然界和人类社会中的不同美妙音符。这些音符向我们发出邀请的信息。它们不断地激励我们走出以自我为中心的隐居生活，进入爱与真理的境界。我们天生就失聪吗？还是因为我们被世界上追求自我的呼声和市场上的喧闹声震聋了？我们听不到至高爱者的声音，我们打架，我们抢劫，我们剥削弱者，当我们能把别人应得的东西占为己有时，我们就对自己的聪明窃笑，我们把来自蓝天、来自大地的爱之溪流拒之门外，使我们的生活变成一片荒漠。

在这个现实生活的领域里，通过打开车间的秘密门锁，你可能会来到那个住着机械师的黑暗大厅，你可以帮助你自己获得有用的东西，但是你永远不会通过这种东西得到最终的结果。这是无数事实的宝库，无论它们多么需要，它们都不是成就的宝藏。不过，结合的殿堂就在那里，在尘世的中心，住着爱人。当你到达那里的时候，你立刻就会意识到，你已经来到了真理之地，来到了不朽之地，你会很高兴，这种高兴是一种结局，但又没有完全结束。

仅仅是由事实构成的信息，仅仅是力量的展现，皆属于外在之物，也不属于事物的内在灵魂。快乐是真理的唯一标准，我们知道，当我们触及真理时，是通过它发出音乐，通过它向我们心中的真理发出的愉悦的问候。正如我之前说过的，它不是以太。这是所有宗教的真正基础。我们接受的光不是蒸汽，早晨我们也不会等待科学家把它介绍给我们。同样，只有我们认识到大爱或善良的纯粹真实之时，我们才能直接触摸到我们内在的无限真实，而不是通过神学家的解释，也不是通过伦理学说的粗陋论述。

我已经向你们承认，我的宗教是诗人的宗教；我对它的一切感觉，都是来自视觉，而不是来自知识。坦率地说，我不能令人满意地回答你们关于邪恶的问题，或者关于死后会发生什么的问题。然而，我确信，在某些时刻，我的灵魂触及了无限，并在欢乐的照耀下强烈地意识到它。我们的《奥义书》中说过，我们的思想和言语对至尊真理感到困惑，可是知道这一点的人，通过自己灵魂的直接愉悦，就能从所有的怀疑和恐惧中解脱出来。

在夜晚，我们被事物绊倒，并敏锐地意识到它们各自的分离，但在白天，我们发现它们是团结一致的。当一个人的内在视野沐浴在他的意识的光辉之中时，他就会立刻认识到，精神上的统一性高于一切种族的差别，他的思想就不会再笨拙地被人类世界中个别的分离事实所绊倒，而接受它们为最终的真实；他认识到和平存在于内心的和谐之中，这种和谐寓于真理之中，而不存在于任何外在的调整之中；这种美承载着我们与现实的精神关系的永恒保证，它等待着我们大爱的完美回应。）

　　诗人泰戈尔在谈到在中国几乎时刻陪伴在他身边的徐志摩时，也谈到了自己的感受，说道："It seemed as though he could not express the pain in his heart. He seemed not to be able to speak freely about his feelings. His smile, unless my mind is too sensitive, was not a true smile. Sometimes we could see it was in the place of tears. 'My evil fate follows me from my country to this distant land. It has not been all sunshine of sympathy for me.' He weighed these words before he spoke them. This was the only point he didn't explain clearly or completely; these words contained unlimited bitter pain, unlimited resentment. At that time I felt very sorry for him ."[①]

　　（他似乎无法表达他心中的痛苦。他似乎不能自由地说出自己的感受。如果不是我的心思太敏感，他的微笑本来就不是一种真正的微笑。有些时候我们可以看到，这种微笑呈现在流泪之处。"我的厄运一直跟着我从我的国家来到这片遥远的土地。对我来说，这并不全是同情的阳光。"——在说这些话之前，他都仔细考虑过了。这是他唯一没有完全解释清楚的一点。这些话里包含着无限的痛苦、无限的哀怨。那时我为他感到很难过。）

---

① কালিদাস নাগ: কবির সঙ্গে একশো-দিন, ৬২-৬৩. 迦利达斯·纳格：《同诗人在一起的一百天》，62—63页。

泰戈尔第一次访华纪实

观看《洛神》和出席饯行午宴

加尔各答〇----仰光〇----马来亚〇----新加坡〇----香港〇----上海〇----杭州〇----南京〇----济南〇----北京〇 太原〇 武汉〇 上海〇

5月18日晚上，中国著名京剧表演艺术家梅兰芳在开明戏院（解放后改名为民主剧场）为泰戈尔一行演出了京剧《洛神》，因为京剧的演出需要很多时间的准备，所以直到夜里11点的时候梅兰芳才登台演出，当时已经疲惫的诗人泰戈尔都过了该就寝的时间。因此在该剧演出的休息时间之后，如果诗人泰戈尔就离开的话，在座的中国人就会认为是不尊重表演者，也是不礼貌，所以诗人泰戈尔一直坚持到演出结束。演出结束后，诗人亲自到后台向梅兰芳表示感谢，并说："我看了这个戏很愉快，有些感想，明日面谈。"

次日即5月19日上午，诗人感到身体不适，没能与梅兰芳交谈。这一天夜里诗人一行要乘火车去山西。中午，梁启超、姚茫父、梅兰芳等人为诗人钱行。诗人穿一双中国黑色布绒鞋来赴宴。梅兰芳问诗人泰戈尔穿这种鞋是否习惯。诗人回答说："中国的鞋子柔软轻松，使双足不受箍勒压迫，是世界上最舒服的鞋子。"他还告诉梅兰芳先生："前几天到小汤山小住，温暖的泉水涤净了我身上的尘垢。在晨光熹微中,看到艳丽的朝霞,蔚蓝的天空,默默地望着地上的绿草,晓风轻轻地摇拂着刚从黑夜苏醒过来的溪边古柳,景色使人留恋。"停了一会儿,诗人若有所思地说:"那天在郊外闲游,看见农民蹲在田垄边,口含旱烟管,眼睛望着天边远处,颇有诗意。"

梅兰芳回忆说:"席间泰翁谈到了《洛神》,他对我的表演做了鼓励,惟对'川上之会'异常的仙岛布景有意见。他说:'这个美丽的神话诗剧,应从各方面体现伟大诗人的想象力,而现在所用的布景是一般而平凡的。'他向我建议:'色彩宜用红、绿、黄、黑、紫等重色,应创造出人间的奇峰、怪石、瑶草、琪花,并勾勒金银线框来烘托神话气氛。'以后我曾依照泰翁的意见,请人重新设计《洛神》的布景,在不断改进中有很大提高,……"①

泰戈尔认为,美术是文化艺术的重要一环,例如,中国的戏剧中服装图案、色彩、化装、脸谱、舞台装置,都与美术有关。艺术家不但要具有欣赏绘画、雕刻、建筑的兴趣和鉴别力,最好自己能画能刻。他还对梅兰芳讲述了他学习绘画的故事,他说:"我一向爱好绘画,但不能画,有几次我在诗稿上涂抹修改,无意中发现颇有画意,打算由此入手学画。"诗人接着继续说,他的侄子奥波宁德罗纳特是印度文艺复兴运动中的先锋,是印度孟加拉画派的创始人。他画过以法显、玄奘到印度取经为题材的《行脚图》。诗人还向大家介绍在场的另一位画家依德拉尔·巴苏,他是奥波宁德罗纳特的继承人,是孟加拉画派的杰出的画家。诗人泰戈尔的书籍装帧、插图都出自他的手。他对中国的绘画很感兴趣。午餐后梅兰芳向依德拉尔·巴苏先生求画,巴苏欣然命笔,用中国毛笔在槟榔笺上画了一幅水墨画送给梅先生。这幅画的内容是古树林中一佛趺坐蒲团,淡墨轻烟,气韵沉古。还在送梅先生的画上题《如来成道图》。

席间有人问诗人泰戈尔,听说诗人对绘画、雕刻、歌唱、音乐

---

① 梅兰芳:《忆泰戈尔》,《人民文学》1961年第5月号。

无所不通,此番听了《洛神》的音乐歌唱有何感想?诗人微微一笑说道:"如外国莅临吾印度之人,初始食芒果,不敢云知味也。"诗人这话是一种比喻,其意思是说,中国的音乐歌唱很美,但是初次接触,还不能辨别其滋味。

梁启超先生问泰戈尔:"这次诗人漫游中国,必有佳句,以志鸿爪。"诗人泰戈尔说:"我看了《洛神》正在酝酿一首小诗,送给梅先生。"诗人凝思片刻。随后在草稿本上起草一首孟加拉文小诗,然后用毛笔书写在一柄纨扇上,又译成英文,签上自己的名字,添赠给梅兰芳先生的字句。随后他兴致勃勃地朗诵起这首孟加拉语小诗。在座的中国朋友虽然不懂孟加拉语,但从他那甜软的声音和鲜明的节奏里都领悟到犹如"月下清梵、泉鸣花底的美感"。梅先生从诗人手中郑重地接过这把纨扇,向诗人深深地鞠躬道谢。后来石真将这首小诗翻译成中文:

亲爱的,你用我不懂的

语言面纱

遮盖着你的容颜;

正像那遥望如同一脉

缥缈的云霞

被水雾笼罩着的峰峦。

这是一首只有两行的孟加拉语韵律短诗,就像我们中国古诗一样押尾韵。石真女士翻译得非常好,将原始的意蕴巧妙地表达出来了,而且用"容颜"中的"颜"字和"峰峦"中的"峦"字押尾韵。诗人非常形象地运用云雾中的峰峦跌宕起伏,来描述中国京剧大师梅兰芳先生所扮演洛神时那种裙袖飘浮、神光绚烂的印象,感受了京剧的美好,可是他又不懂得京剧语言所包含的深刻情感。看起来,诗人有意选择了这种接近中国诗歌风格的创作形式,写下了这首小诗。

泰戈尔第一次访华纪实

太原和武汉之行

加尔各答〇—— 仰光〇—— 马来亚〇—— 新加坡〇—— 香港〇—— 上海〇—— 杭州〇—— 南京〇—— 济南〇—— 北京〇—— 太原〇—— 武汉〇—— 上海〇

5月20日夜里，胡适、梅兰芳、林长民、梁启超、张歆海、林徽因、王孟瑜等到火车站为诗人送行。宾主都有依依惜别之情。梅兰芳先生希望诗人泰戈尔能够再次来中国。诗人泰戈尔回答说："两三年后我还要再来。我爱北京的淳朴风俗，爱北京的建筑文物，爱北京的朋友，特别使我留恋是北京的树木，我到过伦敦、巴黎、华盛顿，都没有看到这么多的桧、柏、松、柳。中国人有北京这样一个历史悠久而美丽的都城，是值得骄傲的。"诗人紧紧握住梅兰芳的手，深情地对他说："我希望你带着剧团到印度去，使印度观众能够有机会欣赏你的优美艺术。"梅先生回答说："我一定到印度去，一是拜访泰翁先生，二是要把我的薄艺献给印度观众，三是去游历。"

夜里11点，火车汽笛长鸣，车轮开始转动，送行的人员向诗人一行挥手告别。列车驶出了北京站，向山西进发。

5月21日下午6点40分，诗人一行抵达太原站。

此前，山西省教育协会就向诗人泰戈尔发出了邀请："The

people of Taiyuan are awaiting your memorable visit and long to see your personality as well as to hear your exalted ideas and accept your challenge to international brotherhood of mankind, both East and West alike."

（太原人民期待着您这次难忘的访问，渴望看到您的个人风采，渴望听到您崇高思想的论述，渴望接受您关于东方和西方两方面人类国际兄弟情谊的考验。）

从1911年起，山西省军事总督阎锡山就以其善于理政而著称。他既保留了古代孔子的社会体制，又在推行现代化，他在发展大工业和城乡建设方面的思想同诗人泰戈尔的理想相似。

5月22日上午，诗人泰戈尔会见了山西督军阎锡山将军，并且同他进行了长时间深入的交谈。阎锡山很赞赏诗人泰戈尔的理想，并且决定拨出一块肥沃的土地由恩厚之来开办印度和中国志愿者合作农场。由于两国动荡的政治局势，诗人和阎锡山开办合作农场的计划根本无法实现。

5月22日下午3点，山西督军阎锡山请诗人在太原的孔子大厦做了一个报告，诗人向3000多名听众宣读他的一篇以《城市和乡村》（*City and Village*）为题的文章。诗人在这篇文章中写道，他并不反对进步，但是对于那种以所谓的进步为名的文明在行出卖人的灵魂之实的时候："Then I choose to remain primitive in my material possessions, hoping to achieve my civilization in the realm of the spirit."

（那就是我选择在物质上保持原始，而希望在精神领域达到文明。）他就是调查研究了城乡关系之后才写了这篇文章。他写道："Cities there must be in man's civilization, just as in higher organisms there must be organized centres of life, such as brain, heart, or stomach…But a tumour round which the blood is congested, is the enemy of the whole body upon which it feeds as it swells."

（在人类文明中必须要有城市，正如在高等有机体中需要有组织的生命中心一样，如大脑、心脏或胃。但是一个周围充血的肿瘤是整个身体的敌人，因为它在膨胀时是以身体为食的。）我们的现代城市以同样的方法在吞噬农村的生命力，建起了辉煌的大厦，在农村只剩下果皮废渣。

诗人泰戈尔的这篇文章是从某些政治观点开始论述的。诗人泰戈尔认为，财富是人们个人能力的展示手段。在个人能力方面人们之间是存在差别的，如果这种个人能力非常强大，也可以称其为利己主义。但是一个人正是以这种能力同别人进行联系交流的，人类历史就是这种个人才能发展的历史。个人是社会的一个单独存在，同样财富也是一种单独的存在。当生活简朴的时候，财富就不会制造任何复杂性，而且个人的财富就会用于社会事业。但是在当今时代由于对财富积累的贪婪，这种状况已经发生变化。印度的往世书中塑造的财神俱比罗形象就是丑陋的贪食者，但是财富女神拉克什米却是美女的形象，她静坐在心莲之上。不幸的是，在当今时代，拉克什米已经丧失她的莲花宝座，在她的位置上却端坐着俱比罗。现在的城市都像是大腹便便的俱比罗丑陋的形象。"贪婪的成长不是真正的进步，而是一种疾病，这种疾病让身体即使在死亡时也还保持着肿胀的状态。"(Its growth is not true progress; it is a disease which keeps the body swelling while it is being killed.)

诗人泰戈尔讲话之后，太原外国语大学的学生们为客人们演出了 Sannyasi（《托钵

熊佛西（1900—1965）

僧》）。夜晚在总督府举行招待晚宴，有50名尊贵的客人出席欢迎诗人泰戈尔的宴会。

5月23日，诗人游览瀛湖公园，并向听众发表了即席讲话，随后游览了晋祠。

5月24日上午，诗人一行乘坐火车前往湖北省武汉。

5月25日早晨，火车抵达汉口站，下榻英国建筑风格的旅游列车酒店，酒店的工作人员大都是英国人。武汉是由汉口、汉阳、武昌三镇组成的"中国的芝加哥"，有常住人口70万人，这座城市是1911年爆发的反对清朝皇帝革命的发祥地。1922年，佛教太虚法师在汉口创办了一所佛学院，成立了青年佛教徒协会（Young Men's Buddhist Association）。

当日上午，应熊佛西[①]的邀请，诗人泰戈尔在汉口辅德学校操场向青年学生们发表了讲话。在这次集会上，诗人泰戈尔谈到了自己这次来华的两个原因：第一，是结识中国青年；第二，是体验中国悠久文明与印度文化交往的关系。他号召他的听众将这两个方面融合起来，通过科学知识既要改善人生的物质条件，又要追求精神文明，将二者联系起来。他说："On your shoulders, my beloved young people, lies this responsibility. Like the dawning of the rising sun, you young people are full of promise. You have a great responsibility, and you should advance with determination. Do not let our Eastern civilization imitate whatever is done in Western civilization. I hope very much that more Chinese students will come to India to study the principles of Chinese and Indian culture, for these two cultures are intimately related. Young people, I urge you to exert yourselves."

（我亲爱的年轻人，这个责任就落在你们的肩上。你们年轻人像初升的太阳一样，充满了希望。你们的责任重大，你们应该坚定地前

[①] 熊佛西(1900—1965)——戏剧家，中国话剧的奠基人之一。

进。不要让我们的东方文明去模仿西方文明。我非常希望有更多的中国学生前往印度学习研究中印文化,因为这两种文化是密切相关的。年轻人,我敦促你们自己要努力啊。)

5月25日夜里,诗人泰戈尔与恩厚之、徐志摩等6人乘坐怡和公司的"吉和"号邮船离开汉口,沿长江水路前往上海。

5月下旬的长江两岸,生机勃勃,鲜花盛开,犹如一幅幅美丽的画卷,展现在人们面前。诗人泰戈尔欣赏着两岸的秀美风光,非常开心,两天来的航行,诗人泰戈尔一直陶醉在大自然的美景之中。

泰戈尔第一次访华纪实

返回上海住进贝纳家里

加尔各答 ○— 仰光 ○— 马来亚 ○— 新加坡 ○— 香港 ○— 上海 ○— 杭州 ○— 南京 ○— 济南 ○— 北京 ○— 太原 ○— 武汉 ○— 上海 ○

诗人一行在长江的船上度过了3个夜晚和2个白天，于5月28日上午10点回到上海。诗人泰戈尔一回到上海，就被侨居在上海的意大利女商人贝纳（G.A.Bena）接到她自己的家里，其他人住进了印度商人拉尔羌德（লালচাঁদ）的家里。贝纳女士热衷于教育事业，所以当天晚上她请求诗人泰戈尔讲一讲教育方面的问题，贝纳还邀请她几位欧洲的朋友也来她家聆听诗人的讲话。在这里，诗人泰戈尔再次讲述了他建立学校的原因和自己的教育理想。他说："I believe that children should surrounded with the things of nature which have their own educational value. Their mind should be allowed to stumble on and be surprised at everything that happens in the life today. The new tomorrow will stimulate their attention with new facts of life. This is the best method for the child."

（我认为孩子们应该被大自然的东西包围，这些东西有自己的教育价值。他们的思想应该被允许对今天生活中发生的一切感到惊讶，新的明天将用新的生活事实激励他们的注意力。这对孩子来说是最好学习的方法。)

诗人泰戈尔讲述当年自己学校生活的体验时说道:"I always had it in my mind to create an atmosphere. This I felt was more important than the teaching of the classroom."

(我一直想营造一种氛围。我觉得这比课堂教学更重要。)

诗人泰戈尔创造了这样的环境,即把自己的诗歌、戏剧演出融入著名画家们的教学工作之中,将这些画家的创作型工作的直接经验直观地展现在学生们的面前。

在诗人泰戈尔讲完这番话之后,几个听众用英语和意大利语提出了一些问题。诗人最后说,他没有想过要去宣传他创办的学校和大学:"我现在还活着,但是没有时间了——我建立的教育机构也会消失,但是我正在发展我所认知的理想,但愿大家都能把这一理想看作是自己的理想。"①

5月29日中午,诗人泰戈尔出席在哈斯克尔路(Haskell Road)上的一所日本学校——同文书院为他举行的送别会。4月17日,诗人曾经在这里发表过关于东方文明的讲话,提到了关于在美国起草的阻止日本及其他国家侵略的法律所进行的讨论。这个建议法案在这期间已经变成了法律,日本人的心态是反对美国和西方的。就是在这种形势下,在这一次前往日本之前诗人泰戈尔在日本这所学校发表了讲话。他说,他第一次去日本的时候受到的关怀,使他永远都不会忘记。日本知道什么叫好客。在那里他住在日本人的家里,就被看作是他们自己的亲人。那户人家的悉心照料,整洁有序,优雅之美,让微小之物都呈现出美好之光——这一切都使他迷恋陶醉。有一天日本与印度建立起亲密关系而且直到今天他们都为此而感到自豪——看到这种情景,诗人就觉得这种关系是真诚的,而

---

① *কালিদাস নাগ: কবির সঙ্গে একশো দিন ১৬২.* 迦利达斯·纳格:《同诗人在一起的一百天》,第62页。

且至今也都是真诚的。诗人泰戈尔至今还赞赏日本人生活中那种英雄气概、自我牺牲精神、自尊和忠诚,日本人可能对印度教心灵修养和佛教都是心存感激的。但愿日本人永远都不要丢弃这些品质。今天日本人面临着一个严峻的考验——对成功和效率的崇拜,也伴随着西方教育进入到日本人的心里。但愿日本不要忘掉古代日本曾经为其而献出生命的那种伟大的理想。所有这一切从童年起就学习遵循并在后来的生活中使其发扬光大,每当在向世界提起此事的时候,他一直心怀这样一种希望,通过日本来发展东方的这种理想,

"你们要像英雄一样为真理和理想而献身!"①——诗人泰戈尔特别喜欢向日本的年轻人讲述这句话。大家都为诗人的讲话而欢呼喝彩。

讲演之后,诗人出席了午宴。在宴会期间,诗人泰戈尔向出席宴会的教授和著名人士提出了几个比较重要的问题。诗人泰戈尔说,在当今时代要完全实现这种理想是困难的。在这个不安宁的动荡时代和平是一个很大的问题,可是除了和平,是没有别的出路的。人类曾经有一个时期诉诸武力,进行暴虐争斗,丧失信仰,相互烧杀。"在政治领域现在依然诉诸暴力。暴力已进入别的地方——但是应该从国家领域将其驱逐,因为它是虚伪,它是野蛮。"当今世界上的很多国家都遭受到这种野蛮的袭击,他们在思考用什么办法将其消除呢?在这个领域印度指出了真理之路,诗人泰戈尔说,印度从来不曾许诺要承担某种责任——出于对生命的深切同情才进行宣传。所以这一点是印度永恒的权利,被迫谴责之人是不存在的。追索所有问题之根源,就会发现病根在哪里。诗人说,曾经赐给我们佛陀和佛教的印度,通过另一种化身又告诉我们这个永恒的真理。为此我们应该怀有感恩之心。②

----

① কালিদাস নাগ: কবির সঙ্গে একশো দিন।৬২. 迦利达斯·纳格:《同诗人在一起的一百天》,第62页。
② কালিদাস নাগ: কবির সঙ্গে একশো দিন।৬২. 迦利达斯·纳格:《同诗人在一起的一百天》,第62—63页。

诗人泰戈尔的这篇讲话全文如下：

"This meeting reminds me of the day I came to China, when I had my first reception in this garden. I had come as a comparative stranger and I hardly knew any one among those who had come to welcome me. I kept wondering whether China was at all like the pictures I had seen and whether I should ever be able to enter the heart of the country. My mind was full of anxiety that day, thinking all the time that your expectation would probably be exaggerated in regard to one who for you belonged to a region of mystery and who had a reputation founded upon rumour. So in order to let you know hat I had my limitations I immediately confessed to you that I was nothing more than a mere poet.

I knew that you have had great men from all parts of the world to visit you, great philosophers and great scientists from across the sea and I felt very humble when I came amongst you, you who had already heard their words of wisdom. I was very shy that day, for I thought that I was receiving your attention almost under a false personation. I was reminded of the woman Chitra in my play who had the boon of beauty given to her by the God of Love. When through this divine illusion she succeeded in winning her lover's heart, she rebelled against this beauty, crying that all the caresses which her heart craved from her lover were intercepted by this disguise.

I have come to the end of my stay in China and if you are still ready to receive me and to shower upon me such kind words as you have spoken I can accept them; for I have been put upon my trial and I have come through. Today I have come ever greedy of your love and sympathy and praise. You may lavish your friendship now, so that when I am away I shall remember this evening of my stay which, like some extravagant sunset, has generously spent its full store of colours. Still, however, I have some misgivings. Those of you who have travelled along with me have not yet spoken.

The speaker of this meeting, who has praised me, has been ill all the time since he met me on the first day. So his imaginations about me had no chance of meeting disaster through my personal companionship. Therefore I am still waiting to hear from the friends who had the unfortunate disadavantage of having been too much with me.

Meanwhile I can say one thing. On the first day I also had my expectations. I had in my mind my own vision of China, formed when I was young, China as I had imagined it to be when I was reading my *Arabian Nights*, the romantic China, as well as the China of which I had caught glimpses when I was in Japan.

My host there had a great collection of Chinese paintings, marvels of beauty, and he would display them casually to me one by one, surprising me into making chance acquaintances with great masterpieces. Thus I built my China on a basis of the great works of your great artists of the older days. I used to say to myself: The Chinese are a great people. They have created a world of beauty. And I remember feeling angry with others who had scant respect for you, who could come to exploit and molest you, and who ignored the debt they owed you for your civilization, for the great works which you had produced.

Of course we know that, such a vision, created from the best products of your history, and your past, does not represent the actual life of your people. Yet I firmly believe that it is from the ideal that we get to know the best aspects of thereal, and that the complete life is given by these two things together. I must admititis difficult for a stranger to discover this innermost truth, but I believe I have caught glimpses of it.

One thing I have felt, and it has often been spoken of by foreigners whom I have met in your land. You are very human. I too have felt the touch of the human in you, and I have come, or at least I hope I have come, close to your heart. I myself am filled, not with a feeling of mere admiration and wonder, but with a feeling of love, especially for those persons with whom I have come into close touch. This personal touch is not an easy thing to obtain.

Some people say that you have the gift of accepting things as they are, that you can take your joy in a naked presentation of reality, which you value, not because it has any association with something outside itself, but simply because it is before you, attracting your attention. May be it is because of this gift that you have been willing to accept me as I am, not as a poet, not, as some foolish people think, as a philosopher or, as still more foolish people imagine, as a prophet, but as very much of an individual.

Some of my younger new friends have become quite intimate with me, and taking me to be of their own age they show but scant respect for my grey beard or for my reputation. There are so many who would deprive me of the contact of reality by trying to turn me into an idol. I feel certain that God himself is hurt because men keep their daily love for their fellow beings in their homes, and only their weekly worship for Him in the church. I am glad that my young friends in China never made these mistakes but treated me as their fellow human being. You have asked me to offer some frank criticisms on this day of my departure. I absolutely refuse to accede to your request. You have critics innumerable, and I do not want to be added to their ranks. Being human myself I can make allowances for your shortcomings, and I love you in spite of them. Who am I to criticize? We people of the Orient possess all kinds of qualities of which others do not approve—then why not let us be friends.

You shall have no criticisms from me, and please refrain from criticizing me in return. I hope my friends in China will not have the heart to probe into my failings. I never posed as a philosopher, and so I think I can claim to be let alone. Had I been accustomed to living on a pedestal, you could have pulled me down and damaged my spine, but since I have been living on the same level, I trust I am safe.

I have done what was possible, I have made friends. I did not try to understand too much, but to accept you as you were, and now on leaving I shall bear away the memory of this friendship. But I must not delude myself with exaggerated expectation. My evil fate follows me from my own country to this distant land. It has not been all sunshine of sympathy for me. From the corners of the horizon have come the occasional grow lings of angry clouds.

Some of your patriots were afraid that, carrying from India spiritual contagion, I might weaken your vigorous faith in money and materialism.I assure those who thus feel nervous that I am entirely inoffensive; I am powerless to impair their career of progress, to hold them back from rushing to the market place to sell the soul in which they do not believe. I can even assure them that I have not convinced a single sceptic that he has a soul, or that moral beauty has greater value than material power. I am certain that they will forgive me when they know the result."

［这次会见使我想起我来中国的那一天，我第一次在这个花园里受到欢迎。当时的我对于你们来说还是个陌生人，而且来欢迎我的人我几乎一个也不认识。我一直在想，中国是否像我所看到的照片一样，我是否能进入这个国家人们的心中。那天我心里充满了焦虑，我一直在想，对于你们来说，我是属于神秘领域、名声建立在谣言之上的一个人，你们的期望可能过高了。因此，为了让你们知道我的局限性，我立即向您承认，我只不过是个诗人。

我知道，在此之前有世界各地的伟人到你们这里来，有来自大洋彼岸的伟大哲学家和伟大科学家。当我来到你们中间的时候，我感到很是卑微，你们已经听到了他们的智慧之言。那一天我很胆怯，因为我觉得我几乎是用假身份来吸引你们的注意的。我想起了我的戏剧中的女人齐德拉，她拥有爱神赐予她的美丽。当她通过这种神性的幻想成功地赢得了情人心的时候，她便反抗这种美了，并哭喊着说，她渴望从情人那里得到的一切爱抚，都被这种伪装遮住了。

我在中国的逗留即将结束，如果你们仍然愿意接待我，并像你们所说的那样对我述说友好的话语，那我是可以接受的，因为我已经受到了历练，并且都经历过了。今天，我越来越渴望你们的友爱、同情和赞美。你们现在可以表达你们的友谊了，这样，当我离开的时候，我就会想起我在这里的这个晚上，它就像一些被展现的日落晚霞，慷慨地耗尽了它的全部色彩。然而，我仍然存有一些疑虑。那些和我一起旅行的人还没有说话。

这次会议上的演讲者表扬了我，自从他（这里指张君劢先生——作者注）第一天见到我就一直在生病，他没有机会陪伴我，所以他没有因为对我的好印象而蒙受攻击。因此，我仍然在等待那些不幸与我相处太久的朋友们的消息。

与此同时，我可以说一件事。第一天，我也有我的期望。我对中国有自己的看法，这是我年轻时形成的，是我读《一千零一夜》时想象的中国，是浪漫的中国，也是我在日本时瞥见的中国。

我在日本时看到那里的主人收藏的很多中国绘画，那些画作美得令人惊叹。主人随意地一幅一幅地拿给我看，让我惊讶地看到了伟大的杰作。因此，我在你们古代伟大艺术家的伟大作品的基础上建立了我对中国的印象。我曾经对自己说：中国人民是一个伟大的民族，他们创造了一个美丽的世界。我记得我对那些不尊重你们的人的愤怒，他们来剥削和骚扰你们，他们忽视了他们对你们的文明和你们创造的伟大作品所欠下的人情债。

当然，我们知道，这样的希冀，这样的愿景，从你们历史和过去的最好产物中创造出来的愿景，并不代表你们人民的实际生活。然而，我坚信，正是从理想中我们了解到现实的最好方面，而完整的生活是由这两者一起展现的。我必须承认，对于一个陌生人来说，要发现这种内心深处的真理是困难的，但我相信我已经瞥见了它。

我有一种感觉，我在贵国遇到的外国人也经常谈到这一点。你们很有人情味。我也感受到了你们内心人性的颤动，我已经来到你们的身边，或者，至少我希望我已经来到你们的身边，靠近你们的心。我自己也体验到了一种友爱的感觉，而不仅仅是钦佩和惊奇，尤其是对那些与我有过密切接触的人的友爱。同这些人接触不是容易获得的机会。

有人说，你们拥有辨别事物本来面目的天赋，你们可以从现实的赤裸裸呈现中获得快乐，你们看重它这种呈现，不是因为它与外在事物有任何联系，而仅仅是因为它就在你们面前，吸引着你们的注意力。也许，正是由于这种天赋，你们才愿意接受我这个人，不是作为一个诗人，不是的，而是被一些愚蠢的人所认定为哲学家，更不是一些更愚蠢的人所想象的什么先知，我只是一个独立的个体。

我的一些年轻的新朋友和我非常亲密，他们把我当成与他们一样的同龄人，对我的白胡子和我的名声却不怎么尊重。有很多人想把我变成偶像，从而剥夺我与现实的接触。我确信天神自己也受到了伤害，因为人们把每天对同胞的爱留在家里，他们只在教会里每周敬拜天神。我很高兴我的中国年轻朋友们从来没有犯过这样的错误，而是把我当作他们的同胞。在我离开的这一天，你们要求我提出一些坦率的批评。我绝对拒绝你们的要求。你们有无数的批评者，我不想加入他们的行列。作为一个人，我可以体谅你们的缺点，尽管你们有缺点，我还是爱你们。我有什么好批评的呢？我们东方人拥有别人不赞成的各种品质，那么，为什么不让我们成为朋友呢？

我不会批评你们，也请你们不要反过来批评我。我希望我的中国朋友们不要深究我的缺点。我从不以哲学家自居，所以我想，我可以宣称自己是不受打扰的。如果我习惯于活在神坛之上，你们可能会把我拉下来，打断脊柱，可是既然我一直与你们是平等的，我相信我是安全的。

我做了力所能及的事情，结交了朋友。我并没有试图去了解太多，而是接受了你们原本的样子，现在要离开的时候，我将带走这段友好的记忆。但是我不能用夸大的期望来欺骗自己。我倒霉的命运跟着我从自己的国家来到这遥远的地方。对我来说，这并不都是同情的阳光，从地平线的角落里，偶尔也会冒出愤怒的云朵来。

你们中的一些爱国者担心，我从印度带来了精神传染病，可能会削弱你们对金钱和物质主义的坚定信念。我向那些因此感到紧张的人保证，我完全没有冒犯他们的意思，我无力阻止他们进步的事业，也无力阻止他们冲向市场去出售他们不相信其存在的灵魂。我甚至可以向他们保证，我没有说服任何一个怀疑论者，使他们相信灵魂的存在，或者使其相信道德美比物质力量更有价值。我确信，他们知道结果后会原谅我的。]

泰戈尔第一次访华纪实

泰戈尔出席告别宴会

加尔各答 — 仰光 — 马来亚 — 新加坡 — 香港 — 上海 — 杭州 — 南京 — 济南 — 北京 — 太原 — 武汉 — 上海

5月29日中午，诗人泰戈尔一行前往徐家汇日本同文书院，参加该书院举行的宴会。下午前往上海的九江路参加印度教会、印度锡克教教会和印度穆斯林教会举行的送别会。

晚上出席在慕尔鸣路37号张君劢先生宅邸举行的送别晚宴。出席宴会作陪的来宾有沈信卿、殷芝龄、瞿菊农、徐志摩，印度人喜司爱、朝鲜人赵素卬以及上海国立自治学院的学生，共150多人。因为人员众多，讲演在室外操场进行。

张君劢主持会议，首先致欢送辞。他说："鄙人自太戈尔先生上次由印抵沪后，即患病。致未曾听过其演说。余之病系天花，人皆谓传染所致。余以为此由太氏带来，盖太氏常言，人当做小孩，故今余患天花。或太氏欲余再做一次小孩欤。又余对于太氏颇为抱歉。有人谓太氏赞助玄学，特别中国帮助鄙人。实则余在其未来华之前从未读过太氏之文章。今读其在京沪之演讲，乃知其有满腔爱与美之心。然则可知他是与余无甚关系，决不会来帮助余。且太氏有高深之学问，更不屑赞助余之玄学。自来人之主张固各有不同，有赞成物质文明者，亦有赞成精神文明者，然均难免受人批评。今太氏系批评赞成物质文明者，又太氏注重美与爱，而人患之若大炮。不亦奇乎。今太氏将去，希望亚洲文明独立。造出一种新时代，并望太氏将中国缺点见告云。"

诗人泰戈尔接着发表了即兴告别讲话，他深情地向中国朋友们表示感谢。

诗人泰戈尔讲完，略进茶点。晚上7点，张君劢在家中设晚宴款待诗人一行。晚上10点，乘车前往汇山码头，乘坐日本轮船，前往日本神户，徐志摩陪同诗人泰戈尔访问。5月30日早晨8点，轮船起锚离港。诗人泰戈尔结束第一次中国之行。

泰戈尔第一次访华纪实

结束语

诗人泰戈尔从1924年4月12日到达上海，直到5月30日离开中国，在中国逗留了49天，先后访问了上海、杭州、南京、济南、北京、太原、武汉等中国7个大城市，实现了他访华的夙愿。师尊泰戈尔在访华期间发表了几十次讲演和谈话，受到中国文化界的真诚欢迎和热情接待。

总体看来，诗人泰戈尔第一次访华是成功的：这次访问重新打开了被历史情势封闭已久的中印友好交往的大门，给战乱中的华夏儿女带来一股温馨的春风，向热情的中国人民敞开了他的大爱胸怀，送来了印度人民的友好情谊。

中国人民一直怀念印度伟大诗人泰戈尔第一次来华的访问。今年4月12日正值诗人访华100周年。为了纪念这个日子，深圳大学在中国对外友好协会、外交部亚洲司、中国驻加尔各答总领事馆的协助下，于4月12日启动中印古典音乐周活动；福州大学于4月26—28日举办了"泰戈尔访华100周年纪念"学术研讨会；在泰戈尔访华100周年之际，以"致敬巨匠百年诗情"为主题的百年丁香诗会于4月17日在北京法源寺开幕；为纪念诗人泰戈尔访华100周年，北京时代华文出版局出版了三本书：《1924年泰戈尔中国行》（子张编著）、《泰戈尔诗画精选》《泰戈尔家书》（后两本为董友忱编译）。2024年5月7日是诗人泰戈尔诞辰163周年，就在这一天我应邀在北京大学红楼二层那间100年前泰戈尔做过讲演的教室，做了一场"泰戈尔厚德人格"的讲演。上述活动表明，中国人民至今仍然怀念100年前来华访问的诗人泰戈尔。

为什么100多年来中国人民一直喜欢诗人泰戈尔？我觉得有两个原因，第一是诗人泰戈尔的作品好，第二是诗人泰戈尔人品好，他是一位具有厚德人格的大作家。他的优美诗句"生如夏花之绚丽，死如秋叶之静美""世界以痛吻我，我要报之以歌"，许多中国文人都能背诵；他的小说《沉船》《戈拉》《喀布尔人》感动过很多中国读者；《独身者协会》《大自然的报复》等他的许多剧本令读者热血沸腾；他的文章《在中国的死亡贸易》《文明的危机》等彰显了诗人泰戈尔的仗义执言、爱憎分明的品格；他在中国的讲演和谈话向中国听众袒露了他的大爱心怀。我说他人品好，是因为他在家庭中真正做到了尊老爱幼，他孝敬自己的父母，关爱自己的子女，忠爱自己的妻子，妻子病故时他不满41岁，为了不让子女遭受虐待，他再没续弦；在外面他善待别人，同情农民的疾苦，并尽自己所能帮助他们，在经营祖传地产的10年间为贫苦农民做了很多好事善事；他的一生言行都在实践自己的理想：做有益于别人的事，绝不伤害别人。他以文笔做武器，坚持战斗，赞美真善美，鞭笞假恶丑。他的作品和人品犹如两股清澈的泉水，滋润着世界读者的心田，净化着人们的心灵。因此在中华大地，人民至今仍然在阅读他的作品，怀念他对中国的访问。

周恩来1957年1月在国际大学授予他荣誉博士学位时深情地说过："来到这个学术中心，不能不令人想起这个大学的创办人，印度的伟大爱国诗人泰戈尔。泰戈尔不仅是对世界文学做出了卓越贡献的天才诗人，还是憎恨黑暗、争取光明的伟大印度人民的杰出代表。中国人民对他抱着深厚的感情。中国人民永远不能忘记泰戈尔对他们的热爱。中国人民也不能忘记泰戈尔对他们的艰苦的民族独立斗争所给予的支持。至今，中国人民还以怀念的心情回忆着1924年泰戈尔对中国的访问。"

周恩来总理的这一番话是代表中国人民对诗人泰戈尔一生所做的高度评价，也是对诗人泰戈尔第一次访华所做的总结，更是对当时那么一点儿不和谐的杂音的否定。

世界屋脊喜马拉雅山犹如一位伟大的母亲，她的左右两侧伫立着她的两个女儿：一对孪生姐妹震旦（中国）和天竺（印度）。我希望并相信，这一对孪生姐妹一定会互帮互助，世代友好相处，为世界文明做出更多的贡献。

参考书目

1. প্রভাতকুমার মুখোপাধ্যায়, রবীন্দ্রজীবনী ও রবীন্দ্রসাহিত্য-প্রবেশক, তৃতীয় খণ্ড, বিশ্বভারতী গ্রন্থনবিভাগ কলকাতা, পুনর্মুদ্রন ১৪০৬（普罗帕特库马尔·穆科巴泰：《罗宾德罗传和罗宾德罗文学入门》第3卷, 国际大学图书部, 加尔各答, 1999年重印。）

2. প্রশান্তকুমার পাল, রবিজীবনী নবম খণ্ড, Ananda publishers private limited ,Calcutta-9.India Second Reprint Jaunary 2004（普罗山多库马尔·巴尔：《罗比传》第9卷, 印度阿侬德出版有限公司, 加尔各答-9, 2004年出版。）

3. রবীন্দ্রনাথ ঠাকুর, চিঠিপত্র, ১৮/বিশ্বভারতী গ্রন্থনবিভাগ কলকাতা, ২০০২（罗宾德罗纳特·泰戈尔：《书信集》第18卷, 国际大学图书部, 加尔各答, 2000年出版。）

4. কালিদাস নাগ, কবির সঙ্গে একশো দিন, কলকাতা （《同诗人在一起的一百天》, 加尔各答出版。）

5. The English Writings of Rabindranath Tagore, 2（《泰戈尔英文

作品集》第2卷）

  6．王邦维、谭中主编：《泰戈尔与中国》中央编译出版社2011年版。

  7．朱纪华主编：《泰戈尔与上海》中西书局2012年版。

  8．子张：《2024年泰戈尔中国行》北京时代华文书局2024年版。

  9．梅兰芳：《忆泰戈尔》《人民文学》1961年5月号。

  10．张光璘编：《中国名家论泰戈尔》中国华侨出版社1994年版。

  11．《梁启超全集》第十六集中国人民大学出版社1918年版。

  12．韩石山编：《徐志摩书信集》天津人民出版社2006年版。